CONVERSION

The Old and the New in Religion
from Alexander the Great to
Augustine of Hippo

BY

A. D. NOCK

OXFORD UNIVERSITY PRESS

Oxford University Press

OXFORD LONDON NEW YORK

GLASGOW TORONTO MELBOURNE WELLINGTON

CAPE TOWN SALISBURY IBADAN NAIROBI LUSAKA ADDIS ABABA

BOMBAY CALCUTTA MADRAS KARACHI LAHORE DACCA

KUALA LUMPUR SINGAPORE HONG KONG TOKYO

First published by the Clarendon Press 1933

First issued as an Oxford University Press paperback 1961

Reprinted 1963, 1965, 1969

To

FRANCIS CRAWFORD BURKITT

PREFACE

No careful student of the life and thought of our times can fail to remark the great and increasing interest which is taken in the history of religion as a whole. Whether that history is regarded as a collection of relics or as a series of milestones marking man's progress towards a fuller and finer understanding of the world and of himself, it is recognized as a thread running through all human development. As a manifestation both of group solidarity and of emergent individualism, it is a sociological phenomenon of the first importance; as making vocal many of the impulses which lie below the level of consciousness and producing a delicate interplay between them and the intellect, it gives to the psychologist some of his most fascinating material and problems. Man does not live by bread alone, and we cannot estimate aright even his attitude towards bread and bread-winning unless we consider also his attitude towards his god or dream or devil.

If we are to do this we must pay particular attention to his passage from one god or dream or devil to another; we must seek to know what first prompted the new interest, what gave to it compelling force, and what its acceptance meant. When Christianity appeared in the Roman Empire, it attracted many who had their own traditional alinement towards the unseen and unknown factors of existence. This process of attraction has in the main been studied from the Christian point of view. What I have here tried to do is to look at it from the outside, and to that end I have devoted a substantial part of this book to a presentation of the advance in this same world of other forms of religion, many of them Eastern in origin, and of other ways of life which also won adherents. We have to inquire into their nature, into the factors limiting and conditioning their success, and into the extent to which they can with justice be called missionary or propagandist. How were religious frontiers crossed in antiquity? What did their crossing involve? And when a man began to take notice of Christianity, how much change in his mode of thinking and living did he imagine that adhesion to it would mean?

From this attempt to discover the presuppositions which a citizen of the Empire would bring to any new approach to the mystery of the universe we shall pass to a study of the attitudes which he might adopt towards this approach in particular. We shall seek to see as a pagan might the Christian Church and the Christian creed. The evidence at our disposal does not admit of complete success in this quest; we can but hope to make a reasonable approximation to the truth and, in the Swedish proverb, 'to put the church in the middle of the village'.

The substance of this book was delivered as Donnellan Lectures at Trinity College, Dublin, in June 1931, and as Lowell Lectures at King's Chapel, Boston, in 1933, and I am very much indebted, both to those who invited me to speak on these matters and to those who listened, for their generous encouragement. I should like to take this opportunity of thanking also all the friends who have helped me by their counsel, and in particular Mr. M. P. Charlesworth, Mr. C. F. Edson, Mr. C. T. Seltman, and Dr. W. W. Tarn.

They have done more for me than I can say; and I should be indeed ungrateful if I were silent on what I owe to the stimulus and sympathy which I have received from my colleagues and my students in Harvard, to the order and resources of its library, and to the unfailing kindness of that library's staff.

A. D. N.

HARVARD UNIVERSITY,
  CAMBRIDGE, MASS.
    June 1933.

CONTENTS

I. THE IDEA OF CONVERSION 1

Nature of religion in general. Primitive religions are social, not looking beyond particular groups, and Not-Reason-Why; prophetic religions are Reason-Why and missionary. Intermediary types created by complex cultures with conquest and migration. Conversion as ordinarily conceived the result of a background of Christian ideas, thanks to which concepts of sin and salvation exist under the level of consciousness in the convert's mind before his experience. Elsewhere conversion lacks these presuppositions but implies a measure of preparedness and a sense of certain needs. Spiritual needs in the Roman Empire. Attractions offered by the mysteries, Judaism, Christianity. Contrast of conversion and adhesion. Why men undertake religious propaganda.

II. THE IDEA OF CONVERSION AND GREEK
   RELIGION BEFORE ALEXANDER THE
   GREAT 17

The worships of a Greek city and of the Greek nation as a civic and national possession, capable of receiving new elements, but not regarded as articles of faith to be imposed on others or recommended to them, other races having their appropriate worships, which deserved the reverence of Greeks living in foreign communities. Greek piety organic, without conflict and missionary zeal, although in the early period the spread of the cult of Apollo, the Dionysiac movement, and Orphism had all involved deliberate propaganda. Relative failure of Orphism, as contrasted with success of Buddhism, typical of the Greek temper in religion.

III. GREEKS IN THE EAST AFTER ALEX-
    ANDER 33

Closer contacts of Greeks and Orientals in the Hellenistic period. The interplay cultural rather than religious, in the main, but resulting in the creation of new mixed forms of worship and of Graeco-Oriental initiations. The rise of Sarapis. The birth of Mithraism. Asoka's mission to Greece.

IV. THE OPPOSITE CURRENT . . . 48

Orientals and orientalized Greeks settling in Greek cities for trade and other reasons. Individuals bringing in cults. The dream of Zoilus. How Sarapis came to Delos. The naturalization of alien cults in Greek cities. Initiations not a predominant feature. Judaism in this world; the resultant give and take.

V. THE PATH TO ROME 66
Worships brought by merchants, slaves, and returning soldiers. Policy of the Roman State; control and Romanization. Cybele. The Bacchanalia. Mithras.

VI. HOW EASTERN CULTS TRAVELLED . 77
Individual propaganda. Processions and other ceremonies. Mendicant priests. Public penitents. Miracle and its record in literary works intended to glorify the deities concerned and to excite interest in their power and worship. Votive offerings. Alexander of Abonutichus. The problem of honesty in religion.

VII. THE APPEAL OF THESE CULTS . . 99
Need for new cults and new groupings arising out of political conditions. Attraction of novelty. Desire for fresh divine protectors in the larger world in which men lived as a result of the conquests of Alexander, and in the still larger and stranger world in which they found themselves in consequence of the dissemination of astrological ideas, which brought the unspeculative man face to face with cosmic universals. Interest in immortality and desire to escape from an uncomfortable hereafter. Inquisitiveness about the supernatural and wish for revelation rather than reason as a guide to the secrets of the universe.

VIII. THE SUCCESS OF THESE CULTS IN THE ROMAN EMPIRE . . . 122
Gradual rise to the death of Nero. Greater rise under the Flavians and Antonines. Connexion between this and the change in the composition of the ruling class. Orientalizing under the Severi. The Roman reaction and the conflict with Christianity. Relative strength of these and of older cults. Absence of theology and hierarchy. Belief and tradition.

IX. THE CONVERSION OF LUCIUS . . 138
The story as told by Apuleius. The confirmation of its trustworthiness by the Oxyrhynchus litany and other evidence. The life of contemplation and obedience in paganism.

X. THE LAST PHASE 156
Conversions back from Christianity to paganism. Porphyry, Julian, and the unknown senator. The continuity of ancient religion.

XI. CONVERSION TO PHILOSOPHY . . 164
The rise of Greek philosophy. Socrates and discipleship. Plato's creation of a permanent home for esoteric study and of an exoteric literature addressed to the general public. Philosophy held a dominant place because (1) it offered intelligible explanations of

phenomena; (2) it offered a life with a scheme, a discipline, and a goal; (3) it produced the saints of antiquity; (4) it had the influence of the living teacher; (5) it made a literary appeal. It evoked repentance and conversion.

XII. THE SPREAD OF CHRISTIANITY AS A SOCIAL PHENOMENON . . . 193

The beginnings of the Church. No out-of-door ceremonial, and nothing to strike the public eye except the type of the martyr, who could captivate the popular imagination because of philosophic analogies and of the general fascination then exerted by striking gestures. Parallels in rhetoric and in the Greek novel. The picture of the movement given by Celsus. Christianity regarded as mass apostasy by those who were repelled, as a society guaranteeing all that was needed by those who were attracted. Its success due to its power to satisfy these needs rather the human personality of Jesus as portrayed in the Synoptic Gospels.

XIII. THE TEACHINGS OF CHRISTIANITY AS VIEWED BY A PAGAN . . . 212

The moral requirements no stricter than those of the popular philosophy of the time, but based on other reasons and reinforced by a promise of new strength to fulfil them. The abandonment of popular worship less acceptable, but in line with speculative thought. Teaching about God the Father not unfamiliar in view of the widespread tendency towards monotheism. The Gospel story of the birth and death of the Son of God intelligible, and the concept of an intermediary divine power common. Idea of incarnation strange. The argument in support of the claims of Jesus from the fulfilment of prophecy then very acceptable. Doctrine of resurrection of body strange and repellent. In general Christianity could be represented as the crown of the best thought of antiquity.

XIV. THREE TYPES OF CONVERSION. JUSTIN, ARNOBIUS, AUGUSTINE . . 254

Conversion in Acts ascribed to the argument from prophecy and to miracles. Justin came to Christianity at the end of a disappointed intellectual quest, Arnobius in a mood of revulsion from paganism. Justin in his account is on the defensive, Arnobius on the offensive. For Augustine, as for modern converts, Christianity was always in the background; he was haunted by it and sought to find whether it could be intellectually respectable. Conclusions.

NOTES 272

INDEX 303

I

THE IDEA OF CONVERSION

MAN is born into a world in which there are some objects and processes which are to him fully comprehensible and others which are not. When he releases his hold on a stone which he has held in his hand and it falls to the ground, the result is always the same, and there is nothing to excite any feeling of dependence on unknown forces. Birth, however, and growth and sexual relations and death and success in fishing or hunting and agriculture are all matters in which man is not his own master and appears to be dealing with something uncanny. This distinction is fundamental, and we can observe it in the behaviour of animals. Where man differs from the animals—so far as we yet know—is that throughout as much of his evolution as is known to us he has normally not remained supine but has striven to take a positive attitude and assume a definite line of conduct towards these mysteries. What he says and does rests on the assumption that the secret workings of nature are capable of being influenced by his actions, and commonly on the further assumption that these secret workings are due to forces which operate in virtue of wills and emotions comparable with those which prompt his own operations.

What he thus says and does makes up religion. Our evidence does not allow us to penetrate into the beginnings of this form of conduct; at the earliest stages of human evolution known to us such activity is already determined by a tradition which embodies

the collective wisdom of the community. Like many
other aspects of social organization, it is often thought
to rest upon some original revelation or revelations,
given by higher powers, or upon the communing of
specially gifted persons with these powers; and like
these other institutions it is commonly conceived as
possessing an inherent fixity. In fact, however, it is
not exempt from the law of change, but such change
is gradual and is not liable to be considerable unless
new needs or new cultural contacts arise. Those who
follow such a tradition have no reason to interest
themselves in other traditions, and no impulse to
commend their own tradition to others. It serves
their own needs, and the members of other social
units have traditions which serve theirs. Within the
group itself pressure may be put upon individuals who
are lax in their participation in time-honoured observances, but that is a domestic matter, and in the last
resort a question of public order and well-being. It
was so, as we shall see, with the Greeks.

Such a religion is part of the whole scheme of life
which each man inherits. It has for him the emotional
value attaching to a thing in which he has grown
up, often intensified by the solemnity of the puberty
ceremonies in which he has learned the weightier
matters of the law. But it makes no sudden imperious
demands—except on any who feel a vocation to be
shamans or medicine men—and it asks of him action
and not belief. The situation changes when a prophet
emerges. By the term prophet we mean a man who
experiences a sudden and profound dissatisfaction with
things as they are, is fired with a new idea, and
launches out on a new path in a sincere conviction

that he has been led by something external and objective. Whereas in religions of tradition the essential element is the practice and there is no underlying idea other than the sanctity of custom hallowed by preceding generations, in prophetic religions the reason is all-important and the practice flows from it and is in a sense secondary even if indispensable.

The prophet has a message which he feels an inward and instant impulse to deliver. He can do nothing else; the truth has been vouchsafed to him, and his fellows have need of it. Let us take an instance from the period under consideration, which is perhaps the more interesting in that it is the record of a prophet whose teaching did not strike firm roots in the world. A tractate called the *Poimandres*, composed in Egypt, probably in the second or third century of our era, and certainly before A.D. 300, tells how an unnamed man who desired to know the truth of things had a vision of the making of the universe and of man in which he was taught the way of the soul's deliverance. His celestial visitant concluded:

'"Now, why do you delay? Will you not, as having received all, become a guide to those who are worthy, in order that the race of humanity may through your agency be delivered by God?" Poimandres said so to me and was made one with the Powers. And I, having given thanks and blessed the Father of all things, was released, having been given power by him and taught the nature of the universe and the supreme vision. So I began to announce to men the beauty of piety and knowledge, saying, "O people, men born of earth, you that have surrendered yourselves to drunkenness and sleep and ignorance of God, sober yourselves, and be no longer as men that have rioted in liquor, and are spellbound by foolish sleep." They heard me and came with one heart. And I said, "Why, O men born of earth, have you given yourselves over to death, although you have power to become partakers in immortality? Repent, you that have trodden with error and been partners with ignorance; leave the light that is darkness, abandon destruction, and take your portion of immortality." And some of them mocked and stood aside, having given themselves up to the way of death, while others cast themselves before my feet and begged to be taught. I made them rise up and became a guide to the race, teaching them the doctrine, how and in what way they should be saved. I sowed in them the words of wisdom and they were nourished by the ambrosial water. And when it was evening and the rays of the sun began to sink wholly, I bade them offer thanks to God; and when they had finished their thanksgiving they turned each to his own bed.'

So the prophet preaches to those who will hear, and some of them are prepared to stake all on the truth and fundamental importance of his preaching. That is the first stage. Of these disciples some are so eager in their adhesion that they seek to convey to others what they have come to regard as saving truths. That is the second stage. From this an institution may develop, in which the experience of what is in time a distant past is mediated to generations yet unborn, as a thing ever fresh, and can harden into a tradition as rigid as the order from which the prophet revolted.

We have so far considered the two opposing poles of man's spiritual history. One is the system of religious observances of a small social unit with elementary needs and interests and no important contacts with other cultures which have either material or intellectual superiority or a cult and belief capable of exciting curiosity and attention—of a unit in which, as a playwright says, nothing happens except hearing three o'clock strike and waiting for it to strike four. The other is the religion of a prophetic movement in the first ardour of the founder. In the first there is no religious frontier to cross, no difficult decision to make between two views of life which make its every detail different; in the other the individual stands before a choice which means either the renunciation of his past and entry into a kingdom, which if the promises made for it are true—and that cannot be proved or disproved—is wholly other here and will be wholly other hereafter, or the refusal of this dream as chimerical.

He cannot wed twice nor twice lose his soul.

Between these two opposing terms, one wholly static and one wholly dynamic, there is a middle country—that of the changes in belief and worship due to political development or cultural interplay. As society advances to more complex forms a particular centre may glorify itself by glorifying its gods and representing its gods as deserving the homage of all the members of the new larger unit; this was so in Egypt, where the rise of Ra and Osiris to national significance is due to their local priesthoods. Conquest and invasion have notable effects.. We expect that under the circumstances the conquered will accept the religion of the conquerors, because our views are formed by the ideas which we have of the sequel of Christian and Mohammedan invasions, but what happened then was peculiar in that the religion of the races possessing military ascendancy was in each case prophetic and

militant in origin and type. In the ancient world the
conquerors were liable not indeed to accept the dogmas
of the conquered—for there were in general no dogmas
to accept—but to incorporate deities and rites of the
conquered in their own system. A conspicuous example
is afforded by the Indo-Germanic invasion of Greece.
Not merely were the conquerors inferior in point of
civilization to the conquered, but it could appear to
them, as to later Greeks, that the gods of a region were,
so to speak, permanent residents who had a natural
right to the worship of any human occupants and
whom in any event it would be unwise to neglect.
Further complication is introduced by the conditions
of a time in which men of different races and religions
are able to move freely over a large range of territory,
whether for trade or otherwise. When this is so, we
find in big cities and elsewhere groups of expatriated
folk living in alien surroundings. Such groups retain
their religious, as their other cultural traditions, often
indeed with changes due to intermarriage and various
contacts; and those among whom they find themselves
are equally exposed to this blending of strains. Exclusiveness in religion is confined to the prophetic type,
and it is natural that there should be give and take
outside it. To take an early example, the connexion
between Egypt and Byblos resulted in borrowings
on both sides. The contacts thus produced by these
foreign groups are the most important, for they led not
only to borrowing but to fusion and to new developments; but there were others, as for instance those due
to military service abroad and to slavery. Naaman
heard of Jehovah through his Hebrew handmaid.

These external circumstances led not to any definite

crossing of religious frontiers, in which an old spiritual home was left for a new once and for all, but to men's having one foot on each side of a fence which was cultural and not creedal. They led to an acceptance of new worships as useful supplements and not as substitutes, and they did not involve the taking of a new way of life in place of the old. This we may call adhesion, in contradistinction to conversion. By conversion we mean the reorientation of the soul of an individual, his deliberate turning from indifference or from an earlier form of piety to another, a turning which implies a consciousness that a great change is involved, that the old was wrong and the new is right. It is seen at its fullest in the positive response of a man to the choice set before him by the prophetic religions.

We know this best from the history of modern Christianity. Here it takes two forms, the turning back to a tradition generally held and characteristic of society as a whole, a tradition in which the convert was himself reared but which he has left in scepticism or indifference or violent self-assertion; and the turning away to an unfamiliar form of piety either from a familiar form or from indifference. Psychologically the two have much in common, since the man who returns with enthusiasm will commonly feel that he has never before fully grasped the import of the faith of his childhood. The bottles are old but the wine is new.

The features of such conversion have been classified by William James as a passion of willingness and acquiescence, which removes the feeling of anxiety, a sense of perceiving truths not known before, a sense of clean and beautiful newness within and without and an ecstasy of happiness; these emotions are sometimes, and in fact often, accompanied by hallucinatory or quasi-hallucinatory phenomena. This type of experience is very well known. We must not, however, expect to find exact analogies for it beyond the range of countries with a long-standing Christian tradition, for in them even when the fact of conversion appears wholly sudden and not led up to by a gradual process of gaining conviction, even when the convert may in all good faith profess that the beliefs which have won his sudden assent are new to him, there is a background of concepts to which a stimulus can give life. When John Wesley preached to the miners in Kingswood few of them can have been obsessed by a sense of sin or filled with a desire for supernatural grace, and yet those ideas were somewhere under the level of consciousness as a heritage from generation after generation of Bible-reading and sermon-hearing forefathers. Such conversion is in its essence a turning away from a sense of present wrongness at least as much as a turning towards a positive ideal. To quote James:

> 'Now with most of us the sense of our present wrongness is a far more distinct piece of our consciousness than is the imagination of any positive ideal that we can aim at. In a majority of cases, indeed, the sin almost exclusively engrosses the attention, so that conversion is "a process of struggling away from sin rather than of striving towards righteousness".'

Primitive religion seeks to satisfy a number of natural needs, to set a seal on the stages by which life is marked and to ensure the proper working of the natural processes and sources of supply on which its continuance depends; it provides also an outlet for certain emotions of humility, dependence, and self-dramatization. Prophetic religion has to create in men the deeper needs which it claims to fulfil. Those to whom the forgotten prophet of the *Poimandres* document spoke had no consciousness of being sunk in sleep and drunkenness, no awareness of the assistance of the divine Mind of which he told them. Acts xvi. 30 represents the jailer at Thessalonica as saying to Paul and Silas 'What must I do to be saved?', but this is in a story told from the Christian point of view. If such a man used phraseology of this sort, he could have meant only 'What am I to do in order to avoid any unpleasant consequences of the situation created by this earthquake?' *Soteria* and kindred words carried no theological implications; they applied to deliverance from perils by sea and land and disease and darkness and false opinions, all perils of which men were fully aware.

Prophetic religion, therefore, does not in general find in men's minds anything like the same unconscious sympathy which modern revivalism has used. Yet it naturally finds men's minds in a measure prepared; it is difficult to see how else it would make serious headway. The receptivity of most people for that which is wholly new (if anything is) is small; tradition suggests that it was long before Zarathustra obtained much following. The originality of a prophet lies commonly in his ability to fuse into a white heat combustible material which is there, to express and to appear to meet the half-formed prayers of some at least of his contemporaries. The teaching of Gotama the Buddha grows out of the eager and baffled asceticism and speculation of his time, and it is not easy even now to define exactly what was new in him except his attitude. The message of John the Baptist and of Jesus gave form and substance to the dreams of a kingdom which had haunted many of their compatriots for generations.

We cannot understand the success of Christianity outside Judaea without making an effort to determine the elements in the mind of the time to which it appealed. The next nine chapters are devoted to a survey of the forms of worship to which men turned although they had not been reared in them and to an inquiry into the ways in which these spread, the psychological factors making them attractive, and the measure of success which they obtained. I may here indicate certain considerations which bear on the whole matter.

In the first place, there was in this world very little that corresponded to a return to the faith of one's fathers as we know it. Except in the last phase of paganism, when the success of Christianity had put it on the defensive and caused it to fight for its existence, there was no traditional religion which was an entity with a theology and an organization. Classical Greek has no word which covers religion as we use the term. *Eusebeia* approximates to it, but in essence it means no more than the regular performance of due worship in the proper spirit, while *hosiotes* describes ritual purity in all its aspects. The place of faith was taken by myth and ritual. These things implied an attitude rather than a conviction. Where there was a conviction it was to be found in those who wished to innovate or to deny, in the men who inaugurated or supported new movements, and in the men who denied the validity of traditional views—occasionally of all views—of the supernatural. Some such denial was common among men of speculative tendencies. Recantation was less common but not unknown. Horace tells how he had been sparing in his attentions to the gods, but was converted by a thunderclap out of a clear sky, a phenomenon for which he could not give a scientific explanation (*Odes* i. 34). Lucretius gives a moving picture of the things which shake a man's unbelief— the starry heaven, sudden disasters, consciousness of weakness before the infinite. Pausanias, writing two centuries later, says of the myth of Kronos and his father (viii. 8. 3):

> 'When I began this work I used to look upon these Greek stories as markedly on the foolish side; but when I had got as far as Arcadia my opinion about them became this: I guessed that the Greeks who were accounted wise spoke of old in riddles and not straight out, and that this story about Kronos is a bit of Greek wisdom.'

Unbelief is not a very important feature of the situation. It did not as a rule excite popular animosity except when it was first voiced with emphasis and publicity, as in Athens in the fifth century B.C. The position seldom became acute, because cult was independent of ideas, which were always fluid. Neglect of worship was due not so much to what we should call irreligion as to self-centred indolence and to carelessness. We know from Rome the story of a young patrician who was qualified for the priesthood of *flamen Dialis* but a wastrel. He was constrained to take office, and became a thoroughly reformed character and a model priest.

In the second place, the feelings which we associate

with conversion or with the acceptance of prophetic
religion were seldom excited by the new forms of
belief and worship to which men turned. These were
as a rule supplements rather than alternatives to
ancestral piety. This is obvious with regard to all the
worship paid to new deities in the ordinary ways—by
sacrifice, by attendance at processions, by making vows
in distress and paying them after relief was obtained.
It needs some explanation as far as ceremonies of
initiation are concerned. What did they offer?
Orphism at an earlier date had indeed maintained
that all men have an inherited guilt which dooms them
to a weary round of reincarnations unless by use of its
means of salvation they win release. But the initiations
which were sought in the world in which Christianity
spread promised something like this: 'We assume from
the fact of your approach to us that you are not in too
bad a state. We will of course give you a preliminary
rite or rites of disinfection which will ensure the
requisite ritual purity. That is to be followed by our
holy ceremony, which will confer on you a special kind
of blessedness which guarantees to you happiness after
death.' This blessedness was secured by a rite in which
the initiate went through a symbolic anticipation of
what was to take place hereafter; it was a piece of
sympathetic magic which ensured safety by a simu-
lation here and now. Death and rebirth have this
meaning and no other—with the exception of a curious
sacrament of auto-suggestion in *Corpus Hermeticum*, xiii,
in which the powers of evil are driven out of a man
and the powers of good take their place, and of the
taurobolium in which he received a new vigour.
Consequently, there is no idea that the sacramental

experiences of the initiate would make it easier for him to live a good life here and now. Further, apart from Orphism and the ancient mysteries of Eleusis, it was never maintained that these rites were essential requisites of happiness hereafter—they were valuable safeguards, on which you could depend—and the rites were actions efficient in themselves as rites and not as the expression of a theology and of a world-order sharply contrasted with those in which the neophyte had previously moved.

Let us set against this the claims of Judaism and Christianity. Judaism said in effect to a man who was thinking of becoming a proselyte: 'You are in your sins. Make a new start, put aside idolatry and the immoral practices which go with it, become a natural-ized member of the Chosen People by a threefold rite of baptism, circumcision, and offering, live as God's Law commands, and you will have every hope of a share in the life of the world to come.' Christianity said: 'You are in your sins, a state inevitable for you as a human being and aggravated by your wilfulness. No action of yours will enable you to make a new start, no effort of yours will enable you to put aside your guilt in God's eyes, and you are doomed to endless suffering hereafter. Turn to us, stake everything on Jesus the Christ being your saviour, and God will give to you the privilege of making a new start as a new being and will bestow upon you grace which will enable you so to live here as to obtain a share in the life of the world to come. By using our sacraments you will here and now triumph over death and will have a foretaste of the joys which await you in heaven. Christ became man that you may become as God.'

This contrast is clear. Judaism and Christianity demanded renunciation and a new start. They demanded not merely acceptance of a rite, but the adhesion of the will to a theology, in a word faith, a new life in a new people. It is wholly unhistorical to compare Christianity and Mithraism as Renan did, and to suggest that if Christianity had died Mithraism might have conquered the world. It might and would have won plenty of adherents, but it could not have founded a holy Mithraic church throughout the world. A man used Mithraism, but he did not belong to it body and soul; if he did, that was a matter of special attachment and not an inevitable concomitant prescribed by authority.

There was therefore in these rivals of Judaism and Christianity no possibility of anything which can be called conversion. In fact the only context in which we find it in ancient paganism is that of philosophy, which held a clear concept of two types of life, a higher and a lower, and which exhorted men to turn from the one to the other. So much for the word. We shall find an approximation to the idea in the story of Lucius (Ch. IX). There it is due to particular circumstances; according to the story he had by Isis been delivered from the shape of an ass, into which he had passed as a result of incautious experiments in magic. Her cult was not new to him; he had prayed to her for the mercy which was thus vouchsafed, but after it his special attachment to her worship assumed a character of deep emotion prompted by gratitude and became a surrender of self with an accompanying element of moral reformation. The writer of the tale, Apuleius, probably felt some such devotion and like others to whom we shall come wrote to glorify Isis. Genuine conversion to paganism will appear in our inquiry only when Christianity had become so powerful that its rival was, so to speak, made an entity by opposition and contrast. Then we find men returning in penitence and enthusiasm to the faith of the past, now invested for them with a new seriousness. At this time there were two mutually exclusive opposites confronting one another; previously there had been Judaism and Christianity, with both of which outsiders had not as a rule concerned themselves much, and apart from them a number of approaches to the supernatural differing from one another and only occasionally in rivalry, none of them appearing useless except to Jews and Christians in whose eyes they were worse than useless.

Nevertheless, although there was no basis for conversion in these worships, men did adhere to forms other than those which they had known from childhood, and did so as a result of deliberate choice. As we shall see, there were spiritual needs to account for this. Men wished to escape from mortality and from the domination of an unbending fate and to win personal knowledge of the secrets of the universe and a dignified status in it. They did not indeed desire to escape from sin, for it was in general assumed that moral evil, in so far as you were conscious of it, was something which of your own initiative you put from yourself before approaching the holy and not something from which you were delivered by approaching the holy. Nor were they concerned to escape from demons, who did not outside the Semitic area trouble the imagination of the ancient world.

There was thus a psychological basis for adhesion, and there were those who sought to promote and secure such adhesion. This is quite intelligible, and is not entirely due to the material interest which some had in seeing to it that the cult of a particular deity should have adherents as numerous and as generous as possible and in making clear to others the greatness of Diana of the Ephesians. You have sufficient reason for disseminating a special form of piety if you are convinced that it affords a means of contact with the supernatural which each and every man needs or can with profit use in addition to those means which he has inherited and uses. While a Jew or Christian held that there was only one true God and that most people around him were given up to idolatry and sin, a devotee of Isis could and did think that his cult was the original and best expression of a devotion voiced by all men in their several ways. On a minimal view he would regard it as a good form of piety and worth recommendation, like the cult of an unrecognized or little recognized saint in the Catholic Church. Each had a reason for urging others to do as he did. The Jew and the Christian offered religions as we understand religion; the others offered cults; but their contemporaries did not expect anything more than cults from them and looked to philosophy for guidance in conduct and for a scheme of the universe. The Jew and the Christian had a stronger motive but a less easy access to the eyes and ears of their contemporaries. Each was speaking to men more preoccupied than most of us are with their inner lives and more inclined to believe in the activity of supernatural personalities. How they taught and with what success we must now seek to determine.

II

THE IDEA OF CONVERSION AND GREEK RELIGION BEFORE ALEXANDER THE GREAT

THE subject of this book obliges us to take a broad view of certain aspects of religious history from the time of Alexander the Great to the time of Augustine. Before we do so it is necessary that we should give some heed to earlier Greek religious development. We must do this for two reasons. First, before the conquests of Alexander there crystallized in Greece attitudes towards traditional and foreign worships which remained very important throughout. Secondly, in the same period certain specific concepts took shape which exercised a wide influence in the later centuries. It has been said that with the time of Alexander the formative period of Greek religious thought is at an end. This is not just; and yet it is true that the earlier time contains within itself the germs of the subsequent development, both in civic religion and in voluntary groupings for worship according to individual choice.

The cults of Greek cities in the fifth and fourth centuries B.C. neither were nor could be missionary. Following tradition, a city honoured certain deities to whom it looked for the satisfaction of its needs. That was its own affair. A friendly city might be empowered, a colony or a subject city might be compelled, to take some part in this worship, but it was primarily a domestic matter. As a city's interests expanded the range of its cults might also be enlarged; to take an example, Athens, which had Thracian connexions,

found a place for the worship of Bendis, a goddess
whom Athenians had met and worshipped in Thrace.
In time Bendis was, so to speak, naturalized and gave
a convenient pretext for an additional torch race.
There was in this nothing more revolutionary than
there was in the introduction of the potato and tobacco
into England from America. Special circumstances
might inspire the addition of a new cult. Thus it was
believed that Pan had appeared to Philippides when
in the menace of 490 B.C. he was sent from Athens to
Sparta and told him to ask why the Athenians paid no
heed to him though he had helped them often and
would do so thereafter, and his worship was accordingly introduced. Again, later in the fifth century B.C.
the Athenians felt the need of a public cult of a special
god of healing to perform functions earlier done by
various deities, and introduced the cult of Asclepius
from Epidaurus.

What has been said of local cults in Greece is
equally true of national cults. Just as an Athenian
qua Athenian turned to Athena on the Acropolis, so
an Ionian *qua* Ionian turned to Apollo on Delos and
a Greek *qua* Greek to Zeus at Olympia or Apollo at
Delphi. There was in all this a natural organic piety
and no element of conversion or tenseness of religious
emotion except in war or famine or plague and again
in the mystery dramas. Piety lay in a calm performance of traditional rites and in a faithful observance
of traditional standards.

Further, the object of piety for a Greek was something regarded as a possession of the Greek race, but
not as a unique phenomenon. Just as in describing
a strange people you spoke of *chresthai nomois* (using or

having customs), so you spoke of *chresthai theois* (having gods). The gods of a people were one of its attributes. It was commonly held that the gods of different nations were identifiable, that the Egyptians worshipped Athena and Zeus and Dionysus under other names. And yet that was a matter of speculation, however widespread, but on the face of it people used different selections from the list and different names and there was no reason why we Greeks should desire a Lydian to sacrifice to Zeus by that name rather than to his own god, unless he happened to be staying in our city. The Lydian might do it if he wished: Croesus consulted Delphi, and Darius in his letter to Gadates speaks of Apollo as the god who has proclaimed complete truth to the Persians: that means that his reputation has made its way, just as the oracle of Ammon in Libya acquired a reputation in Greece and was consulted like Delphi or Dodona.

While some foreign habits in religion, as for instance animal worship, appeared strange to the Greeks, there was among them no prejudice against alien worship, and a Greek in a strange country ordinarily paid homage to its gods. When the Athenians sent settlers to the Thracian city of Brea, shortly before 441 B.C., they ordered them to leave the consecrated precincts as they were and not to consecrate others. This indeed was probably not common practice in Greek colonies, and was partly due to the close connexions of Thracian with Greek myth and religion. Thus the Greek settlers at Naucratis in Egypt had their own precincts, the greatest being called the Hellenion, and made dedications 'To the gods of the Greeks'. In Egypt, and during the national crisis of the Persian war, the gods of the Greeks were strongly felt to be an aspect of their nationality. But there was no permanent feeling of superiority. The Greek point of view comes out very well in a legend inscribed in the temple of Athena at Lindos on Rhodes. When the Persian Datis was besieging Lindos in 490 the inhabitants came near the end of their supplies of water. Athena appeared in a dream to one of the magistrates and bade him to be of good cheer, for she would ask Zeus for water. The inhabitants asked for an armistice of five days, the period which their resources would last. Datis laughed and gave it, and the next day abundant rain fell on the acropolis, and the Lindians had enough while the Persians came to be in need. Datis in admiration dedicated all his personal ornaments to Athena. In a Christian legend he would have permanently transferred his religious allegiance.

The commercial importance of Athens brought with it a large influx of resident aliens. They were allowed to have their own associations to worship their deities: we possess the record of a permission granted in 333–332 B.C. to the merchants from Citium in Cyprus resident in Athens to acquire land to build a temple of Aphrodite (that is, their Semitic Aphrodite, often called Ourania), *just as the Egyptians have built the temple of Isis*. Contacts with such groups of foreigners, like foreign travel, might introduce individual Athenians to foreign cults. In one of these two ways certain privately celebrated rites of initiation and purification in the name of Zeus Sabazios and of Cotytto came to Athens from Thrace; those of the latter attracted attention enough to be the subject of mockery in comedy. Again, such rites were pursued in private, often through associations for worship, a form of organization which already existed for certain old traditional rites. Aristophanes refers to lamentation in 415 B.C. for Adonis (*Lysistrata*, 389 ff.). But serious development along this line does not come till later. Although private domestic cultus was free, the city-state did not tolerate serious interference with its religious homogeneity, as we see from the prosecution of Socrates for not believing in the city's gods and for introducing new daemonia.

This picture of piety without conflict and without missionary zeal represents an equilibrium reached at the end of a process. In the establishment of the known order after the collapse of Minoan–Mycenaean civiliza-tion, the Dorian invasion, and the Ionian emigration there was not a little conflict. To study that would take us too far from our present inquiry: we may, however, consider certain instances in which the prestige of a divinity was in historical times deliberately promoted.

Apollo was clearly an incomer: at Delphi and else-where his cult has imposed itself on earlier worships. The missionary zeal which accompanied this process appears in the fact that in many parts of Greece Apollo is not given local epithets but is called *Pythian* or *Delian* from the focal centres of his cult, in the existence of his *exegetai* or local representatives at Athens, and in the legends of his saints, Abaris, a Hyperborean, or citizen of the god's own Never-Never-Land, who carried the god's arrow about in different lands, and the equally mysterious Aristeas.

This enthusiasm produced a powerful institution which took care to emphasize its merits by sacred legend, as for instance the story of the deliverance of Croesus, the pious man saved at the last moment by the god, and the miracles whereby Apollo defended his shrine against the Persians, the bad end of Glaucus who tempted the god, and again an almost creedlike statement of the god's oracular power: 'I know the number of the sand and the measures of the sea: I understand a dumb man and I hear one that speaketh not.' Delphi could excite a warm personal devotion such as we see in Pindar, who never tires of praising Apollo, and it recognized such devotion: the poet enjoyed certain honours after his death. All this is the forerunner of the later religious propaganda by literature. But the current of feeling which produced the institution was canalized: and the dubiously patriotic tone of the oracle in the Persian war, and the rise of rationalism, weakened even the resultant product, though a crisis like the Celtic invasion in the third century B.C. could evoke a fresh awakening of religious emotion.

A remarkable illustration of literary propaganda in support of an immigrant deity is probably afforded by the curious hymn to Hecate inserted in the *Theogony* of Hesiod (411 ff.). She is the only daughter of Zeus: any man whom she favours acquires distinction in the market-place and victory in war. Her cult was probably an importation from south-west Asia Minor, and the hymn is written in its support. We see such deliberate promotion again in the case of the mysteries of Demeter at Eleusis. They are in origin agrarian rites belonging to a small community and administered by a small number of families. Such a rite would originally be limited to citizens of the community, but the Homeric *Hymn to Demeter*, which does not mention Athens and is almost certainly earlier than the end of the seventh century B.C., speaks to humanity (480 ff.): 'Happy is that mortal who has seen these things; but he who lacks the holy rites and has no share in them never enjoys a like happiness when dead and in the murky gloom.'

The collection of the Homeric hymns to which this belongs comes in the main from the seventh century B.C. and is of particular significance as showing the rise of other cults at that time. Of course any hymn must glorify the deity to whom it is addressed, but it is noteworthy that the recipients of elaborate hymns are Apollo, a new-comer, Dionysus, another new-comer of whom a miracle is here recorded, Demeter, whose mysteries are clearly lauded in a spirit of propaganda, and Hermes, who receives this special emphasis perhaps because his emergence as a dignified personal god from a heap of stones was relatively late. Further it should be remarked that these hymns are nearly contemporary with the movement of temple building which belongs to the seventh century (earlier there had been in the main private chapels in palaces and places for sacrifice in the open), and with the making of large cult-images as part of the normal furniture of worship, again a feature of the seventh century. For these two developments various causes can be suggested. The dissemination of the Homeric poems had crystallized anthropomorphic thinking, and Greeks were now moving freely as traders and mercenaries in the Near East and saw the gigantic temples and cult-images of Egypt, where they had a settlement at Naucratis, and Babylonia. Perhaps they felt that it would be well to give their own gods houses and shapes of equal dignity (might it not improve their power to aid?). In any case there were now greater economic resources than in the period immediately preceding and a greater instinct for self-expression. The Homeric hymns belong to the world of these changes: thus the *Hymn to Demeter* stresses (l. 270) the need for a big temple at Eleusis, and this did not exist till the seventh century. In any event there are clear signs of an upward movement of enthusiasm and vigour in religion, and this comes soon after the probable date of Apollo's establishing himself at Delphi.

Dionysus above all is gaining in this period, and the story of his cult as a whole affords the most manifest example of religious conquest. It represents a religious invasion from the Thraco-Phrygian stock. The adherents of Dionysus, mainly women, wandered on mountain sides. They were called by various names, such as Maenads and Bacchae, indicating their spiritual union with the god. In ecstasy they danced and rent animals and devoured the flesh raw: for them milk and honey seemed to gush from the ground,

> and all the mountain side
> Was filled with moving voices and strange stress.

The coming of this into Greek life seems to have produced one of those outbreaks of religious frenzy which at times spread like fever (such for instance was the Flagellant movement). It was new, and perhaps at the same time old: I mean that it may have meant the revival of ideas and even of rites current in Greece in the Minoan–Mycenaean age and possibly existing throughout in a subterranean way. This movement also was canalized by Delphi, itself now the bulwark of religious conservatism: Dionysus was given three months of the year at Delphi itself, and different cities had their regular Maenads.

All the same, the memory of the original character of the movement did not wholly die. Legend told of the resistance which Lycurgus and Pentheus offered to the god, and the *Bacchae* of Euripides gives a unique picture of the spirit of the faithful. The disguised god speaks before Pentheus like a Christian saint before a Roman magistrate: like many a saint he is vindicated by miracle. And Dionysus claims to have made his conquests not only among Greeks but also among barbarians; he has established his worship in Lydia, in Phrygia, in Persia, in Bactria, in Arabia, and throughout Asia. He wants homage and submission from every man young and old (206–9). 'The god will lead us thither and we shall not grow weary' (194). The tale of his birth as the chorus sings it is no piece of mythology: it is a *credo*, a *credo* of 'the things ever held' (71), sung by the god's willing servants who would fain see others be even as they are. This service means ecstasy and liberation and a curious sense of holiness which goes hand in hand with fierce hatred of the man who 'fights against god' (45, 325) and 'kicks against the pricks' (795). This is of that passionate temper of the Thraco-Phrygian stock which flames up later in Montanism. We feel for the moment in contact with a religion which could produce a church when we see in an inscription at Cumae 'No one may be buried here except one who has become a Bacchant'. Ordinary humanity felt the spell for the moment; but it had to return

To the old solitary nothingness.

What had been a liberation for all became a formal annual performance by a few women, taking its place in the ordinary cycle of regular rites. It retained indeed more interest in the private ceremonies conducted by cult associations for the god's honour. These included initiations and in the Hellenistic age and later had a substantial following. We shall find something like the early enthusiasm again in Italy in the second century B.C. (p. 71).

We have considered certain forces which had in the main spent themselves by the fifth century. We must pass to Orphism, in which salvation and personal religion emerge. By Orphism we mean a theology and a way of living which claimed to be based on a sacred literature passing under the names of Orpheus and Musaeus, singers of the mythical past. In the fifth century B.C. we hear of the *Orphic life* (abstinence from eating animal flesh and wearing woollen clothes, and contact with birth and death, respect for the holy writings, contempt for the body as the soul's tomb, and a general preoccupation with the expectation of a future life in which the soul will enjoy happiness thanks to discipline and initiation on earth). The early sacred literature appears to have taken shape in the sixth century and largely at Athens. Its emergence is the product of social unrest and of a religious anxiety which showed itself in a desire for purifications: of this we have a record in the puzzling but not entirely legendary story of Epimenides, the Cretan who was said to have been called in by the Athenians to give advice in time of plague. It was a period of sick souls. The tone of the literature is prophetic in the Jewish sense of the word: it addresses humanity as foolish, misled, offspring of earth, and the like. A curious reflex of this character of Orpheus is seen in the plot as we know it of the lost *Bassarai* of Aeschylus. Orpheus would not honour Dionysus, but regarded the Sun, whom he called also Apollo, as the greatest of deities. He rose at night and would wait on Mount Pangaion to see the first rays of dawn. As a result Dionysus caused his worshippers to tear him limb from limb. Here Orpheus is the lonely prophet.

This literature exercised wide influence. Obscure as the chronological evidence is, we may with fair confidence hold that it influenced Pythagoreanism. Its ideas exercised a fascination on the mind of Pindar. In his second Olympian ode and in fragments of his *Laments* (probably all from one) he gives a picture of the after life which is in the main Orphic, though like Plato later he has substituted righteous conduct for initiation as a qualification for happiness, and though again a comparison with his other utterances on the topic shows that he is employing pictorial language which must not be taken literally as a statement of conviction. Euripides, though not a believer in these things, shows time after time that he felt their attraction, and Plato reveals no little knowledge of Orphic literature and something like that mixture of fascination and abhorrence which Catholicism inspires in some to-day. More important for our purpose is that Aristophanes in the *Birds* parodies some of the ideas and the style of Orphic cosmogony (which implies that a reasonable proportion of his audience would see the point of the parody), and Alexis, a fourth-century writer of comedy, says in describing the contents of a bookshop, 'There is Orpheus, Hesiod,

Epicharmus, and writings of all sorts'. At the same time it must be observed that Plato in the *Apology* makes Socrates put before the jury two views of what may be expected after death, either dreamless sleep or converse with the wise men who have gone before. There is no hint of reward or punishment, and in the funeral oration of Pericles there is no word of any hereafter.

This literature could lead to a rejection of one's old life and the entering on a new life, which is conversion. Did it generate a sect? The question requires a definition. When we speak of a sect the idea which arises is that of a stable community. This idea is based first on the established schools of philosophers beginning with Pythagoras, who founded a sodality with a real feeling of solidarity, and then on the organization of cult-societies and of the Christian Church. What is certain is that there was this literature with its prescriptions for life and for rites, that there were the rites, and that there were priests to perform them, and both devotees who lived an Orphic life and others who while not doing so came to or employed an Orphic priest from time to time.

Theophrastus, in his character of the Superstitious Man, says that he goes once a month with his wife and children (if his wife is too busy, he takes the nurse) to the Orpheotelestai *telesthesomenos*, which would ordinarily be translated, 'to be initiated'. There, however, we have to remember the more general use of *teletai* for any kind of rite and in particular for purification: that is no doubt the sense here, for while initiation admits of grades it is not normally capable of repetition, and what we know of Orphic ceremonies points to a purification of the soul by ritual rather than a reconstitution of it by sacrament. This professional ministrant is known to us also from Plato's description of the way in which people with books of Orpheus and Musaeus swarm at the doors of rich men and undertake by spell and rite to put away their sins and their ancestors' sins, making much of a heaven of perpetual drunkenness and a hell of perpetual mud (*Republic*, p. 364): a papyrus fragment of one of their books has been found at Gurob. It is clear that many might have recourse to such ministrations on occasion without being formally members of a special sect. The ordinary Greek was familiar with the idea that under certain circumstances a purification was necessary: the superstitious man was the man in whom this became an obsession. Just so to-day the ordinary man knows of germ life and is aware that vaccines and inoculations are necessary under certain circumstances, and a hypochondriac might conceivably frequent quacks for continual inoculations. It is noteworthy that Theophrastus does not speak of the Superstitious Man as going to take part in the monthly services of a confraternity: had it been so he would hardly have failed to enlarge on the point with ridicule such as that which Demosthenes heaps on the processions connected with the initiations (probably the initiations in honour of Sabazios) conducted by Aeschines and his mother.

Is the continued existence of the professional type of initiator possible without some kind of sect? The answer is probably *yes*. Such knowledge can be handed from father to son (or mother to son, as the analogy of Aeschines reminds us), or passed from one man to another (sometimes bought, as magic is from any one other than one's father in the Trobriand Islands), or acquired straight from the books and experience. The rarity of professional clergy to consult in antiquity left an opening all the time for private quacks, oracle-mongers (who could, of course, be employed by a city as well as by an individual), purifiers, exorcists, and the like: and it was extremely easy for cults to be handed down in families and for private mysteries to arise and to continue.

Nevertheless, there are certain indications pointing to the possible existence of Orphic communities. Porphyry preserves a fragment of the lost *Cretans* of Euripides in which the spokesman of the chorus of prophets of Idaean Zeus says:

> 'I have lived a pure life ever since I became an initiate of Idaean Zeus and celebrated the thunders of night-loving Zagreus and his meal of raw flesh, and held on high the torches for the Mountain Mother and, being hallowed, was called a Bacchos of the Curetes: I wear raiment of pure white, and shun human birth: no coffin I touch: all food with life in it I have kept from me.'

This is an idealized picture of a supposed antecedent of Orphism: perhaps the reality was something like it. The Gurob scrap includes an invocation of the Curetes and the password *There is one Dionysus*. Again, certain gold lamellae (pieces of inscribed foil) found in graves of the fourth and third centuries B.C. at Petelia in south Italy give quotations from an Orphic poem telling the dead man what to say and do and the formulas recur in texts of the second century A.D. They remind us of the burial-place for Bacchic initiates. Further, we have a book of Orphic hymns which refers to the officers of a sodality. It is almost certainly Imperial in date and may be a purely literary product of the Pythagorean revival, or again (since the terms of membership are Dionysiac, and Dionysiac cult-societies flourished then) it may well belong to a Dionysiac society which has appropriated Orphic ideas and phrases: it is notably un-Orphic in its thought, which shows no trace of otherworldliness. The fixed organization of these as we find them over a wide geographical range, their fixity of usage (Apuleius can say of a symbol that the initiates of Liber present in court will know what he means; p. 114 later) are most naturally explained as resting on a sacred literature, and some of that literature could be Orphic. *Hieroi logoi*, sacred books, are expressly mentioned in a Ptolemaic text about those who initiate for Dionysus: and a roll perhaps representing one appears in the pictures of the Villa Item at Pompeii. There is so far no unquestionable evidence of an organization or a spirit in Orphism comparable with that of the Pythagoreans. One Pythagorean could recognize another by certain signs and passwords, like those required for admission to certain mystery worships, and any Pythagorean knew the standard 'The master said'. At the same time the ideas of Orphism involved an awareness of otherness from the world and might here or there at any time generate a sect. But it never conquered the nation or any large part of it. It never had the success of Buddhism. The Greek temper was not the right soil for such a seed to grow to its own maturity. Instead it absorbed certain things, the idea of the soul as a unity, the same in life and after life, fundamentally different from the body, and perhaps immortal, the hope of a hereafter (conditioned now by individual merit rather than by ceremony), and for the most part it discarded the theology as an alien thing for which it had no use.

To sum up, Greece knew civic and national worship in which the individual had his part automatically, and also personal worship of choice. Delphi produced a seat of authority, Dionysus a religion which became stereotyped and sterile, Orphism an idea of conversion and a sacred literature but no church

III

GREEKS IN THE EAST AFTER ALEXANDER

IN the centuries which we have surveyed most Greeks were living in Greek surroundings, either in old Greece or in the colonies which had the normal civic life and were politically concerned with one another and with the motherland, the natives around them affording a field for trade or exploitation. Some Greeks were abroad as individuals, whether as mercenaries or as traders, and a few of these at Memphis intermarried with Egyptians and produced a mixed race, but in general a Greek was very eager to come home and end his days in familiar and loved surroundings. That is why exile, even while spent in another Greek city, was so heavy a penalty, and why those who had suffered it would go to any lengths of treason to secure their return. When Odysseus preferred his return to Ithaca to immortality on Calypso's island he was true to the spirit of the Ionian Greek, the most travelled of all the Greeks.

In the fourth century more and more Greeks had to go abroad to earn a living, and the old order in politics was visibly bankrupt. Philip set the seal on this bankruptcy by his victory at Chaeronea in 338, which marks the end of a chapter.

Alexander's conquest of the Persian Empire opens another. The new order required thousands of Greeks as soldiers or officials. Many of them married women of the land and settled. Their descendants would have more and more native blood in each generation, and might in time become wholly un-Greek in physical type and law and custom, as for instance at Doura-Europos, a military colony on the Euphrates known to us from the excavations of Cumont and Rostovtzeff. We must not, however, generalize from this: at Susa the Greeks remained Greeks, although the chief deity was the native goddess Nanaia, who was also Artemis. Greek culture commonly remained dominant because of its social status. Its language, its art, to some extent even its divine names had prestige because they were those of the governing classes.

Greek and Oriental ways and beliefs were thus brought into intimate contact. Some Greeks became completely absorbed in native *milieux*, some natives in Greek. On both sides cult was a part of culture. Accordingly the normal Greek attitude was one of intelligent interest and acceptance while on the spot, the native was one of indifference, at most of acceptance of name-equivalents and language. On both sides religion was essentially static. Greek religion was a possession of the race but not, like Judaism, a unique possession and, unlike Judaism, it was not fostered and guarded by a professional class. Other Eastern religions had such classes but not the same spirit nor the same diffusion of interest through the nation. In Egypt, Babylon, and Persia, in the priestly principalities of Syria and Anatolia, the individual was a member of a social unit whose relations with the supernatural were a collective interest in the hands of the king or of hereditary specialists. His wants were thus satisfied. Why should those of others be? The prophetic zeal of Zarathustra, the revolutionary enthusiasm of Akhnaton, the systematization of Hammurabi, are just incidents, momentary ripples on the placid sea of Eastern thought. The Persian Empire had in religious matters no policy save toleration. Artaxerxes II set up images of Anahita in Babylon, Susa, Ecbatana and established the cult in Persia, Bactria, Damascus, and Sardis, but there is no word of compulsion or propaganda, and on the other side there is the letter of Darius reproving his satrap Gagates for raising tribute from the holy gardeners of Apollo and the sympathetic attitude of Darius towards the rebuilding of the temple at Jerusalem, the favour later shown to Ezra, and the homage paid by Cyrus to Marduk and by Cambyses to Neith at Sais.

If the Persian Empire thus possessed no deliberate policy in religious matters, the same is true of the successors of Alexander except in so far as cultural policy carried with it religious policy. Some attempt to find a religious point of union is perhaps to be seen in the first phase of the cult of Sarapis, to which we shall come, and in the numerous cults of 'all the gods' in new cities. The Seleucid dynasty which ruled Syria and the hinterland and much of Asia Minor sought to base their power largely on the Greek city-state. Consequently they built large temples to Greek gods and at one point attempted forcibly to hasten the process of hellenization which had gone far in Judaea, at that time from a cultural standpoint an alien corridor in their dominions. They had, however, no bigoted policy, as we see from their liberality to priests and temples in Mesopotamia. Their policy was natural and (apart from Judaea) easy, for Syria and Asia had long been open to Greek influences and in neither was there any sort of national unity or religious organization. In both the unit was local and not ethnic, and

unification could proceed on a Greek basis. Hellenization in religion therefore made great headway. The language of cult commonly became Greek. At Palmyra
later the vernacular was used but the architecture
was Graeco-Roman. New cult-legends were made
bringing these worships into relation with Greek myth
and history. Old religious forms survived—ritual
prostitution, sacred stones, fish and dove taboos,
castration and other self-mutilations, hereditary sacer-
dotalism and a dependent feudalism, but a Greek
veneer was superimposed.

The Ptolemies in Egypt ruled a narrow strip on
each side of the Nile which was essentially a unit in
which religion was in the hands of a closely organized
hierarchy. The situation had to be accepted and
regulated. The Ptolemies patronized and controlled
the priesthood and in Alexandria and Ptolemais
fostered Greek culture. For a moment, in the establishment of the cult of Sarapis, they appear to have sought
to find a meeting-place for the two racial elements:
but this policy was not continued. There was of course
a certain amount of convergent development; the
native priests commonly learned Greek and accepted
equations of Egyptian with Greek deities, giving the
names side by side in their calendars of festivals (there
is one at Sais of about 300 B.C.) and in Greek forms
of temple oaths. The Greeks in their turn built
few substantial temples for their own deities outside
Alexandria, Ptolemais, and Naucratis. In these and
in private cult associations they worshipped Greek
gods but commonly they paid their devotions to the
native gods. That is to say, they offered sacrifice or
caused it to be offered for them, they made votive

offerings in bronze or terra-cotta (a habit which called forth the production of new art types), they sought cures and oracles and made acts of homage, often engaging in pilgrimages for the purpose. But there was little real interpenetration. The Greeks (that is to say the settlers and those of the later generations whose cultural orientation was Greek) accepted Egyptian cults in a matter-of-fact way: the priests made official returns in Greek, but their liturgy was conducted in Egyptian and as early as the end of the third century B.C. a nationalistic spirit is apparent in them.

In all this development there is no element of conversion, none of self-surrender. Usually we have simple adhesion involving little emotion. There is in this one feature of interest for us, that it implies a piety of individual relationship and not of corporate relationship, not that of a citizen to his city gods. The only phenomenon involving a self-surrender would be the occasional Greek who being at Hierapolis in Syria at the time of the great festival might take full part in it, like the native pilgrims, and brand himself or even in a sudden enthusiasm castrate himself and become a servant of the goddess like her local eunuch priests; Catullus (poem LXIII) tells of a young Greek who castrated himself in honour of Cybele and Attis. For the subsequent expansion of cults from the Near East in Greece and in the West no worships are of great importance except those which were substantially translated into Greek and remade with Greek elements into cults which retained an Oriental flavour but were divorced from their original cultural and religious setting.

The chief of these is the cult of Sarapis, who carried

with him as associates Isis and (in a minor capacity) Horus and Anubis. The name Sarapis indicates that the god is a hellenized form of Osorapis of Memphis, the dead Apis calf believed to have become an Osiris after death and after the due funeral ritual (just as any man might). He was worshipped earlier at Memphis, perhaps in an anthropomorphic type, and known to Greeks there before the Ptolemaic régime. Ptolemy I with the Egyptian priest Manetho and the Eleusinian exegete Timotheus as advisers made from this the cult of Sarapis in Greek form at Alexandria, originally perhaps as a meeting-place for Greeks and Egyptians, perhaps as a suitable concomitant of the new dynasty (we must recall not only Akhnaton but also the temples which each Pharaoh built to honour the gods and to commemorate himself). A liturgical book in hieroglyphics is mentioned by Apuleius, *Metamorphoses* xi. 22, as used in the mysteries at Corinth and the ritual awakening of the god each morning was done in Egyptian, but paeans were composed for him in Greek by Demetrius of Phaleron and remained in use long afterwards. The new god was given the associates of Osiris (Isis, Anubis, and Harpocrates), and the group attained widespread worship. Sarapis soon attracted attention: Menander, who died in 293/2–291/0 B.C., says 'Sarapis is a holy god'.

Furthermore Isis acquired new mysteries. These are to be distinguished from the old drama of mourning for the dismemberment and disappearance of Osiris and of joy for his finding by Isis and her putting together of his scattered limbs, of his solemn obsequies, trial and acquittal and installation as king in the underworld. This was in the new temples done annually: in Egypt it had been performed in certain temples or chapels daily in a ceremony of twenty-four hours, each of which commemorates the story. This drama was performed before all who cared to be present and not before those being initiated on a special occasion. Juvenal speaks of 'the cry of the people when Osiris is found', and we know a number of parallel rites so performed before the whole body of the faithful, who have assisted at them before and will do so again. With reference to this celebration it should be noted that only one of the Egyptian dramatic festivals, that in Athyr, passed into general use outside Egypt. Sarapis has a separate festival on 25 April at Rome, in April at Naxos. Our one full source for the newer mysteries is Apuleius, who describes in a veiled manner other ceremonies of initiation in which an individual believer, after preparation and purification, passed through the elements, saw the underworld, was reborn, was dressed as the Sun and, being presented to the body of the faithful (not present during what preceded), was adored by them as for the moment divine (Ch. IX). That is novel. There is in old Egypt no initiation of individual laymen: those 'admitted to the adyton' are apparently, with rare exceptions, priests, and it must not be forgotten that happiness in the hereafter depended on the ritual performed after death and not on the fact that the dead man had taken part in the ritual dramas in his life. The actual rites used are perhaps related to those performed on the king succeeding to the throne of Egypt: they are certainly related to those thought to be performed for the benefit of a dead man. All three mean in a sense 'this mortal must put on immortality'.

We do not know when or where these mysteries arose: but it is likely that they arose at Alexandria, and it is not improbable that they did so early in the Hellenistic period. This Graeco-Egyptian blended cult, and the cult of Agathodaimon (the Egyptian Kneph, worshipped as the patron deity of Alexandria, who unlike Sarapis was not destined to become important in the world at large) are the only known cases of religious fusion in Egypt. They represent deliberate action by some one: the general cultural conditions here did not make for the spontaneous generation of such products. The difficulty which we have in relating the new mysteries to the Egyptian background suggests that they were not a natural unconscious growth; this is the first instance of such a development and lacked precedent. Further, we have a document giving the praises of Isis and Osiris in Greek which appears in inscriptions of Ios and Cyme, in poetic paraphrases on Andros and at Cyrene, and in a summary in Diodorus Siculus i. 27. It represents an accommodation of the Egyptian style to Greek ideas; in it Isis speaks of herself as having written down the sacred story or rite which the initiates hold in reverent dread. I suspect that in all this we have to see the influence of Ptolemy, Timotheus, and Manetho, and it must not be forgotten that the last wrote a history of Egypt for Greeks. There was a particular religious need to meet. The Greeks were familiar with initiatory ceremonies which guaranteed to the participant happiness hereafter: their own ceremonies—as those which Timotheus knew so well at Eleusis—were, apart from private initiations, bound to particular spots in the motherland. The Greeks were impressed by

Egyptian religious tradition and anxious to know its meaning and use its sanctities. So a new cult was needed. The process is in a sense comparable with the development of Christianity. There, too, events conspired to detach an effective element of Eastern religion from its periphery: after its detachment it could grow in the outer world.

Sarapis is a classic instance of a process which we cannot yet elsewhere follow in the same detail. Yet it is clear that Adonis, who had already shown himself at Athens, became fully hellenized. In another case a process which had begun before the Hellenistic period was completed in it. The Greek Mother Cybele was known to the Greeks from early times; her ritual might excite hostility, as perhaps at Athens, but it could be hellenized, as early at Ephesus. Similar figures appear all over Asia Minor (for example, Ma in Cappadocia) and to a Greek were all recognizable. Her consort, Attis, became familiar early in the Hellenistic period, and his legend was discussed by Timotheus (possibly the Eleusinian whom we have met in Egypt): Attis also acquired mysteries, and a formula which survives from them indicates the presence in them of Eleusinian influence. The chief seat of the cult was Pessinus. When the cult of Cybele and Attis moved westwards Greek was its liturgical language: Greek acquired a canonicity which it retained in the Roman world, in which the cult was to play so great a part to the end of ancient paganism.

We may now consider another composite product, Mithraism, for though in its familiar form it does not appear before Roman times its origins clearly go back to this period. The Persian rule had brought groups of Magi into those towns at least in Asia Minor where satraps or garrisons were placed, for the presence of a Magian was necessary at every sacrifice. In Cappadocia, Commagene, and Pontus (just as farther East in Armenia, to which the Greeks did not penetrate extensively in the Hellenistic age) there must have remained a not inconsiderable Persian element, for an inscription in Cappadocia speaks of the wedding of Bel (the local god) to 'his sister, the Mazdyasnic religion', personified, and this may point to an actual festival commemorating the official acceptance of Iranian worship and we know of the presence of Magi in this region; in Commagene there is on the Nemrud Dagh the funerary monument which its king Antiochus I erected for himself 'in accordance with the ancient teaching of Persians and Greeks': the gods honoured have both their Persian and their Greek titles. In Pontus there is the great temple of Anaitis, Omanos, and Anadates at Zela, and the royal dynasty bears the name Mithridates from the god. In these kingdoms Persian religion is, so to speak, the Establishment—or rather *not* Persian religion in its entirety as it existed in ancient Persia, but the religion of the priestly caste with Greek and other accretions. There were other Magi scattered over Asia Minor and in Egypt. They and their descendants were not repatriated: they would live on and have children. We learn under the Empire of the cult of the Persian Anaitis at Hierocaesarea and elsewhere in the land of Lydia, as again of the great temples at Zela in Pontus and at Akilisene in Armenia, both distinguished by extensive temple prostitution, which suggests a considerable Babylonian or other alien element in the cult or fusion with local deity and custom; we know *Lydians called Persians* at Hypaepa and Hierocaesarea: they did sacrifice, wearing tiaras and uttering Persian prayers, it being thought that the wood for the offering caught fire when their spells were spoken over it.

The phrase italicized implies that these men were not of Persian blood but men adopted into the nation, just as no doubt in the Mithraic mysteries initiates were when they reached the grade of *Persa*: again at Aria-ramneia in Cappadocia an inscription of the first century B.C. or A.D. records that one Sagarios son of Magaphernes 'became a Magos for Mithras'. Dion of Prusa (xxxvi. 39 ff.) quotes a 'song of the Magi': it is a legend of the repeated destruction of the universe, containing Stoic elements and probably due to a Magian (born or adopted) who seized on elements capable of being combined with his own beliefs, just as Philo seized on Logos speculation. This Magianism is detached from its national and cultural setting: its representatives can do their sacrifice and perhaps practise a little of what *we* call magic for private persons (the interpretation of dreams, necromancy, and spells to secure the affection of others or to do them harm). They may remain, so to speak, simple practi-tioners of the occult with a reputation for special power. Or they may develop a message. We have references to Magian asceticism and in particular to their abstinence from meat, which is clearly at variance with Zoroastrianism, which regarded any mortification of the body as evil and worthy of punishment. We are naturally inclined to discount these as due to the Greek tendency to predicate such practices of the holy men of any nation sufficiently remote, or to the impression made by the obvious otherness of Magianism, but they may well describe genuine development on alien soil.

Development there certainly was, for under the Empire we find mysteries of Mithras, in which he is detached from his Persian setting and made the central figure of a cult centring in initiations with a priesthood of the type, common in cult-societies, of men who have passed through the various grades. This product has something from Babylon (the concept of the heavenly zones through which the soul passes), something from Greece (as for instance its art-type, and the framework of the cult-society), and has almost certainly come through Asia Minor, where Greek and Persian ideas could fuse. It was notably capable of variation and of assimilating rites (as sometimes the *taurobolium*), contacts with other deities (as Hecate, and, in the Rhineland, occasionally local deities) and legends. It spread quietly: according to Plutarch, *Pomp.* 24, its first known appearance was as practised by the Cilician pirates in Lycia. What it owes to its Persian origin is not quite clear: the communion certainly, the washings, the concept of cosmic opposites, the figures of Mithras and Ahuramazda and occasionally Ahriman, and Aion, perhaps the animal masquerading. Here, as with Sarapis and Isis, we have to reckon with something picked out of a foreign ensemble and adapted for wider circles.

These products of genuine fusion had a great and important history which will concern us later. Here I would emphasize again their Greek character. The older ideas were not dead: there were waves of conservation, as for instance the emotion which grew up after Apollo's supposed defeat of the invading Gauls. We may conclude this chapter with a record of the attempt which one Eastern religion possessed of a theology and a will to conversion made to influence the Greek world. The Indian king Asoka says in the thirteenth of his rock edicts:

> 'And this is the chiefest conquest in the opinion of His Sacred Majesty, the conquest by the Law of Piety, and this again has been won by His Sacred Majesty both in his own dominions, in all the neighbouring realms as far as 600 leagues where the Greek (Yona) King named Antiochus dwells, and north of that Antiochus to where dwell the four kings severally named Ptolemy, Antigonus, Magas, and Alexander; and in the south the realms of the Cholas and Pandyas, with Ceylon likewise.'

The kings have been identified as Antiochus II or possibly I of Syria, Ptolemy II, Antigonus of Macedon, Magas of Cyrene, and Alexander of Epirus. Magas gives the *terminus ante quem* 258. Asoka goes on to say:

> 'and here too, in the King's dominions, among the Yonas and Kâmbojas, among the Nâbhapamtis of Nâbhaka, among the Bhojas and Pitinakas, among the Ândhras and Pulindas (all in the North or Northwest of India), everywhere men follow His Sacred Majesty's instruction in the Law of Piety. Even where envoys of His Sacred Majesty do not penetrate, there, too, men hearing His Sacred Majesty's ordinances based on the Law of Piety and his instruction in that Law . . ., practise and will practise the Law. And again the conquest thereby won everywhere is everywhere a conquest full of delight. Delight is found in the conquests made by the Law.'

Again, in the second rock edict we read:

> 'Everywhere within the dominions of His Sacred and Gracious Majesty the King, as well as among his

neighbours, such as the Cholas, Pandyas, the Satiyaputra, the Keralaputra, as far as Ceylon, Antiochus the Greek (Yona) King or the kings bordering on the said Antiochus, everywhere has His Sacred and Gracious Majesty made curative arrangements of two kinds, curative arrangements for men and curative arrangements for beasts. Medicinal herbs, also, wholesome for men and wholesome for beasts, wherever they were lacking, everywhere have been both imported and planted. Roots, too, and fruits, wherever they were lacking have been both imported and planted.'

What was the effect of this remarkable propaganda? We do not know exactly what the religion of Asoka was, though it was clearly influenced by Buddhism. The adhesion of Yonas, Greeks, within the king's dominions need not be doubted, whether we do or do not believe the statement in the *Mahavamsa* that the missionary Dharmaraksita, sent to the Aparantaka country, was a Yavana. There is the Graeco-Buddhist art of Gandhara to show us the employment of Greek artists in the service of this religion, and it is likely that Greek settlers in the frontier provinces of India would be culturally absorbed, and that Buddhist influences reached the Greek dynasties ruling on the fringe of India.

But did these emissaries reach the West, and did they exercise influence? We have no direct evidence. The Oxyrhynchus invocation of Isis (discussed p. 150 later) equates her with Maia (i.e. Maya) in India and makes her mistress of the Ganges. There were considerable trade relations with India, and in consequence Indians reached the West: an Indian embassy came to Augustus, and we have a mime, with what purports to be an Indian dialect, but there are no dedications to Indian deities in the Graeco-Roman world and no terra-cottas reproducing their forms, easily as they might have appealed to the Hellenistic taste for the exotic. Brahman asceticism was known, and in fact became a literary commonplace, but Indian religious thought was not, in spite of the philosophic tendency to find concealed wisdom in all or any non-Greek traditions. Similarities have been noted between the mysticism of Plotinus and Buddhism, and influence is possible, but must at the moment remain very questionable. The Greek had like other men little ability to get under the skin of any alien people and he was only too ready to see in them merely those features which he had come to regard as typical of all races on the circumference of the world. Cultural contact is shown by Indian borrowings in astrology and art (Asoka's father had asked Antiochus I for the visit of a Greek philosopher, unfortunately in vain), but the only certain debt of Greece to India is in folk-tale, above all in animal fables, and here Greece received what it did early, certainly by the third century B.C., perhaps by the fifth, and it is possible that Persia was the intermediary. Buddhism was known in Mesopotamia in the time of Mani, but there is no sign of knowledge of it farther West till later.

On the whole, it is likely that Asoka's missionaries never reached their goal, or if they reached it effected nothing. The history of religion is the poorer for the loss of what might have been an epoch-making contact of ideas.

IV

THE OPPOSITE CURRENT

WE have considered the contacts of individual Greeks and of Greek dynasties with Eastern religions in the East. We have now to pass to the results of the settlement of Orientals and orientalized Greeks in the older Greek world. There is a radical difference between the acceptance by a Greek living on alien soil of the cults which he there found and his adhesion to such cults if transplanted to his own soil. The first need not be more than *noblesse oblige* and conformity: the second involves deliberate choice.

Merchants settling in a foreign port tended to form a compact group. We know the 'Romans' (really Italians) at Delos, the Tyrian community at Puteoli, the *stationes* of various nations at Rome and at Ostia, and other associations of the same type. Such groups would commonly carry on their hereditary cults: we have noted how permission to do this was at Athens given to the Egyptians and to the Cypriots. It was no doubt in this way that Isis was brought to Eretria: a dedicatory inscription of the third century B.C., or at latest of the beginning of the second, in the Iseum there runs thus: 'The Egyptians to Isis.' The bearers of the cult would often be Greeks who had lived in Egypt or men of mixed stock: the actual Egyptians would at least be men who used Greek and thought in Greek, and like their predecessors at Athens would have to pay their devotion to figures of their Pantheon like Isis in an individualistic way. They could not transfer the system with its great temples devoted to groups of deities. A little later, in 128/7 B.C., Achaeus of Hierapolis in Syria built a small temple for Hadad and Atargatis on Delos, from which a civic cult developed. At Rome the cult of the Syrian deities on the Janiculum was in the main a cult by Syrian immigrants living near at hand.

A cult may be introduced in this way. It may again be brought by an individual and sometimes with the conviction of a divine command. Thus in 258/7 B.C. one Zoilus of Aspendus wrote to Apollonius, the powerful finance minister of Ptolemy II, saying that Sarapis had more than once ordered him in a dream to sail over to Apollonius and tell him that a temple of Sarapis must be built and a priest established in the Greek quarter of a city whose name is lost. Zoilus begged Sarapis to excuse him and then fell sick and undertook if healed to do as he was bidden. He recovered and then a man came from Cnidus and set about building a Sarapeum on the spot in question, but was forbidden by Sarapis. Zoilus went to Alexandria and still shrank from speaking to Apollonius; so he had a relapse for four months. He now urges Apollonius to do what is necessary 'that Sarapis may be gracious to you and may make you much greater with the king and more glorious and give you also bodily health. Do not therefore be afraid of the cost, thinking that the matter will involve you in great expense: you will be able to do it on a very profitable basis, for I will assist in supervising the whole affair.' How much or how little religious sentiment there is in this we cannot say, though we can hardly doubt that Zoilus hoped to bring himself to the notice of the authorities and perhaps to secure profit out of his helpfulness in the building operations.

Two points deserve particular attention. First, the story which Zoilus tells is notably like the legend of the bringing of the image of Sarapis from Sinope to Alexandria. According to it, Ptolemy I had a vision of a divine figure commanding that his image be brought to Alexandria: then, says Tacitus, Ptolemy took advice but did nothing till the vision reappeared and threatened him and his kingdom with destruction unless he obeyed. Then Scydrothemis the ruler of Sinope refused to give up the image, in spite of tempting offers, and he in his turn was visited by a threatening dream: as he still delayed, various disasters and sicknesses befell him. Finally, thanks to another miracle, the statue was brought away. This is no doubt the official story. Of course dream commands are common in this and in other cults (for instance, the hero Naulochus and the Thesmophoroi appeared thrice to a man of Priene *c.* 350 B.C., enjoining the worship of the hero and indicating the spot) and divine chastisement for delay is a familiar motif: but the coincidence here suggests that Zoilus is playing off on Apollonius a variant of the canonical legend.

Secondly, this competition with the Cnidian is instructive. We shall consider later the selectivity which Isis shows (only those to whom she indicates her will may be initiated, or may go into the holy of holies of her temple at Tithorea): the story of David and Solomon affords an analogy for the inacceptibility of a particular man as temple-builder. What is most significant is that the new cult had in two generations acquired such momentum that in this port there were two rival temple-builders.

Another story of the introduction of the cult by an

individual is preserved by an inscription of the last quarter of the third century B.C. on a column in the first Sarapeum of Delos:

'The priest Apollonios made this record on the god's order. Our grandfather Apollonios, an Egyptian of the priestly class, brought his god with him when he came from Egypt and continued to serve him in accordance with tradition. He is believed to have lived ninety-seven years. My father Demetrius succeeded him and continued in the service of the gods, and for his piety was honoured by the god with a representation in bronze which is dedicated in the god's shrine. He lived sixty-one years. When I inherited the sacred things and devoted myself busily to the observances of piety, the god gave me an oracle in my sleep. He said that he must have a Sarapeum of his own dedicated to him and that he must not be in hired quarters as before, and that he would himself find a place where he should be set and would show us the place. And so it was. Now this place was full of dung, and it was advertised as for sale on a notice in the passage through the market-place. As the god willed it, the purchase was completed and the temple was built quickly, in six months. But certain men rose up against us and the god and laid a public action against the temple and me, for the infliction of punishment or fine. And the god made me a promise in my sleep: *We shall win.* Now that the trial is over and we have won in a manner worthy of the god, we render due thanks and praise the gods. Here is the poem of Maiistas on this theme.'

Then follows his hymn in sixty-five hexameter lines. It speaks of the countless miracles done by Sarapis and Isis, the constant protectors of the good, and passes to the story outlined in the prose preamble. This Apollonios ' sang of thy miracles every day and continually prayed thee to tell him clearly by night in his sleep where he should build thy temple, that thou mightest abide for ever established in thy shrine and not stay on alien soil'. The story proceeds as before with emphasis on the ease with which the structure rose, the earnest prayers of the priest to Sarapis to ward off the fates of death, and the god's reply:

> ' "Cast care from thy mind. No human vote shall destroy thee, for this action affects me myself and no man shall say that it prevailed against me: so be no longer downcast." And when the time for the trial came, the whole city hastened to the temples, yes, and all the multitudes of strangers from many lands to hear divine justice. Then did thou and thy spouse perform that dread wonder. Thou didst paralyse the wicked men who were bringing the action, making their tongues speechless within their mouths, so that no one praised their ability or the evidence which they had to give in support of their case. In truth by divine operation they stood like heaven-struck phantoms (*or*, idols) or stones. *And all the people in that day marvelled at thy power*, and thou didst bring great glory to thy servant in heaven-established Delos. Hail, blessed one, thou and thy consort who are the gods of our temple: hail much hymned Sarapis.'

Here we have a small cultus in an alien land, brought by an individual who at first conducts worship in hired quarters. Then the cult grows sufficiently to need an independent temple. The hymn does not mention it, but there was a society of worshippers, *Therapeutai*, who contributed: we have not merely inscriptions on the stone benches given by particular men but also a dedication, no doubt connected with the trial, 'The priest Apollonios and those of the *therapeutai* who contributed, to Victory'.

The way in which the opposition is described reminds us vividly of the way in which opposition to St. Paul's preaching is described in Acts. Its motive may well have been conservatism: its legal strength probably rested on the fact that Apollonios had not obtained from the popular assembly the authorization necessary for buying land for a foreign worship. Incidentally it should be remarked that the cult is said to have been introduced and carried on in accordance with ancestral custom. Yet it is clear that the worship introduced was not the original Memphite cult of Osorapis but the hellenized cult of Sarapis and Isis: even at this early time it took the credit of possessing immemorial antiquity.

Sarapis has vindicated himself by miracle: to be sure no one is converted. But the new god has now the cachet of success, and we find another private Sarapeum (the Sarapeum B) arising with various sodalities attached, *therapeutai, melanephoroi* (probably people who wore black during the mourning for the dead Osiris), and *Sarapiastai*. Towards 180 B.C. the cult became public: the offerings made in the official Sarapeum and Iseum went into the sacred treasury administered by the *hieropoioi*, and in 179 B.C. the alms given to Sarapis equalled those given to Apollo and far surpassed those given to Asclepius, Artemis, and Aphrodite. Further, now that the cult is civic we find as with most Greek cults (except mystery worships: a qualification to which we must return) priests who hold office for one year at a time. Sodalities made offerings in the public temple (the so-called Sarapeum C) as well as in their Sarapeum B: and the descendants of Apollonios still remained lifelong priests of the god in the original shrine, the Sarapeum A, as we know from an inscription which tells us how, after the Athenians became masters of the island in 167/6 B.C., the closing of this temple was ordered, but Demetrius, the priest at the time, obtained a favourable decision from the Roman Senate. This shrine then retained its character, and another text records the coming of one Horus from Kasion near Pelusium as assistant in the rite. But the civic cult was thoroughly Greek. Athens sent out a citizen of position each year as priest of Sarapis. There were also a *kleidouchos*, again an Athenian and a man of dignity, a *zakoros* or sacristan (who naturally could hold office for a number of years), *kanephoroi*, maidens of quality with processional functions, an *oneirokrites* who interpreted dreams, and an *aretalogos* who celebrated the god's wonders. The last two roles could be combined. They are functions directly related to the cult in Memphis and Alexandria: from the former we have the sign of a dream interpreter, 'I judge dreams, having a command from the god: good luck: it is a Cretan who judges these things'. Yet they do not form a discordant element in the thoroughly Greek appearance which the cult had assumed: at Epidaurus the priesthood both interpreted the dreams of sick persons sleeping in the temple and recorded the miraculous cures, and temples elsewhere preserved records of miracles and epiphanies (pp. 90–92 later).

The story of Delos is clear in its main lines, thanks to the exploration of the sites and to Roussel's study. Elsewhere in the Greek world things probably went in very much the same way except that there is no other evidence of conflict. The introduction of the cult into a city was no doubt generally due to immigrants (in which case there was first a cult-society, then a public cult by the side of which the society continued to exist), sometimes to the action of the city. This action has been thought to be inspired by political considerations, in fact by Ptolemaic influence; and it certainly does appear that Agathocles introduced the worship in Sicily on marrying Ptolemy I's daughter; but the Ptolemies did nothing about it during their period of influence at Delos, where the private cult emerges under Antigonid suzerainty. At the same time, while the Ptolemies did nothing from above, it was natural that the cities should take action of their own to win favour: this seems a probable explanation at Rhodes, Miletus, Halicarnassus, Athens, Ceos. Yet it is likely that the cult was often imported as filling a gap.

At Magnesia on the Maeander we have a law of the beginning of the second century B.C. regulating the civic cult of Sarapis: whether it actually describes its introduction is uncertain in view of the mutilation of the opening: we have a similar law at Priene of about 200 B.C. This is of special interest, for after prescribing the sacrifices and torches to be offered by the priest to Sarapis and Isis and Apis, it says (ll. 20–1) 'And let the temple administrator provide also the Egyptian who will join in performing the sacrifice in an expert way. And let it not be permissible to any one else to perform the sacrifice to the goddess in an inexpert way or without the priest's aid.' The cult is hellenized so far as may be, but technical competence is required: so we have a subordinate for the purpose, like the Etruscan *haruspices* whom a Roman magistrate would consult but would treat as hirelings. It means much that the priest is appointed by the city, as he is again at

Magnesia in Thessaly. At Eretria and at Athens the priesthood was an annual office.

Now this is particularly important as an indication that the cult was absorbed in the ordinary run of civic cults and also that it was not commonly in the wider Greek world at this time a mystery cult. A mystery generally demands permanent clergy, such as we know at Alexandria and such as Apuleius describes at Cenchreae and at Rome. All our references to the Isiac priesthood at Rome suggests a professional clergy living in the temple precincts. The conclusion to be drawn is, I think, that, while individual Italians returning from Delos might bring back with them an interest in the cult, the form which it took came from Alexandria. Under the Empire we find also a priest for life of Sarapis at Termessus, though we do not know whether his position was special and personal. It is not clear that initiations of the later type had formed a part of the cult outside Egypt in the Hellenistic period. The absence of a mention in the texts at Magnesia and Priene may of course be due to their fragmentary condition, but the nature of the priesthood is clear evidence to the contrary. Even the drama of Osiris at Athens may have been introduced, and was at least reshaped, as late as A.D. 63, and in Rome under Caligula. In any case the use of Soter and Soteira (Saviour god and goddess) for Sarapis and Isis refers to deliverance from perils by sea and by disease, and the deities are *saviours of all good men*.

Further, when we find the ceremonies of initiation described by Apuleius, they are not ceremonies for every one interested in the cult: they were expensive: Lucius spent all his money. The many who frequented the temples would know of such initiation as a privilege available for those whom the god or goddess designated by dreams and who could afford it: they would have seen the glorified initiate come forth to receive their adoration, or again watched the initiates of both sexes walk in procession at the Ploiaphesia (the ceremony of the opening of the sailing season) after the flute-player and before the priest, radiant with the pure whiteness of linen garb, the women with hair bound in translucent nets, the men clean shaven with shining heads, 'the earthly stars of great religion', making a clear sound with *sistra* (rattles) of bronze and silver and gold. They are like a confraternity with its special place in a procession of the Host.

Initiation was thus a restricted privilege. So again the *taurobolium*, of which we shall speak later, was expensive, and the men who recorded their initiation in a variety of mysteries were men of means. It was left for Christianity to democratize mystery. It expected liberality of the wealthy but gave its rites to the poor and needy, just as it gave to them the advantages of burial guilds and more: even a poor man's guild required subscriptions and was in danger of liquidation.

To sum up, the cult was for the majority of its worshippers not a mystery cult, and in many places in the Hellenistic period proper it was not a mystery cult at all. The uninitiated devotee might attend the public worship, might pray for help, might make his vows in sickness and pay them in health, might have sacrifice offered by the priest, might wear a ring with representations of the gods as an amulet, might put up private shrines or join in a cult association, might dine 'at the god's couch'. Isis was able 'to save the universe'. Such a claim of universalism can of course be made by a religion which at the same time holds that its means of grace are indispensable; *peace on earth to men of goodwill* can exist side by side with *he that believeth and is baptized shall be saved: he that believeth not shall be damned*. It was hardly so with the Egyptian deities. When Firmicus Maternus speaks of Isis and Osiris, he discusses the cult drama and not initiations; when he speaks of Sarapis, he mentions only sacrifices and prophecy (*Concerning the Error of Profane Religions*, 2. 13). Initiation in fact corresponds not to baptism but to some additional act of special devotion, such as joining the third order of St. Francis.

In the main the worship was a powerful cult which had approximated to the ordinary framework of life: this is exemplified by a dedication to Isis, Anubis, Bubastis, and Zeus Ktesios, the domestic god, on Delos, and by dedications to Zeus Kynthios associated with Sarapis and Isis in the Sarapeum C there. In Boeotia in the second century B.C. the temples of Isis and Sarapis were commonly used in the manumission of slaves, so often done in the form of a ceremonial dedication or sale of the slave to a deity; again, Pausanias, although he uses 'the Egyptian goddess' as a synonym for Isis (x. 32. 13) refers to her temples as though they were not exotic. Nor must we forget that at Tithorea Isis took over an old festival celebrated twice a year. No less Greek was the private cult in societies, which often started before the civic cult and commonly continued side by side with it. Such societies acquired legal personality and the right of owning property.

So Isis and Sarapis held the place of two new saints, with the attraction of freshness, the power of which we see now in the popularity of the cult of the Little Flower, St. Thérèse of Lisieux. Where there was conflict, as at Delos, there would be a situation in which something like conversion could take place, but in general there is no more than acceptance of what was brought in by immigrants or returning natives, or again copying of other neighbouring cities.

Our evidence shows that the Alexandrian cults obtained in this way a sure if hellenized position in Greek worship. Phrygian Cybele had in many places such a standing well before the beginning of the Hellenistic period. To what extent native practices and the new initiatory ceremonies and the *taurobolium* grafted themselves on the cult in the mainland and islands of Greece during the Hellenistic period we do not know: our information is much fuller for the Empire. The worship of Men, a moon deity from Asia Minor, in Attica is attested before the end of the third century B.C. by the presence of names derived from him.

There is now very interesting evidence for the rise of the so-called Syrian goddess (Atargatis) to civic importance. At Beroea in Macedon we have a dedication of the end of the third century B.C., 'Apollonides the son of Dexilaos, priest, to Atargatis the Saviour', and in A.D. 239 and 261 we have records of manumission 'to the Syrian maiden goddess', as she was then called. At Phistyon in Aetolia we have evidence of the cult in 204/3 B.C. It was perhaps brought back by Aetolian mercenaries returning home. Here again she was concerned with manumissions, and commonly bears the title *Aphrodita Syria Phistyis*, which indicates that it was felt that in spite of her foreign origin she had become Our Lady of Phistyon. Then there are two decrees of Thuria in Messenia of the earlier part of the second century B.C. The first relates to arbitration with Megalopolis: if it is successful, the names of all the *syndikoi* or representatives are to be inscribed on a stone pillar in the temple of the Syrian goddess. The second is in honour of Damocharis of Sparta, a benefactor of the city. He is granted various privileges and among them a front seat on the days of the mysteries and a leading place in the procession with the officials called *hieromnamones* and a share in all the amenities.

'Moreover, since, honouring both the worship of the Syrian goddess and our city, he promises to provide throughout his life the oil for the days of the mysteries, let the ephors who are colleagues of Menestratos dedicate a painted representation of him in the temple of the Syrian goddess with the following inscription: "the city of Thuria honours Damocharis".'

These texts are extremely important. Firstly, they show that the temple of the Syrian goddess was, so to speak, the cathedral of Thuria. Secondly, they are the first explicit evidence for mysteries of hers. Thirdly, the *proedreia* at the mysteries explains the theatres possessed by the goddess at Delos, at Baalsamin-à-Si, and elsewhere. We may with probability infer a dramatic re-enacting of some part of the legends told by Lucian. We know the cult of the Syrian goddess at Delos, Athens, and Aegeira, but though she became a familiar figure she did not bulk as large as Isis in the world as a whole.

Mithras seems not to have been thus brought by foreign groups; perhaps this is purely accidental and due to a paucity of contacts with Cappadocia and

Commagene. Slaves came thence, but Persian religion may have belonged mainly to a higher caste.

A stranger phenomenon in the Greek world was the Jewish Dispersion. The prophetic movement and the experience of the exile had created a conviction that Gentile religion was idolatry offensive to God, and at the same time that the day would come when God would be acknowledged and served by all mankind. The contact with Persia had generated or stimulated in many the belief that there was a world to come: in this there would be room not only for Jews but also for Gentiles who abjured their pagan ways, either by becoming proselytes (that is naturalized Jews) or, on the more liberal interpretation, by simple observance of the so-called Noachite commandments, which were held to be binding on all men. There resulted from this a missionary idea which is illustrated by the book of Jonah. Written probably towards the end rather than the beginning of the period 400–200 B.C., it describes the irresistible vocation of a Jew to preach repentance to the people of Nineveh (now a ruin, but good as a type of heathenism). The sailors of Joppa who manned Jonah's ship are Gentiles praying every man to his own god, but the storm causes them to fear God exceedingly and to make vows to him. Jonah's message is one of repentance, and its inherent rightness is vindicated against his peevish anger.

The Jewish Dispersion talked Greek and Latin (Greek predominated in the inscriptions of their catacombs in Rome) but was unique from its normally exclusive attitude towards alien religion which involved serious social bars (non-participation in festivals and in meat and wine which might entail idolatrous contamination) from its cohesion, in many cities from its numbers (certainly so at Alexandria and Apamea, and in those parts of Phrygia and Lydia where Antiochus the Great had about 200 B.C. settled 2,000 Jewish families); unique also from its possession of the synagogue with its sermons which would remind outsiders of a philosophical school rather than a temple. Under these conditions it could not be indifferent to its environment. Commonly it grew in the consciousness of the value of its peculiar beliefs which had arisen in prophetic teachings and in the experience of the exile: often it developed an eager desire to proselytize. We hear of many proselytes in Antioch and we know elsewhere of many 'fearers of God', who conformed with those commandments binding on all mankind and participated in the sabbath worship of the synagogue without either the privileges or the obligations of the real Jew and without the social condemnation which commonly rested upon the Jew. Acts xiii. 43–4 implies that many Gentiles might come to a synagogue when a famous preacher was expected, just as they would rush to hear Dion of Prusa or Lucian. Again, Judaism might take a quietist tone and live its life either in isolation or in recognition of cognate elements in contemporary thought.

But we find also, what we have learned to expect from the contact of Greeks with an Oriental national religion, first the recognition by Greeks of the god of the Jews as a fit object of worship and as capable of equation with a deity of their own (Zeus or Dionysus or Attis); secondly, the formation of new composite products as a result of give and take on both sides.

The god of the Jews (under the name Iao) is

prominent in magic papyri and in ancient curses as a god of power. Further, many who were not Jews respected some Jewish observances, notably the Sabbath, but also fasts, lamp-lighting, and some food rules. A normal pagan might well feel that there was something of value and use in customs so strenuously maintained, without being prepared to go to the drastic length of becoming a proselyte, which meant a complete renunciation of his past, an acceptance of heavy obligations previously not incumbent upon him, and not a little social disapproval or ostracism. The dedication of a *proseucha* or prayer-house in 102/1 B.C., found at Alexandria, was made 'to the great god who hears prayer' with the characteristic Egyptian 'great' (familiar of course also as an epithet in the Old Testament). At Tanais in the Bosporus, in Mysia (second or first century B.C.), and elsewhere there is a cult of Hypsistos, the Highest God (a common epithet of God in the Septuagint), by cult societies including in the Bosporus 'adopted brothers' and so probably by implication originally entirely composed of Jews and yet by now sufficiently assimilated to their environment to use once a formula of manumission ending with the common Greek phrase, 'under Zeus, earth, the sun'.

At Tanais the names are, except for Sambation and Azarion, non-Jewish and mostly barbarian: further, the group had priests (as well as the regular *presbyteroi*) and perhaps therefore a sacrificial cultus (which would to an orthodox Jew be illicit), and in texts of the third century A.D. it is sometimes called 'The association around the highest God and the priest N', which involves an un-Jewish intimacy with deity. Late in the fourth century A.D. we hear of a sect of *Hypsistarii* in

Cappadocia, survivors of this movement. The father of Gregory Nazianzen belonged to this before his conversion, and his son characterizes it as a mixture of Hellenic (i.e. Gentile) error and the humbug of the law, honouring fire (probably from the Persian element in Cappadocia) and lamps and the Sabbath and food regulations while rejecting circumcision. Similar believers existed in Phoenicia and Palestine, and even in the West. Again, we know in Cilicia a society of *Sabbatistai*, and there is evidence that a certain fusion took place between the cult of Jehovah as conceived by some of the Jews settled by Antiochus in Phrygia and the native cult of Zeus Sabazios. Such fusion was not then out of the question; the Maccabee movement had not yet come to heighten Jewish self-consciousness, and even the hierarchy at Jerusalem was very ready to compromise; in later times Philo had to complain of Jews who felt themselves to be emancipated. The Jews in Phrygia married Gentiles, and we later find the descendants of such marriages as priests of the Emperor's worship. This connexion with Sabazios is probably due to the similarity of name with Sabaoth, which to a man speaking Greek seemed to be a proper name in the nominative and not the genitive 'of hosts'. There are indications of this fusion at Apamea and in Rome.

In the last chapter we saw the formation of blended worships with a capacity for success in the world at large. We have here considered the way in which they were carried by migrants, commonly just as their own form of worship, and how in the Hellenistic period some of them acquired an important position even among the official cults of the city. One cause which has been noted, the desire to please the Ptolemies, applies only to the worship of Isis and Sarapis in areas where Ptolemaic favour was worth winning. There must therefore be other factors. At times it might be that the immigrant group if it attained full civic rights would surpass the old inhabitants in wealth and would therefore hold magistracies. Yet more often the issue must have turned on the attraction of novelty, and on the feeling that the old cults were in a measure outworn and ineffective, and the old deities unable to protect you in the immense new universe which had taken the place of the limited horizon of the city-state world, unable again to protect you against the universal power of Fate or the capriciousness of Fortune. Men of conservative temper were always restoring and enlarging old ceremonies, but it is doubtful whether except in Arcadia the populace shared their enthusiasm, and the new cults were presented in such a way as to have the merit of novelty without the defect of being too strange. To these problems we shall return in Chapters VI and VII.

V

THE PATH TO ROME

'AND so they journeyed towards Rome.' As Rome became first a world power and then the world power, merchants came in their hundreds, slaves in their tens of thousands, and others again who had gone forth from Rome as soldiers or traders returned with new ideas and beliefs. Let us take two concrete examples, which though later than the beginning of this development throw light upon it. An inscription at Puteoli dated 29 May, A.D. 79, says: 'The god Helios Saraptenos (that is the Baal of Sarapta between Tyre and Sidon) came on ship from Tyre to Puteoli. Elim brought him in accordance with a command.' Elim is like Apollonios of Delos. Again we have an inscription giving a letter sent by the Tyrians at Puteoli to their mother city in A.D. 174, which refers to the expense of the worship of their national deities as heavy on them with their now shrunken numbers. Inscriptions from the Syrian temple on the Janiculum show that its cultus was mostly an affair of Syrian immigrants, and this is true also of the priests and officers of the Roman cult society of Juppiter Dolichenus.

The part which slaves can play is familiar from the story of Naaman's Jewish handmaiden. We may recall the Syrian Eunus in Sicily, who claimed to have special revelations from the Syrian goddess and to know that he would be a king, wherefore his master brought him in to amuse guests after dinner by his prophecies, and the guests made him small presents, asking him to remember them when he should become king. Again, the returning soldiery sometimes carried back strange cults with them, as Sulla's soldiers perhaps carried Ma from Comana: it is said that their commander had a vision of her on his first march to Rome. Tacitus tells how as day broke on the desperate struggle before Cremona in A.D. 69, the soldiers of the third legion saluted the rising sun; 'That is the way in Syria' (*Histories*, iii. 24). The influence of trade appears in the fact that the Syrian festival of Maioumas became a civic celebration at Ostia and that as early as 105 B.C. there was a public temple of Sarapis at Puteoli: whether this is in any large measure due to returning Italians is however doubtful, for, although we have records of their interest in the worships of the Levant, the evidence on Delos indicates that the mercantile colony of Italians living there was at least in its domestic cultus fairly conservative.

New cults when they came to Rome entered an atmosphere different from that of the Hellenistic cities in which they had previously found acceptance. In those cities, indeed, as in Rome, public worship was a public concern, and we have seen occasional interference by the authorities against unwarranted innovation. In Rome this was far more systematic and thoroughgoing. The religion of the republic was a relationship between the State and the gods. The State did its part and looked confidently to the gods to do theirs. Further, the State took over the responsibilities of individual citizens and freed them from *religio*, uneasy fear of the supernatural, an emotion always latent and liable from time to time to break out in panic. The attitude of the State towards individuals was exactly like the attitude then of the head of a household to its members. The elder Cato, in his treatise on agriculture, gives this advice about the bailiff's wife, 'Let her not perform ceremonies or bid another do so for her without the command of her master or mistress. Let her know that her master does worship for the whole household' (ch. 143).

Rome's range of worships was not, however, fixed once and for all. In early days the cults of various conquered communities were absorbed, and other cults were from time to time introduced from abroad to satisfy popular emotion in time of panic: so for instance the Greek practice of putting the images of the gods on couches and setting a banquet before them, so again in the plague of 293 B.C. the cult of Aesculapius, in 217 B.C. Venus Erycina from Sicily, and in 205 B.C. the cult of the Great Mother Cybele from Pessinus. It is characteristic of the Roman instinct for government that there was a special commission (ultimately of fifteen) in charge of all foreign worship. In a time of stress men were liable to think that the traditional proceedings were inadequate: this feeling is exemplified by the burying alive of a Greek man and woman and a Gaulish man and woman in occasional crises. When the Great Mother came, what was imported was strictly speaking just a rite. The eunuch priests of Phrygian stock performed their ceremonies privately and the State derived the appropriate benefit. No Roman citizen might become a eunuch priest, and we hear of the banishment of a slave who castrated himself. At the same time the goddess received official sacrifices from the praetor who presided at the games given in her honour, and banquets for her festival were conducted by aristocratic Roman societies. (This corresponds to the annual civic priests of Isis in Greek cities noted earlier.) The Trojan legend helped to give her importance, and the *lauatio* or washing of her image in the Almo on 27 March certainly became a public ceremonial of the state in the time of Claudius, when the cult was fully naturalized. Thenceforward the *archigallus* was not a eunuch and was a Roman citizen. The public procession and dramatic ceremonies of the Mother's consort Attis were in time celebrated with great pomp as part of the State's religious calendar. The festival occupied six days. On 15 March 'the reed entered', on 22 March 'the tree entered', the 24th was the day of blood, the 25th that of joy, the 26th that of rest, the 27th the washing, but the first certain evidence for days other than the *lauatio* does not come till the time of Marcus Aurelius.

The calendar of Philocalus adds *Initium Caiani* as the name of the 28th. This may refer to the sanctuary of Cybele on the Vatican, perhaps to mysteries attached to the cult: it does not appear to have been an integral part of the cycle. In any case, we are in the dark as far as such mysteries are concerned, though there are undeniable indications that initiations existed. We know more of the *taurobolium*. The recipient descended into a hole dug in the ground and a bull was slaughtered over him: its blood dripped over him and he saw to it that it fell on cheeks and ears and lips and nose and eyes, actually catching some on his tongue. He was then adored by the onlookers. The rite may originally have been the sequel of the lassooing of a bull, as the term has been thought to indicate. The first inscriptional records tell us nothing of the meaning of the act, except that it was done on behalf of the

Empire: later we read that the recipient was 'reborn for twenty years'; later still 'reborn for ever'. Whatever the original meaning was, the rite was there as something which a devotee could undergo if he could afford the necessary bull (as also the *criobolium* if he could afford the necessary ram). Here again as with Isiac initiation there was the idea that it could not be done without divine sanction: the phrase *ex uaticinatione archigalli*, 'in accordance with the divination of the archigallus', occurs not merely in numerous records but also in a legal text (a *taurobolium* so conducted in Portus, the harbour of Ostia, for the Emperor's safety excused one from the duties of guardian, a fact which reveals anew the official recognition of this worship). At the same time it is to be noted that this ceremony was attached to the *Frigianum* or sanctuary on the Vatican and not to the old temple on the Palatine.

Around this rite there crystallized a great deal of feeling in the last days of paganism: an inscription on an altar found near St. Peter's records how a man performed the *taurobolium* and *criobolium*, scattered the darkness of twenty-eight years, and brought light again—the darkness being no doubt the time of Constans and Constantius, and the text a document of the Julianic revival. A modern man cannot but feel that the performance of so distasteful a rite must be the product of considerable religious devotion. But we have only to contemplate ancient superstitions regarding relics from gladiatorial contests to realize how intense was belief in the efficacy of blood, and the medicine of the Empire as of later times is full of nauseating remedies, composed of excrement and the like. Further, it must be noted that the earliest recorded *taurobolium* in the West (at Puteoli, A.D. 134) was in honour of Venus Caelesta (that is, Atargatis) and the rite occasionally attached itself to Mithraism. So, though Cybele's, it was not hers exclusively; and it had no basis in her myth and did not always take place during her festival. It was an act like sacrifice. People were attracted by having seen it (it drew a crowd), by the hope of getting special grace, by the desire to show loyalty to the Empire, by a desire to have prominence for a moment; perhaps at times by a desire to show that they could afford it.

We see here the gradual development of a cult which the State had accepted, its full expansion being in and after the Antonine period. It belonged to the *sacra publica* controlled by the commission of fifteen. This centralized authority is illustrated by inscriptions which show them as conferring the insignia of priesthood on priests of the Great Mother in towns other than Rome.

This is the perfect story of the Romanization of an alien cult. Other strange religions came in unobtrusively and if they attracted attention were liable to be suppressed by a magistrate acting on the Senate's advice, as what we should call a police measure. There was a particular zeal to prevent any sort of religious professional quack, of the type discussed earlier in connexion with Orphism, from getting a hold upon the popular imagination and disturbing the public tranquillity. The classic instance is that of 186 B.C., when a religious movement, suddenly discovered and thought to be a grave menace to public order and safety, was suppressed. According to Livy's account (xxxix. 8 ff.) a Greek had brought Dionysiac rites into

Etruria: he is described in the familiar way as making money out of popular superstitions, and performing nocturnal ceremonies. The ceremonies were originally given to a few and then spread widely with the added attraction of wine and banquets and mixed company by night. From Etruria it spread to Rome. There it was discovered through a chain of circumstances. The mother and step-father of P. Aebutius desired his undoing and the mother told him that when he was sick she had vowed that she would initiate him in the Bacchic mysteries as soon as he recovered. For ten days he must be chaste: then, after he had dined and bathed, she would take him to the sanctuary. His mistress Hispala Fecenia saved him from this, telling him of the dangers which would threaten him there, and then word having reached the consul, she was constrained to tell him all about this cult, though she avowed fear of the gods and much greater fear of the other devotees. Her account was that the temple had originally been one frequented only by women, to which no man was admitted and in which initiations took place on three fixed days in the year and different matrons were priestesses in turn. Then Paculla Annia from Campania changed everything, claiming that she did so on the advice of the gods. She initiated her sons, she transferred the ceremonies from the day to the night, and she substituted five initiation days a month for three a year. (It will be noticed that Hispala's account is different from that first given by Livy, in which the movement was from the beginning one in which the sexes were mixed.) Hispala then told of nocturnal licence (a characteristic of sects persecuted or suppressed), of prophesying in wild ecstasy, of miracle (torches dipped in the Tiber and brought out alight), of supposed carrying off of men by the gods. She said that there was a great multitude of followers, *almost a second people*. The authorities in fact feared that they had to face a mass-movement: the *second people* is very reminiscent of Christianity.

The guilty were punished, all temples which could not claim antiquity were destroyed: no such meetings were to be held in future at Rome or in Italy: but, if there were any who said that it was necessary for them to have a Bacchanal (a site given up to the cult), they should come to the praetor urbanus at Rome and when their case had been heard the Senate should decide (a quorum of one hundred present being obligatory during the discussion): no man was to approach the Bacchae without consultation of the praetor urbanus and a decision given by him with the approval of a quorum of the Senate. In the ceremonies which would thus be permitted for conscience' sake not more than five must be present, there must be no common chest, and no president of the rites or priest. The suppression was not complete in 181 B.C.

We see here a real movement of religious enthusiasm, with an idea of divine compulsion which even the State recognizes. The suppression was not for ever. A recent find at Tusculum has given us the list of the members of a college of initiates there in the first half of the second century A.D. arranged according to their religious rank; the list includes nearly five hundred names and the head was Julia Agrippinilla, her slaves and freedmen being among the members. Such associations existed commonly in the Empire, and the influence exercised by their ideas is shown by the predominance of Dionysiac imagery on sarcophagi and its importance in Pompeian paintings and art and in the decorations of the Casa Farnesina at Rome.

The policy of checking the intrusion of alien elements, unless sanctioned and in fact introduced by the *quindecimuiri*, continued. As early as 181 B.C. certain supposed books of Numa Pompilius, said to have been found on the Janiculum, were burnt in public with the approval of the Senate, since the praetor adjudged that they tended in the main to the break up of beliefs; in 139 Chaldeans, that is astrologers, and Jews making proselytes were banished, as were astrologers and magicians in 33 too (when Agrippa took action). So long as new cults of this type kept quiet, no action was taken, but when altars of Isis were put up on the Capitol they were destroyed in 59, 53, probably 50, and 48 B.C.: in the last year a temple of Bellona was destroyed. The triumvirs voted a public temple to Isis in 43 B.C., perhaps to conciliate the masses, but it was probably never built. In the war against Cleopatra, Augustus was compelled to assume a strongly nationalist pose as the champion of the Roman order and Roman religion, and under his régime even private shrines to the Egyptian deities were excluded, first in 28 B.C. from the *pomerium* or official city bounds, then, when they were again entering in 21 B.C., from a circle of a mile outside it. Under Tiberius as a result of a scandal (p. 153 later), in A.D. 19 a temple was destroyed, the image thrown into the Tiber, and 4,000 freedmen addicted to this cult or to Judaism, against which another piece of sharp practice was charged, banished, others being given a time limit to recant. But under Caligula the cult became official and Isis and Sarapis obtained a public double temple in the Campus Martius (still outside the *pomerium*): two centuries later, under Caracalla, Sarapis obtained a public temple on the Quirinal. So the African Liber and Hercules received their public temples under Septimius Severus, Sol Inuictus Elagabal his (temporary) temple under Elagabalus, Dea Suria hers under Alexander Severus, Sol Inuictus (in a Roman form) under Aurelian, and Bellona Puluinensis probably, Juppiter Dolichenus possibly, in this century. Elagabalus and Aurelian acted from personal motives, but otherwise the final step of canonization is the culmination of a process of private growth.

Mithras alone remains private and yet fully approved, for (1) Mithraism was primarily, what the others were only secondarily, a mystery religion and had no public ceremonies: a civic cult would have had little *raison d'être*; (2) Mithraism was unquestionably loyal and also markedly successful with the official class; (3) there was no shade of impropriety in the cult; (4) it could seem to be a specialized form of the Sun worship which became official; (5) it had not a professional priestly class without secular activities. So it continued its existence in small cryptlike temples, having sometimes porticoes, on ground privately owned (by individual benefactors or *collegia*).

Of course many of the incoming cults did not succeed in establishing themselves. The Syrian gods seldom won such a place as Isis did: their worship was often just an affair of the local Syrian group, or of the mendicant priests of the Syrian goddess who drew alms from all and sundry. We can imagine people feeling that there probably *was* something in this exotic devotion and a small gift would not hurt, also that the priests were liable to curse and a curse was a terrible thing. Again, the attempt of Elagabalus to make the worship of his god Elagabal the central worship of the Empire provoked a reaction: when Aurelian introduced the Syrian cult of the Sun it was in strictly Roman form, as part, if a predominant part of the Pantheon: it was an addition changing the balance of power, not a change like those effected by Constantine or Julian.

In general Rome was receiving: but she gave something. Wherever a colony was founded there was a miniature Capitol; there was one at Oxyrhynchus, and Zeus Kapetolios was worshipped in various cities in the Eastern provinces. Any such influence was no doubt fairly superficial. It is quite a different story in the Western provinces. Here Latin was the language of the superior culture, as Greek was in the East, supplanting native tongues, and native deities were identified with Roman gods.

VI

HOW EASTERN CULTS TRAVELLED

Many of these various cults succeeded in different degrees in attracting outsiders. We must here ask, How were they presented? and how far can we speak of missionary activity and propaganda? reserving for the next chapter the further question, What psychological needs did they answer? Here we shall be concerned with the following modes of presentation: individual propaganda, teachings, external cultus and processions, mendicant priests, public penitents, and miracle and its record in literary propaganda and in art.

Mithraism, Christianity in its various forms, and small private mysteries must have depended for new adherents mainly on the bringing in of one individual by another to the *collegium* or temple. Literary allusions make it clear that any one would have heard of Mithras and would probably know that there were mysteries connected with him: some feeling of the effective otherness of the cult may have been inspired by the sight of a Mithraist at a banquet refusing the wreath offered to him, as, if he had reached the grade of *miles*, he was bound to do. Many of us owe our first acquaintance with Catholicism to some parental explanation of why So-and-so did not eat meat on Friday. There must also have been some general idea that these rites affected the future of your soul: certainly this was so with the Dionysiac societies.

Judaism must have attracted men largely in this way through individual propaganda in households by slaves and freedmen or casual acquaintances: Juvenal, vi. 542, mentions a Jewess among the various religious quacks battening on women's superstition. Judaism appeared as something like a philosophy. Its monotheism would incidentally free you from a number of religious expenses, though of course if you took it seriously it would at the same time exclude you from festivities. This teaching was presented in the synagogue, with its reading of the Scripture in Greek and its sermon. Nothing in paganism before the Julianic revival corresponded to this: in a mystery there was a *prorrhesis* or proclamation, warning the unfit not to present themselves and the rest of those present to purify themselves, and during the ceremony a certain amount was said, but it was in the nature of the text of a liturgy and apparently without much explanation. This teaching was the more effective by reason of its exclusiveness and absoluteness: it was sure of itself. Judaism had no outdoor processions, but it had a certain amount of appeal to the eye. Persius, v. 179 ff., when inveighing against superstition, says:

> 'But when the days of Herod are come and the violet wreathed lamps, set in order in the greased window, have poured a thick cloud of smoke and the tail of the tunny-fish curls round the red dish and is afloat, and the white jar is bursting with wine, then you move your lips without speaking and grow pale with fear before the Sabbath of the circumcised.'

It may be asked whether literary propaganda is to be reckoned among the ways in which Judaism was spread. Writings of Artapanos and others in later Ptolemaic times sought to show that the origin of Egyptian culture was Jewish, and Josephus dedicated his *Jewish Antiquities* and *Against Apion*, an apologetic for Judaism, to the rich freedman Epaphroditus. Certain works of Philo, as for instance *On the Contemplative Life* and *That Every Virtuous Man is Free*, are definitely addressed to Gentiles, and the latter is in substance based on popular Hellenistic diatribe: it is remarkable that in the forty-second section (ii, p. 452 M.) he speaks of the companions of kings and the companions of the Olympian gods and adds, 'The lawgiver of the Jews goes even farther'. But there is no evidence that Philo's intention had any success: there is one citation of him in Heliodorus, and that is all in pagan literature. Certainly there is no indication of substantial knowledge of the Septuagint except as heard by those who frequented synagogues or were concerned to write polemical treatises against Christianity: as a book it was bulky, expensive, and inaccessible. The quotation of Moses in the treatise *On the Sublime* (probably first century A.D.) may be due to chance knowledge or to the ethnographic observations of Posidonius: at the same time it is notable that Posidonius did not know of the Jewish prophets when he enumerated specimens of the type all over the known world. Again, there is no evidence that the Judaizing redaction of the Sibylline oracles and of certain Orphic texts exercised any influence outside Judaism and Christianity, though it is noteworthy that a Jewish story about Alexander's visit to Jerusalem and another about his shutting out of Gog and Magog found their way into the popular redaction of the legendary history of Alexander passing under the name of Callisthenes. The use of Genesis i in the cosmogonies of *Corpus Hermeticum* i and iii is familiar: the first quotes a supra-Hebraized form, 'increase with increase, and multiply with multiplication', and both represent an unmistakable fusion of Jewish and other ideas.

We may pass to the direct appeal to the eye. Isis and Cybele had this in a marked degree. Isis had such visible rites as the *Ship of Isis*, the blessing of sailing at the opening of the season, and solemn processions which we find represented in art as well as described in literature, and again imposing ceremonies in the temple from which the public was not excluded (the morning ceremony of opening the temple and the toilet of the images, sacred dances, the adoration of the urn of supposed Nile water as shown in a painting from Herculaneum, the drama of Osiris, the coming forth of the initiate dressed as the Sun-god). Moreover, there was something to strike the imagination in the whole aspect of these ostentatiously exotic temples with niches in front, often no doubt with elaborate precincts and pious residents. At Pompeii the priests lived in the Iseum: at Corinth Lucius before his initiation spent a period of retreat in an abode within the temple precinct: at Smyrna, just as at Memphis, there were *katochoi* living there, men on whom there lay some divine constraint compelling them to abide in the temple.

The eye was struck also by penitents sitting as suppliants before the temple of Isis or shouting through the streets, 'for my sins my sight was taken from me', or doing strange penances. The shorn priests and the daily services, the noisy hymns of the faithful, the incomprehensible hieroglyphic inscriptions might give a sense of continuous religious life and otherness; and their residence in the temple and absorption in its business might create an impression of professional skill. Traditional worship, carried on generally by men whose priestly functions were incidental, might in comparison seem easy-going and amateurish, though I must confess that I know no direct evidence for such an attitude, and we could hardly expect to find it expressed by men of the literary class; in their eyes this sort of religious professionalism when in their midst belonged to vulgar superstition, ready as they might be to idealize the native priesthood of Egypt and Persia.

So it was with Cybele. She had her anger. In 38 B.C. it was reckoned as a portent that certain persons, becoming possessed by the Mother of the gods, declared that the goddess was angry with them. And she had her public ceremonies. Lucretius (ii. 608 ff.) gives a striking picture of how 'The image of the divine mother is carried in dread fashion through mighty lands. Various races according to the ancient custom of the rite call her the Idaean mother'; the Galli walk in the procession to the sound of timbrels and cymbals and horns and flutes, they carry weapons as signs of their mad frenzy, able to overpower with fear of the deity's might the thankless hearts and impious breasts of the crowd. 'So when first she rides through mighty cities and with closed lips showers an unvoiced blessing on mortals they strew all the way with silver and bronze, offering liberal alms; roses fall from them like snow on the Mother and the throngs of her attendants.' Lucretius closes his account in accordance with his principles, 'Although these things are well and excellently arranged, yet they are far removed from the true view', but he has for a moment made even us feel the thrill of the crowds, the still majesty of the image: we can hardly fail to think of the atmosphere which surrounds a procession of the Host. Under Claudius the dramatic processions and visible ritual became part of the State's round of festivals and acquired new splendour. So also Bellona had processions and a cult society called *hastiferi*.

> These hot long ceremonies of our church
> Cost us a little—oh, they pay the price.

Again the populace was reminded of several of these cults by begging priests. We find these attached to the cult of Cybele and of the Dea Suria and to that of Isis, and know best those who exercised their profession for the Syrian goddess. They went everywhere, carrying around her image, dancing as dervishes do, cutting their arms with knives, accusing themselves in frenzy of sins against her, scourging themselves, and then begging alms for her, able on occasions to prophesy and to invoke celestial pains and penalties on their mockers. We have the dedication of one of them saying that on twenty journeys he had filled forty sacks, and we have a grim picture of their life drawn by Apuleius, *Metamorphoses*, viii. 24 ff. His enthusiasm for Isis may have added some blackness to the picture, but they were no doubt a despised class. Still, their threats inspired fear in a world which ascribed great power to the spoken curse: they spoke in the name of a deity. The fanatics of Bellona were similar.

Cicero in his treatise *On Laws*, ii. 40, forbids all such begging save for Cybele on a few days, 'for it fills men's minds with superstition and drains their resources'. But there is no reason to believe that their activities were directed towards the influencing of those who heard and saw them to the practice of regular personal devotion to Cybele or Dea Suria. They wanted money for a religious purpose, and they had a technique, religious in their eyes, for securing it. Marius had a Syrian prophetess whom he took about with him and he performed sacrifice at her bidding, but it did not change his personal attitude, any more than the consultation of a medical quack would have changed his views, if any, of the physical nature of the universe. Celsus tells of many prophets who went about in Syria and Palestine begging and moved as in prophecy.

'It is easy and usual for each to say, *I am God, or the son of God, or a divine spirit.* I have come, for the world is already perishing and you, O men, are going to destruction because of iniquities. I wish to save you, and you shall see me coming again with heavenly power. Blessed is he who has worshipped me now; on every one else, on cities and lands, I shall cast everlasting fire. And men who do not know the penalties which they incur will in vain repent and groan; but those who have obeyed me I shall keep in eternity.'

He says that he had himself confuted these men. This picture seems to owe some of its features to Celsus' hostility to Christianity: the threat of cosmic destruction so put is applicable only in a Messianic context.

There was another means of winning adherents which is particularly important to students of the rise of Christianity. I refer to the supposed miracles done by these gods and the literary propaganda which made them known and enhanced their value. These miracles would be largely miracles of healing, but were not limited to that. Aristides, who tells us at length elsewhere about the various divine graces bestowed on him in his illnesses, says in his prose hymn to Sarapis (written towards the middle of the second century A.D.), 'Who the god is and what nature he has may be left to the priests and the learned among the Egyptians to say and know. Our praise will be sufficient for the moment if we tell of all the varied blessings which he is shown to bring to men, and through these very things his nature can be seen.' Aristides mentions miracles of various kinds and stresses wonders performed by Sarapis for sailors. As the god of the greatest port in the Mediterranean he might well care for them: this development is probably late Hellenistic if not Imperial, for in the early Hellenistic period the Cabiri of Samothrace were actually more worshipped than before the time of Alexander. Aristides says:

> 'He it is who is really steward of the winds much more than the islander in Homer (Aeolus). He has power to still and rouse which he will. He it is who has sent up drinkable water in mid sea, who has raised the fallen, who has caused the clear light of the sun to shine on beholders, *whose achievements fill countless volumes on the sacred shelves.*'

Now we possess on a papyrus of the second century A.D. the end of a short record of the type to which Aristides refers:

> 'He said, For your sake I will grant the water to the men of Pharos: and having saluted him he sailed out and gave the water to the men of Pharos and received from them as a price one hundred drachmas of silver. This miracle is recorded in the libraries of Mercurium. Do all of you who are present say *There is one Zeus Sarapis.*'

There follows the book's title, 'The Miracle of Zeus Helios, great Sarapis, done to Syrion the Pilot'. By the time Aristides came to Alexandria this had become a typical achievement of Sarapis. A similar miracle has been inferred by Vogt. An inscribed altar of the year A.D. 108/9 at Wâdi Fatîre in Upper Egypt speaks of *the most fortunate water-finding named in honour of Trajan Dacicus*. A well had been found and a well station made. Now a coin of Alexandria of 111/2 shows Sarapis sitting by a water-basin, which is being filled from a lion's head (the regular mouthpiece for a spring): the standard of a company of soldiers is behind. This coin type, repeated under later emperors, probably means in its first use that the finding of the water was regarded as a special mercy of Sarapis. The priesthood at Alexandria could in all good faith regard the accidental as providential (mere coincidence was not a popular hypothesis in antiquity) and was in close enough contact with the Roman authorities to secure the expression of these ideas in coinage, which in those days served purposes now served commonly by postage stamps and occasionally by postmarks.

Miracles of healing would be numerous. Thus Sarapis gave orders in sleep to a blind man and a lame man to go to Vespasian, and they were cured of their infirmities. Ovid tells the story in *Metamorphoses*, ix. 667 ff., of Telethusa, a woman of Phaestus in Crete. Her husband had told her that if the child she was about to bear was a girl it must be exposed. Isis appeared to her by night, attended by the other Egyptian deities, and said: 'O Telethusa, who art one of mine own, lay aside your heavy cares and elude your husband's bidding. And do not hesitate to rear whatever offspring there shall be when Lucina relieves you by a birth. I am a deity strong to help. I bring

aid when invoked; you will not complain that you
worshipped an ungrateful deity.' A girl Iphis was
born, reared as a boy, and in time betrothed to a girl.
The mother invoked Isis, reminding her that she had
obeyed her commands, and Iphis immediately became
a youth. This story is probably based on the legend,
intended to explain a Phaestian festival, the Ekdysia, of
Leto, to whom the mother called Galatea had directed
her prayer; it has been changed in Ovid to an areta-
logy. The work by Artemon of Miletus on dreams
included an account of commands and cures by
Sarapis.

There is a most important parallel text in honour
of Imouthes, an Egyptian deity commonly identified
with Asclepius and forming part of the circle of deities
round Sarapis at Memphis. This, a papyrus of the
second century A.D., tells us how the (unnamed) author
had often intended to translate into Greek a book
connecting the god's worship with Menecheres (Men-
kaura, the Mycerinus of Herodotus: of the fourth
dynasty), supposed to have been found by Nectanebus,
the last independent ruler of Egypt and a popular
figure in legend. This book was said to have been
a factor in causing the god to be greatly revered (29 f.).
The writer had, however, been hindered by the greatness of the story, 'for it is within the reach of gods alone
and not of mortals, to describe the mighty deeds of the
gods' (40 f.). As he lingered, fever came upon his
mother. She and he went to the god as suppliants, and
Imouthes appeared to her in a dream and cured her
by simple methods, and she and her son sacrificed in
thankfulness. Then the writer was seized with a sudden
pain in the right side and hastened to the helper of

human nature. He received mercy and tells us how (90 ff.):

'It was night, when every living thing save those in pain was at rest, and the deity appeared to me in special power. I was afire with a violent fever and convulsed with difficulty of breathing and cough from the pain arising from my side. Yet in a stupor of pain I was drowsing into sleep, and my mother in great distress at my tortures, as mothers will be for a child (and indeed she is by nature affectionate), sat by me enjoying no sleep at all. Then of a sudden—not in a dream or sleep—for her eyes were immovably open, but they did not discern precisely, for a divine vision came on her, inspiring fear and preventing her from discerning readily, she saw the figure (whether it was the god or his attendant)—anyhow it was some one passing high, of more than human stature, clothed in radiant linen, with a book in his left hand. He did but contemplate me from top to toe twice or three times and vanished. And she came to her senses and, quivering as she still was, tried to waken me. She found me rid of the fever and streaming with sweat, so she gave glory to the god for his epiphany and wiped the sweat off me and brought me to myself. She would fain have told me of the god's miraculous goodness, but I spoke first and told her all: for a dream had revealed to me all that she had seen with her eyes. The pains in my side ceased and the god gave me yet another remedy stilling distress, *and I proceeded to proclaim the benefits which he had done to me.* And when we had again propitiated him with the sacrifices which were in our power, he, through the channel of the priest who serves him in the life of discipline, asked for the promise made to him long ago. We knew that we had not failed to render what was due in sacrifices and votives but nevertheless besought his favour with them again. But when he frequently said that his pleasure was not in them, but in that which had been

previously undertaken, I was baffled, and with difficulty
did the divine obligation to write prevail over my dis-
paraging of it. However, as soon as I recognized, O
master, that I was neglecting the divine book, I invoked
thy providence and being filled with thy divinity I hurried
to the inspired task of thy record and I think that I shall
sanctify it, telling in prophetic way thy intention, for in
another book I set forth truly the story of the making of
the universe put in a reasonable way on a physical theory.
Through the whole writing I have supplied what was
lacking and removed what was superfluous and I have
told shortly a tale sometimes long, simply a story which is
complicated. Accordingly I reckon, Master, that the book
has been completed in accordance with thy favour and
not with my intelligence; for such a writing suits thy
divinity. . . . *And every Greek tongue shall tell of thy story and
every Greek shall reverence Imouthes the son of Phtha.* Come here
together, O men of good will and virtue, go hence, O
envious and impious, come here all . . . who having served
the god have gained release from diseases, all who handle
the art of healing, all that will come as seekers after virtue,
all that have been prospered with great abundance of
blessings, all that have been saved from peril by sea. *The
power of the god has gone into every place to save.* I am about
to tell of his marvellous epiphanies, and of mighty blessings
of his power.'

Then the story starts and the papyrus soon breaks off.
Here a present-day miracle is combined with supposed
wonders of the past. It should be remarked that, while
the book may have been an adaptation of an Egyptian
text, it may equally be an original composition like
the Dream of Nectanebus in a Leiden papyrus, or the
literature current under the name of Thrice-greatest
Hermes (that is, Thoth).

Now it is of the utmost importance that these miracles were written down in book form. The papyrus which has just been quoted addresses itself to a wide public. The story of the water-finding professes to be a record made for archives but is a copy found up country, and there must have been others. Its conclusion with the acclamation to Sarapis is most significant. An acclamation by those present at a miracle is very common in popular stories of Christian wonders; thus in apocryphal Acts of Apostles the crowd generally exclaims 'Great is the god of the Christians' (or 'of Peter', 'of Andrew', &c.). Such an acclamation before an expected wonder (not fulfilled) is ascribed to pagans in the Confession of St. Cyprian of Antioch. But this is an imperative, *Do you say*, and an imperative plural addressed to hearers. In effect it corresponds to *Laus tibi Christe* after the Gospel in the Mass to-day. It presupposes a public which hears such holy stories recited. This tradition revived in the *libelli* recording miraculous cures, the composition of which became usual in the African Church in the time of St. Augustine; here, however, the *libellus* was read only once (in one case it was composed within twenty-four hours and read within forty-eight hours of the event).

In fact we know that such recitation existed. There was attached to the cult of Sarapis and Isis a class of men called *aretalogi*, tellers of the god's wonders; we find them in Egypt at Memphis, and in Delos. Even at the end of the fifth century A.D. we find a miracle claimed for Isis at Menouthi, the giving of a child to a childless man after priestly interpretation of his dreams; the Christian account is that it was the illegitimate offspring of a priestess.

This propaganda is important as an analogy for our study of the advance of Christianity and was no doubt effective; much later the cult of St. Cyrus and St. John of Menouthi was brought to Rome by those who said that they had been healed at their shrine. One feature of the time was a marked credulity. Anything reported on any authority was to the man of education possible and to the man in the street probable or even certain. The parody of this attitude in Lucian's *Lover of Lies* is not exaggerated. We have only to look at the letters of Pliny, and to read his story of the dolphin which took a boy to school, or glance at the writers known as *paradoxographi* who told of miracles and other unnatural history.

The recording of wonders and epiphanies in temple inscriptions was an old Greek practice; we have remarked it at Lindos and Epidaurus. It was a matter also of civic pride: the local historian of Chersonesos on the Black Sea, Syriscus, at the end of the third century B.C., was thanked by his fellow citizens for having laboriously written an account of the manifestations of the Maiden and read it aloud, and this gratitude was immortalized on stone. We know in this context the acclamations noticed earlier. There is at Panamara in Caria an inscription describing the miracle which defended the shrine from an attack, probably that of Labienus in 41/0 B.C.; it speaks of the people as shouting loudly, *Great is Zeus Panamaros*. Furthermore, in and after the Hellenistic period writers composed general works on such topics, as for instance that of Istrus (about 200 B.C.), *Epiphanies of Apollo*, and that of Phylarchus, of about the same date, *On the Appearance of Zeus*, and in the second century A.D.

Aelian's *Concerning Divine Manifestations* and *Concerning Providence*, both books being elaborate refutations of scepticism by reference to miracle. To this century belongs a papyrus dialogue between a man believing in oracles and a doubter, in which the argument appears to have ended in a *coup de théâtre*. From the beginning of the next century we have the *Heroicus* of Philostratus, which describes the conversion by a vine-tender devoted to the hero Protesilaus of a Phoenician trader who is sceptical but sympathetic (the vine-tender does it by telling what the hero had done for him and told him). The same writer's work on Apollonius of Tyana is a justification by miracle and sanctity of the special position claimed for Apollonius. Lives of Pythagoras written under the Empire are similar: and Lucian's *Alexander* is the parody of such writing.

The recording of miracles for the benefit of private individuals appears to be confined to Asclepius, the Egyptian deities and Christianity, though we find the recording of punishments for sin (equally wonders) by the Mother goddess in Lydia and by Anaitis and Men at Sardis. At the same time, while a miracle did not necessarily attract all who saw it to new worship, the principle was fully accepted that miracle proved deity. 'I make you a god in his eyes: I tell of your *virtues* (which can mean virtues or miracles),' says a character in the *Adelphi* of Terence (535 f.), and a curious papyrus catechism includes, 'What is a god? That which is strong. What is a king? He who is equal to the Divine.'

Further, this recording of miracles, expressly so described, is only a special form of the general glorification of a deity before others by hymns and votive offerings and works of art. The hymn told the world at large of the greatness of a god. Let us take an illustration from the third century B.C. Artemidorus of Perga settled on the island of Thera and put up inscriptions to Hecate and Priapus:

> 'Artemidorus set up this Hecate, of many names, the light-bringer, honoured by all who dwell in the land. Artemidorus made these steps as a memorial of the city of Thera and stablished a black stone. I, Priapus of Lampsacus, am come to this city of Thera, bearing imperishable wealth. I am here as a benefactor and a defender to all the citizens and to the strangers who dwell here.'

Under the Empire there was a considerable production of hymns in verse and prose. The fact that the leading rhetoricians, men who enjoyed a very high standing in the public eye, wrote these hymns no doubt gave a certain prestige to the cults thus favoured: it made it clear that they were in the fashion. Hymns acquired yet greater significance when they were put in the service of dogmatic religions and expressed their tenets in a form which could reach the popular intelligence: this was notably so with gnostic sects and Manichaeism, but is illustrated also by St. Augustine's *Psalm against the Donatists*, in which by the use of a non-literary measure he addressed himself to the people. The religious revival of Augustus was not dogmatic in character; but the *Secular Hymn* of Horace is very definitely didactic.

Any one who thought he had received favour from a deity or wished to show his piety might set up an inscription or a votive work of art. This was an ancient custom in Greece and Rome and Egypt and Syria.

The individual's record was primarily directed to the god; it was a transaction between the two of them. But it also had a certain value as visible to the world at large. The pictures of those who had been saved from shipwreck by Isis and Sarapis or the Samothracian deities, the records of those who had made *taurobolia*, the epitaphs which described the religious dignities which the dead man had enjoyed, could all excite interest and curiosity and imitation. How this served a religious purpose is clear from the way in which the Augustan restoration of older Roman religious ways found artistic as well as literary expression. The reliefs on the Altar of Peace taught the same lesson as the *Aeneid*.

We have discussed the ways in which a cult was spread by the obscure activity of scattered individuals. We may conclude this chapter by considering how one determined man disseminated a worship in which he had a strong personal interest. About the middle of the second century of our era Alexander of Abonutichus, a small city in Paphlagonia, came before the notice of the public in general. He had when young been the pupil of a doctor who had been a follower of Apollonius of Tyana, a famous Neopythagorean and what we should call a prophet. From him he learnt, says Lucian, magical tricks to aid people in their love-affairs and in the finding of buried treasure—and no doubt some rather more serious religious ideas. Then he struck up a partnership with one Cocconas, a writer of choral songs, and they bought a large tame serpent, and decided to found an oracle as a means of enriching themselves. They went to Chalcedon and buried bronze tablets, stating that in the near future Asclepius and his father Apollo with him would migrate to Pontus and settle in Abonutichus. These tablets were found and the people of Abonutichus, who had already a cult of Asclepius, at once voted to build a temple and set about digging the foundations. Cocconas was left behind in Chalcedon, composing ambiguous prophecies, and there died. Alexander went on first, and appeared dressed like Perseus and declaiming an oracle which proclaimed that he was a scion of Perseus and of the blood of Podalirius. A Sibylline prophecy of his activity was also produced.

Thus the stage was set by prophecy, a factor the importance of which we shall see in Chapter XIII. Alexander proceeded to create the impression of the miraculous by foaming at the mouth and then contrived the discovery of an egg in the temple foundations; the idea was spread abroad that a small snake which emerged was in very truth Asclepius. After a few days he displayed his original large snake, into which the baby snake had supposedly grown with wondrous speed; its head was concealed and instead there was a linen head showing beside his own beard. The simple folk filed past in wonder. The god had come in the freshness of young vigour to a world in which the traditional divine figures appeared old and remote. The news spread, and people from Bithynia, Galatia, and Thrace poured in and the making of paintings, statues, and cult-images began. The god acquired a new name, Glycon. A supernatural figure could acquire a new name; according to the late myth Hippolytus, when restored to life and settled in a fresh existence at Nemi, was known as Virbius. There is perhaps some influence here of Pythagorean ideas; just as a human being when reincarnated took a new name, might not Asclepius in this new snaky form?

Alexander now announced that from a particular date the new god would make prophecies. People were to write in a scroll what they wished to know and to tie it up and seal it. He then took the scroll into the holy of holies, summoned by herald and priest those who had presented the scrolls, and gave back the scrolls sealed as before, with answers appended. This involved a little elementary trickery; but everything was organized, and now Alexander sent abroad men to create rumours among various races about the oracle and to tell of his successful predictions. People then came from all sides with sacrifices and votive offerings and liberal gifts for the prophet himself.

This is a point of peculiar interest. Undoubtedly the fame of the oracle would have spread on its own merits, but we cannot doubt that the prophet left nothing to chance and engaged in real propaganda. The good communications which the roads of the Roman Empire provided and the mutual intelligibility which prevailed within it made such work possible and fruitful. Further, Alexander is said to have polemized against the unbelieving attitude of Epicureans. In time he won the allegiance of Rutilianus, a Roman of high rank and the governor of Asia, who married the daughter whom Alexander had, as he said, by the Moon. The prophet's ambitions rose. He sent emissaries to cities throughout the Empire, warning them against perils of plague and fire and earthquake and promising to them help which could not fail.

In this we see the widespread desire for direct supernatural information which will be discussed in the next chapter. Alexander met other religious needs also. He established an annual celebration of mysteries which lasted three days, and enacted the birth of Asclepius, the manifestation of Glycon, the union of Podalirius and his own mother, and finally the love of the Moon for himself and the birth of their daughter. In these ceremonies the faithful could see his thigh, made to look golden, as though he were connected with Pythagoras; the exact relation was declared in an oracle. In this we see the popularity of the visible showing forth of a sacred story and of the presentation of myth in act.

In due course the prophet died. Some of his associates hoped to succeed him, but Rutilianus decided that the post of prophet must remain Alexander's. The cult of Glycon remained in honour at Abonutichus, as we learn from the presence of the man-headed snake on its coins till minting ceased; we have evidence at Nicomedia also and a dedication at Apulum in Illyria. In this way a cult, which blended old and new ideas in a skilful manner and knew how to employ methods of publicity, won an enduring position in the world of its time. The will to accept and, if not quite in our sense, to believe was strong.

This is a perfect example of the methods by which a cult could be commended to the attention of the public. Alexander certainly has many of the marks of a charlatan, although a certain caution is needed in considering what Lucian wrote, for Lucian was deeply out of sympathy with popular religion and in the tradition of ancient invective some very unpleasant charges were conventional. Nevertheless, Lucian here speaks with a depth of feeling which is unusual in him and which suggests that he was deeply shocked with what to him seemed very successful but very palpable fraud.

Better established cults did undoubtedly produce artificial miracles. The incense which at Gnathia melted without the application of a flame, the bowls of water annually turned into wine at Elis, the spring of wine which annually appeared in Dionysiac festivals in Andros and Teos required manipulation, and what may be evidence for the technique has been found at Corinth; and we have reason to believe in the existence of certain deliberately produced supernatural effects in Egyptian temples under the Empire, though it is not clear that the ingenious devices of Heron to cause a shrine to open when fire was lit for sacrifice, close when it was extinguished, to make a trumpet sound when the temple doors were opened, and so forth were in use. Even in dealing with these phenomena we must beware of being over free with charges of deliberate bad faith. Ancient Egyptian magic and ritual rested on the assumption that material objects and persons could be given a new and supernatural content and significance: and the Dionysiac wonders were dramatic ceremonies, presenting under conditions of time and space what the god and his ideal followers were thought to have done in the early days. In any case men could and can adopt a position in which they never allow themselves to ask just what they mean by what they are doing.

Further we may apply the old legal test, *Cui bono?* The priests of Isis, as also the mendicant servants of Dea Suria or Cybele, had an interest in the amount of alms which they could collect, and in the general principle, 'Nothing like leather'. But there can be no doubt of the sincerity of those who recorded the miracles by which they believed themselves to have benefited, or of Aristides or Apuleius.

So in these forms of propaganda we must recognize what we should call a religious spirit, even though we cannot in our sense give the name of a religion to the things in the service of which it was spent. Religious spirit does not need to be deliberately purposeful or dogmatic: in this as in so much else the reasons which we ourselves give for our actions are often merely rationalizations of our conservatism and of our impulses.

VII

THE APPEAL OF THESE CULTS

WE have surveyed some of the methods by which cults and beliefs brought themselves before the notice of individuals and communities. What were the psychological factors of attraction which caused these methods to bear fruit? Difficult as it is to answer this question, we must make an attempt. The acceptance of Roman cults by the conquered peoples of the West is a simple phenomenon, much more so than the acceptance of Christianity by natives in modern colonies. There was little at stake except the use of Roman names in place of Celtic, and the Roman name had the authority given by cultural and political superiority. The acceptance of the other cults which we have surveyed is more complicated, and in its development the formative impulse came largely from the recipients of new cults. How was this?

Some of the relevant factors are clear. The conquests of Alexander broke old ties and associations, and created a consequent demand for new groups. We have seen earlier the attraction of new cults *qua* new and of mysteries not tied to a particular place. We must now consider (1) the picture of the universe which arose, above all from astrology, (2) the interest in immortality, (3) an inquisitiveness about the supernatural resulting in a general increase in the tendency to believe.

(1) Political events had changed the world out of all recognition. Zeus and Athena had been good protectors for the citizen of a town which was one of a number of towns living as it were in a small luminous

area. But now this little world was swallowed up in the *oikoumene*, the inhabited world as known, and a vast uncertainty had come into men's lives. This was no neat little world in which Zeus or the providence of the gods saw to it that the just man had a reasonable measure of prosperity and the unjust man of punishment. It might be ruled by a blind Fortune, or again by an unchangeable Fate written in the stars or determined by them. This last doctrine, commonly called astrology, made a great change in the outlook not merely of the studious but also of the man in the street. In native Greek ideas the stars have their influence on weather: the Watchman in the *Agamemnon* tells how in the course of his duties he has become familiar with 'those who bring winter and summer to mortals, the bright rulers shining in the firmament', and the natural connexion of the moon with birth and growth is found in earlier Greece as elsewhere; so is a conception of fate, and in philosophers an idea of natural law. But it was reserved for the time of contact with Babylonian observations and calculations concerning the movements of the heavenly bodies and determinations of the future from their position to accept the system which we call astrology and to find a visible embodiment of this fate in the courses of the heavenly bodies. Destructive criticism was levelled at astrology: nevertheless for the plain man it acquired an axiomatic validity which it retained everywhere till the seventeenth century, and which for some it still has.

The general importance of this change is clear and the desire for some sort of deliverance from this determinist order was natural. What is here to be emphasized is that now for the first time the man in the street found his existence and well-being related to cosmic universals. Earlier he had had dealings with Zeus and Athena and Artemis, accessible and placable Greeks of a larger build. Now there happened to him in this sphere something even more revolutionary than the political transformation of the times, whereby his city had been for all practical purposes swallowed up in a larger entity. He was under a universal law. The logical inference was that stated by a technical astrologer, Valens Vettius, 'It is impossible for any man by prayers and sacrifices to overcome what is fixed from the beginning and to alter it to his taste; what has been assigned to us will happen without our praying for it, what is not fated will not happen for our prayers' (v. 9). The Emperor Tiberius, says Suetonius (*Tiberius*, 69), neglected worship as useless in view of the certainty of astrological predestination. That was not a popular attitude: the effective answer was to make the gods lords of the stars. We find under the Empire not merely a general rise in the importance of celestial divinities but also the investing of Attis (earlier a figure connected with the fruits of the earth) with a starry cap on the coins of Pessinus and his invocation as 'shepherd of the white stars' in a popular poem of the second century A.D.

Man was committed to relations with a universal order, and he was as we have seen an individual facing it.

> I a stranger and afraid
> In a world I never made.

A deity who commands his homage must be superior to this order. So Bel is *Fortunae rector*, lord of Fortune and able to change its decrees. We shall meet later the statement of Isis to Lucius that she can prolong his life beyond the term fixed by Fate. One text describing a miracle of Sarapis includes an overruling of *Moira*, Destiny, though not of astral fate, for the disease is transferred to another man born under the same constellation. It is particularly notable that the quasi-canonical *Praises of Isis and Osiris* mentioned earlier says, 'I conquer fate and fate obeys me'. The strength of the desire which lies behind these beliefs is shown by the regularity with which its satisfaction is promised in the esoteric ceremonies which came into being. The so-called Chaldaic Oracles, professedly translated from Zoroaster and perhaps a product of the second century of our era, promise that *theurgoi*, practitioners of the occult rites prescribed in them, do not fall under fate: a Hermetic fragment promises as much to the 'pious': Servius knows of certain 'consecrations' which protect men against the attacks of fortune and which unless taken from them prevent them from dying.

(2) We have seen earlier the attraction at Eleusis of a guarantee against an uncomfortable hereafter. That continued to be important: it was clearly emphasized in Dionysiac private mysteries (and it must not be forgotten how large a part Dionysiac symbols play in funerary art under the Empire), in Mithraism, in Isiac initiations, and in the private magical rites of which we shall speak later. Augustine in his summary of Books VI to X of his *City of God* (*Retractationes*, ii. 43) gives as one of his purposes the refutation of the idea that sacrifice to pagan gods was useful because of the life that there would be after death: the wife of Vettius Agorius Praetextatus is in

her epitaph represented as saying to him that he freed
her from the allotted fate of death (by initiations).

In the first century A.D. the educated commonly
doubted survival, but the strength of Pliny's protest
indicates that this was not universal, and many feared
a cold disconsolate shadow life, like that portrayed in
Odyssey xi, or positive pains and penalties. It was not
a wholly imaginary bogy from which the Epicureans
sought to free mankind. Immortality, on the other
hand, sometimes appeared as a sort of prize to be won.
Christianity was taunted for its appeal to rewards and
punishments, but the taunt shows that the appeal was
not wholly ineffective.

Now there was a demand for more comprehensive
promises, for sacraments or faith able to give to the individual a new and dignified relation to the dangerous
realm outside. The esoteric rites just mentioned illus-
trate this best: man wants 'to become possessed of a
nature like god': it is so in the promises of magic
in the *taurobolium*, in the statement (Eph. vi. 12) about
the relation of Christians to the *Kosmokratores*, the
planetary lords, in the Marcosian sacrament (Irenaeus,
i. 14), in the account of the transformation of the elect
described in *Corpus Hermeticum* i and xiii, and in the
final prayer of the *Asclepius*, in Philo's class of 'men of
vision', and in his remarks on the prophetic vocation
of Moses.

'Since when the prophetic intellect has become initiated
in divine things and a bearer of god, it is like unity, not
being fundamentally commingled with any of those things
which show communion with duality. He indeed who has
come into close attachment to the nature of unity is said
to have approached god by a closeness of kinship, for

having left all mortal kinds, he is transmuted into the divine, so that he becomes akin to God and really divine.'

The desire is negative ('Defend me against every superiority of power both of spirit') and positive, and it is not limited to any one cult or circle. One of the really significant things is the popularity of elaborate gnostic systems: this is so for instance in Egypt, where there are such important manifestations in Coptic, the special language of a backwater. If you really knew how the wheels went round, you could in some measure control their revolutions.

I have spoken of the significance of this idea of Fate and of desires for some sort of liberation from it. Writers on the rise of Christianity have commonly referred also to a desire for protection against the activity of demons and possession by demons. It is certain that exorcism was a Christian curative activity which impressed the popular imagination: that we know from the remarks of Celsus. But Celsus rightly calls attention to the fact that there were other contemporary exorcisms. The significant thing about Christian exorcism was that it was a deliberate and official activity and not, like that of the sons of Scaeva at Ephesus, a private trade pursued for profit: in Christianity it was an activity that was an integral part of a religion. In any case it does not bear on the topic of this chapter, for there are no indications of exorcisms as religious practices of the other rival faiths, except Judaism, and the promises of security made by Isis and her priest to Lucius say nothing of this. No doubt if you were attached to one such cult you looked to its deity or deities for protection in general. In any case it would be wrong to picture Graeco-Roman

society of this period as demon-ridden. The phenomenon of possession was known and the practice of
exorcism not unfamiliar, and there was a fear of the
evil eye and of bewitchment: but superstition provides
its remedies, just as a populace exposed to infectious
diseases sometimes develops its immunities, and there
was a traditional apparatus of amulets and purifications which was used by all except the few who held
a rationalist point of view. Paganism had plenty of
deities who were to be feared if you did not take the
right steps to appease them, but paganism knew the
right steps to take.

Greece and Rome had not (like Persia, Judaea under
Persian influences, and Egypt) an existing organized
celestial opposition, and as we shall see in Chapter XIII,
daemones were for them neither good nor bad. The
antithesis of God and the angels over against daemones
as necessarily evil was spread by Judaism and Christianity, to whom the gods of the pagans were devils.

(3) We may pass to the factor of religious inquisitiveness. This could be casual. Horace, idling in Rome,
stood by the soothsayers as one might listen to a
cheapjack hawking his wares (*Satires*, i. 6, 114). It
could take a purely speculative and intellectual form,
with an antiquarian or ethnological colour. Thus we
know of Varro's great work on the religious antiquities
of the Roman people, Apion's on the symbolic meaning
of Egyptian hieroglyphs and rites, Chaeremon's on
Egyptian priestly life, Pallas and Eubulus on Persian
religion: we possess more popular works drawing on
them, as for instance Plutarch's *Isis and Osiris*, *Greek
Questions*, and *Roman Questions* and parts of his *Table
Talk* (which includes remarks on Jewish religious

customs), and incidental digressions in historical works by Posidonius (for instance that on the religious fanaticism of Eunus) and Julius Caesar and Tacitus (in the *Germania*, and again in *Annals* xii. 13 on the Parthian hunter god, in *Hist.* v on the Jews), and Nicolaus of Damascus, and Mnaseas of Patara, and again in poetry (as for instance Lucan's treatment of Celtic religion). Josephus hoped for and perhaps had Gentile readers for his *Jewish Antiquities*, and certainly directed his *Rejoinder to Apion* to a Gentile public. We know again the interest in the exotic as such: examples are Nero's interest in the Persian rites which Tiridates brought from Armenia and his passing devotion to an image of the Syrian goddess, and the fashion which in Pliny's time made rings with representations of Harpocrates common, and again the questions which Lucan makes Julius Caesar address to the aged Egyptian priest (x. 176 ff.), and the remarks made by Statius to a friend about to sail to Egypt (*Siluae*, iii. 2, 107). It is an invocation to Isis:

> 'Under thy protection let him learn whence comes the fruitful freedom of the marshy Nile, why the shallows subside and the bank marked with mud laid by Attic swallows restrains the waters, why Memphis is envious, or why the shore of Therapnaean Canopus is sportive, why the Doorkeeper of Lethe holds the altars of Pharos: why common animals are on a par with the great gods: what altars the long-lived phoenix prepares for itself: what fields Apis, adored by eager shepherds, deigns to inhabit, or in what eddy of the Nile he lays him.'

The learned interest in alien belief and practice might be detached: or it might assume a theological tone, in the common view that all worships were directed under different names to one deity (which view became official in Graeco-Egyptian piety), or in the theory that the phenomena so studied contained primitive wisdom veiled in allegory, or in the refinement thereof according to which there was in most beliefs a superimposition of priestcraft and false subtlety on this wisdom.

But the religious curiosity of the time was not satisfied with these intellectualist answers. There is a widely attested desire for information coming straight from the sanctuary and even from the god, for enlightenment in its fullest sense. An excellent illustration by parody is the opening of the *Menippus* of Lucian. The Cynic hero professes to have come back from the underworld. He had been brought up on the popular myths, and had then found them at variance with the ideas of right and wrong contained in the laws. Next he had gone to philosophers and found them at variance with one another and acting in a manner diametrically opposed to their principles. So he decided to journey to Babylon and there to consult one of the Magi, the disciples and successors of Zoroaster, 'having heard that with certain spells and rites they could open the gates of Hades and take in whom they would and bring him back': there he could consult Teiresias. There follows a parody of the ceremonial required and an account of the journey and of the return by way of the sanctuary of Trophonius at Lebadea. The central idea of consulting Teiresias goes back to the *Odyssey*, and its humorous use no doubt to Menippus (another parody is found in Horace, *Satires*, ii. 5). But the opening is most significant.

As has been often observed, it is extraordinarily like

the beginning of the Christian romance called the Clementine Homilies. There Clement is represented as (like Justin) so distressed by puzzling on death and on the nature and origin of the world that he grew pale and wasted away, but could not keep his mind off these topics. Having visited in vain the schools of the philosophers, he decided to go to Egypt and seek a Magian who could bring up a soul from Hades to settle the question of immortality. Circumstances put him in the way of Barnabas and salvation. There is a parallel of extraordinary interest. Prefixed to an astrological work on botany is a letter of Thessalus to the Emperor (probably of the famous doctor and astrologer Thessalus of Tralles to Nero or Claudius). This letter relates how the author after receiving his schooling in Asia Minor went to Alexandria and there pursued his studies. He was unsuccessful in his attempt to use a (supposed) writing of King Nechepso and came to a despair which seemed to him harder than death. So he went into the interior of Egypt, his soul prophesying to him that he would have converse with the gods. He continually held up his hands to heaven in prayer that there might be vouchsafed to him by a vision in sleep or by divine inspiration something which would send him back in exultation to Alexandria and his homeland. Everywhere he asked if there was anything of magic force left. Finally, when he found an honourable old priest who said that he would show visions in a dish (of water), he fell at this man's feet and wept bitterly till he was promised a revelation. After a three days' fast by both of them (which seemed to Thessalus to last for years) the priest gave him the choice of intercourse with a spirit or with a god. He chose Asclepius in spite of the priest's reluctance. Meanwhile the priest had prepared a 'house'. Thessalus sat in front of the god's throne and the priest went out and shut him in. Immediately the god appeared *alone to him alone* in marvellous beauty, lifted his right hand and greeted him with these words, 'Blessed Thessalus, who art already honoured by God and wilt in the future be revered by men as a god when thy success is known; ask what thou willest; gladly will I grant thee all'. Thessalus, who had smuggled in paper, asked why he had obtained no success with Nechepso's recipes on the powers of plants, and heard that Nechepso gave them not from divine revelation but from his knowledge, excellent in itself: what he did not know was when and where they should be gathered. These facts were now revealed by Asclepius and taken down by Thessalus.

The general schema is found in a number of other parallels. One is afforded by the Rabbinic type of true proselytes, Joshua, Naaman, and Rahab, who go through all heathen cults and schools without finding peace, but they find rest and satisfaction in the haven of the Bible and the Prophets, because the sacred Word alone can ensure peace of soul and knowledge of God. Here we have a striking parallel to what Augustine said he found. Another is an inscription in the temple of Mandulis, the solar deity at Talmis (Kalabscheh) in Upper Egypt, giving a visitor's record of his experience:

'O ray-shooting lord Mandulis, having seen certain radiant signs of thee I pondered on them and was busied therewith, wishing to know accurately whether thou art the Sun-god. I made myself a stranger to all vice and all godlessness, was chaste for a considerable period, and made an incense offering for holy piety. I saw thee and found rest. Thou didst grant my prayer and didst show thyself to me, going in thy golden boat(?) through the heaven, when, washing in the holy water of immortality, thou appearest anew. Thou camest making thy rising in due season, giving breath and great power to thy image and temple. There I knew thee, Mandulis, to be the Sun, the all-seeing master, king of all, almighty Eternity. O happy people that dwell in the city beloved by the Sun Mandulis, even holy Talmis, which is under the sceptre of fair-haired Isis of the countless names.'

This is written in vulgar Greek, and proves the penetration of such ideas into popular circles. A third is the Confession of St. Cyprian of Antioch, a Christian romance not later than the fifth century A.D. recording the conversion of a supposed magician. He recounts *his* experiences. His parents wished him to know the occult virtues of all things, so he passed through all available initiations, including a private initiation on Mt. Olympus (probably invented), and studied magic with the experts of various lands. A familiar and popular motif is thus elaborated with a wealth of detail largely drawn from the writer's imagination.

Such a religious quest was often no doubt a real experience, as for Justin Martyr and for St. Augustine. The Thessalus letter is of peculiar importance, since it takes back the attitude and the literary form to the first century A.D. It may seem surprising to find these ideas coming from a doctor of eminence, but after all the work of Pamphilus on herbs, as we know from Galen, used Hermetic revelations. The first century A.D. is, further, the century back to which we can trace the kernel of the contents of our magic papyri. And we may recall I Cor. xiii. 2, 'though I understand all secrets and have all *gnosis*'.

The most authoritative guidance comes direct from the gods, as to Nechepso or Thessalus or the writer of the Revelation or Hermas or the *Katochoi*: ecstasy is another way. Again, we may turn to the oracles. Their function had earlier been limited to the answering of practical questions and to the giving of advice on ritual and religious institutions. But in the third century Porphyry as a young man wrote a work *On the Philosophy to be drawn from Oracles*, giving oracles from Apollo of Claros and shrines of Hecate which not merely prescribed cultus but also defined the nature of god and asserted the existence of one Supreme Being who is Eternity (Aion), the ordinary gods of paganism being his 'angels': another oracle saying that the Supreme Being is Iao (that is Jehovah), identified with Hades, Zeus, Helios, is quoted by Cornelius Labeo, who probably belongs to the early part of the same century. Now, while these oracles have a perhaps suspicious resemblance to a literary work probably of the second century, the Chaldaic Oracles, which answered a similar need and became a holy book to later Neoplatonism, the connexion of some at least of the supposed Clarian utterances with Claros is rendered very probable by the dedications *To the gods and goddesses in accordance with the interpretation of the Clarian oracle* found on the Roman wall in England, at Nora in Sardinia, in Dalmatia, and in North Africa. Apollo had apparently ordered this universalizing piety. What is of particular importance for us is that the inscription at Nora is on grounds of lettering ascribed to the first century A.D. If this is trustworthy, the oracle's interest in theological questions goes back to that time, to the age when Germanicus on his visit to the East turned aside to visit it; and we have another indication of this attitude then. But the oracles can hardly have counted for much in that age as answering man's questions. Cicero speaks of the decay of Delphi, Lucan speaks of its silence. This may be regarded as rhetorical exaggeration, but the treatise of Plutarch *On the Decay of the Oracles*, which is of real weight in view of Plutarch's connexion with Delphi and the priesthood which he held there, bears witness to the reality of the decline. Further, Maximus of Tyre, writing in the second half of the second century A.D., says: 'Would that there were an oracle of Zeus or Apollo not giving obscure or ambiguous answers! . . . let Apollo of Delphi give me one clear answer on the subject of Zeus, or let Zeus give it himself!' It is hard to believe that theological oracles were then widely current, although in the second century some oracles were rising in importance, as we see from the sudden emergence of the oracular shrine of Glykon at Abonutichus in Pontus with Alexander as its prophet, and the record by Nearchus of his pilgrimage to Libya 'where Ammon gives oracles to all men'. It is not surprising that Claros rather than Delphi should benefit from this revival of interest. There are fashions in religion as in everything else. Again men might turn to the individual with supernatural gifts. Philodemus, a contemporary of Cicero's, says of the masses, 'wherefore they think that not the advice of the sage but all the injunctions of the men called divine should be received'.

Further, men could and did turn to mysteries for enlightenment. This does not to us appear justified by the facts. Aristotle said that those being initiated were not to learn something but to go through an experience and to be put into a state of mind. It has been remarked earlier that what an initiate carried away was the impression made by the liturgy: in interpretation he had a wide field left to himself. Now the commonplace that we find in a religion what we bring to it applies here also. There is a special cause operant in our period, which is the conviction that the various mysteries were founded very early by prophets of deep wisdom: Orpheus, Musaeus, and the other creators of rite and legend were philosophers, using symbols suited to a humanity for which pure truth

> sears too much
> The sense of conscious creatures to be borne.

The idea is strange to us, to whom the past is something interesting and in respects perhaps worthy of imitation, but essentially the past, for to us the notion of progress is axiomatic. To the ancients it was not so: individual philosophers held such views, but their ideas did not command general sympathy. Most men were ready to accept the concept of the wisdom of the past and many held that what we call progress was in fact decline from a Golden Age of noble simplicity. The political ideals of antiquity are static constitutions with careful safeguards against change. The fundamental difference lies in certain facts. First, the geographical horizon had not widened as ours has. There was not between Plutarch and Solon the gap which there is between us and Dr. Johnson (to Claudian, for instance, the typical

globe-trotter is the man who goes to farthest Spain).
Secondly, the advances of experimental science had
not really changed the outlook even of speculative men
and had not seemed to make a new world. Thirdly,
at all times the common goal of Greek thinkers was
a simple key to the understanding of phenomena. The
generalization was more dignified than the individual
fact, and in the Hellenistic age the philosophic centre
of interest became primarily ethical. Ancient speculation never lost the conviction that there was a
straightforward explanation of the universe.

Men turned then to the mysteries. Up to a point
they could do this by reading books and theorizing,
like Plutarch (though he had been initiated in Greek
mysteries), or like the author of the Naassene theology
preserved by Hippolytus. Logically, on the theory that
the various divine names belonged to one unity, one
mystery might suffice. But initiates were bound to
secrecy and what was divulged was not the whole story.
So if a man was to get to the heart of the matter he
must be initiated in as many mysteries as possible.
Thus Apuleius in his defence against a charge of magic
says (ch. 55):

'In Greece I took part in very many initiations. I keep
carefully certain symbols and memorials of them handed
to me by the priests. What I say is nothing unusual or
unknown. Those of you present who are initiated in the
rites only of Father Liber, for instance, know what you
keep concealed at home and worship far from all profane
persons. But I, as I have said, learnt worship on worship,
rites beyond number, and various ceremonies *in my zeal for
truth and in my dutifulness to the gods*. This is no tale put
together to serve the moment: it is something like three

years since in my first days at Oea in a public discourse on
the majesty of Aesculapius I made the same declaration
and recorded all the rites known to me. That speech is
very well known; it is read commonly; it was not so much
my eloquence as the mention of Aesculapius which made
it dear to the pious men of Oea.'

That is it, *studio ueri*, the motive pretended by Menippus, described by Clement and Cyprian in the
romances; and Apuleius was and claimed to be a
philosopher. This was no doubt one of the motives of
the other enthusiastic pagans who took initiation after
initiation, like Julian, of whom Libanius says that he
'consorted with *daimones* in countless rites (*teletai*)', or
Vettius Agorius Praetextatus, whose wife says to him
in his epitaph, 'Thou didst witness my initiation in all
mysteries'.

Such a man turned to the normal civic and private
mysteries of the time and was initiated in some or all
of them. What he found we do not often know: but it
was probably for the most part ideas which he already
had of the nature of the soul and its hope of bliss and
of the symbolic expression of natural processes, and
he gained a sense of intimate and special personal
relationship to the universe and the spiritual forces
underlying its operations. The interpretation of mysteries as veiling fundamental truth we know from
Plutarch, and we find strikingly set out in a document
preserved in Hippolytus, *Refutation of all Heresies*, v, and
professing to give the views of a Christian sect called
the Naassenes. This document takes the form of an
exegesis of a hymn to Attis sung in theatres by men
who know not what they do say. It expounds the
content of various legends on the first man, throws

light on the triple nature of the soul from 'Assyrian mysteries' (the cult legend of Adonis), and refers to Phrygian, Egyptian, and Greek mysteries, the Phrygian and the Greek both giving the concept of a bisexual Heavenly Man—all in this style. What is particularly to be noted is that it does not confine itself to matter which we might expect it to draw from learned books on the mysteries or from any literature which respected the discipline of silence; at least this is true of Eleusis, for the solemn and secret act of the holding up of the corn ear and the hierophant's cry are described. Here this view is combined with a symbolical interpretation of Jewish and Christian texts used just as in Philo or in Clement of Alexandria.

Demand creates supply, and this demand was met by the rise of private mysteries. We have seen earlier the popularity of Orphic rites and their continued existence (p. 26): we have seen also the popularity of private Dionysiac rites, and we may remark here on the rise of Neopythagorean societies in the first century B.C., for these also were really cult-sodalities. Here lies one of the roots of the vogue of the costly individual initiations in temples of Oriental gods in the world at large. From the same root came also private mysteries celebrated in private houses (as we saw the Egyptian cults start at Delos, and as Mithraism no doubt started; it remained a cult 'on private soil') or lonely spots. Philo in his polemic against mystery devotees asks, 'Why, O initiates, if these things are fine and useful, do you shut yourselves up in deep darkness and do good to three or four only when you could do it to all mankind by setting the source of benefit in the market-place, in order that all might be able freely to obtain a share in a better and happier life?' The criticism is to some extent a Jewish commonplace against mysteries, but fits this type well. As instances of it we may adduce (a) the *Chaldaic Oracles*, a work in Greek hexameters supposedly translated from Zoroaster, outlining a theology of the sanctity of fire and the soul's ascent to Heaven, and prescribing private cultus and private mysteries of Hecate (dated on general grounds in the second century of our era); (b) the piety represented by parts of the so-called Hermetic literature (supposedly translated from Thoth, an Egyptian god called by their writers 'Thrice-greatest Hermes'). Much of it is nothing but the commonplace of Hellenistic philosophy put in this authoritative form, and unconnected with any cultus. But the first tractate of our—probably fortuitous—collection, the so-called *Poimandres*, while saying nothing of sacrament or church, records a prophetic message of salvation which could have produced a community (pp. 3 f.). In tractate IV there is a metaphorical baptism, in XIII a rebirth by auto-suggestion: at the end of the *Asclepius*, another work from this school, there is a 'spiritual sacrifice' and we find specified times of prayer and specified forms of prayer and praise, one of which (from the end of the *Poimandres*) passed into a Christian collection of prayers by the end of the third century and a gnostic gem, another into a magical papyrus. Whether genuine communities were or were not formed, we have here something doing the work of a sect; the mode of operation would be that described by St. Augustine, *for from one loving heart another is kindled*. Further, we have, in the tractates named, a feeling of otherness from the world and a concept of conversion. The latter bears a relation to the analogies from philosophy to which we come in a later chapter: the former is very striking. The *Asclepius* says (22), 'There are not many, or rather there are very few who can be called truly religious, so that even in the world they could be counted'. *Corpus* xiii says: 'I have become ready and have manfully turned my soul from the deceitfulness of the world.'

(*c*) Further indications of the genesis of private channels of grace and illumination are afforded by our Greek magic papyri. They are texts found on papyrus, dating from the second century A.D. to the fifth, but for the most part from the late third to the early fifth. They are collections of recipes mainly for the attainment of practical objects and above all for success in love, the harming of one's enemies, and the curing of ailments, and so far correspond to similar texts in Demotic and Coptic, with which they are combined. We must regard them as the working copies of practical magicians: in fact a number of them almost certainly belong to a single ancient library. To such an expert the private man turned for a spell as he needed it, and it may be remarked that the texts contain numerous indications of the comparatively humble character of the clientèle. The surprising thing is the presence in these of methods of securing less trivial advantages, as for instance, personal introduction to the Sun-god and immortalization. These texts indicate what are in effect private mysteries, and they have the characteristic features of the official mysteries of the time, rebirth, the guarantee of the hereafter, the intimate personal relation to deity.

Further, the setting in which we find them indicates thay they were used by popular circles, and this is confirmed by vernacular Coptic works of Christian gnostic sects in Egypt, such as the *Pistis Sophia*. We may recall 2 Tim. iii. 6 f. (quoted by Origen, *Contra Celsum*, vi. 24, à propos of the Ophites), 'men who worm their way into houses and captivate women filled with sins, led about by various desires, always learning and never able to come to a recognition of truth'.

The memory of these gnostic sects reminds us of an important fact: their desire for information had a strongly practical side, the safety of the soul hereafter. Some sort of passport for the after life was a common thing (Orphic and Egyptian parallels occur at once). But the astrological scheme of the universe, if coupled with Jewish or Christian ideas of a fall of man, introduced new terrors. How is the *animula uagula blandula* to get past? Hence the complicated diagram of the Ophites. The very difficulty (as we see it) of visualizing the details of these schemes probably appeared to indicate their inspiration.

To resume, curiosity was widespread—an eagerness to penetrate the mysteries of the universe. The aim of this curiosity, whether pagan or Christian, is *gnosis*, special knowledge of the nature of things giving to man special privileges here and hereafter. Piety will give you knowledge. This is the attitude of those who trusted cults rather than speculation. The harder thinkers held the opposite proposition, which we find in Hellenistic philosophy, that knowledge, and above all knowledge of God, is or produces piety: that is to say, you cannot have a right attitude to the supernatural unless you are in the way of right thinking.

This can be mystical, as in Plutarch's *Theology is the goal of philosophy*, but it can be quite hard and intellectual. Few books are more unemotional than the *Summary of Greek Theology* by Cornutus: for him the gods are simply natural forces, and their qualities and attributes explicable either thence or as a disease of language. Yet Cornutus states his purpose thus (ch. 35):

'Concerning these things and the service of the gods and all that is fitly done in their honour in accordance with ancestral custom you will receive the perfect explanation. It is only so that the young are led to piety and not to superstition and are taught to sacrifice and pray and swear correctly at the right times and in the suitable order.'

The contrast of these two attitudes shows to us a very significant development. From the fifth century B.C. to the end of the first century A.D. Greek and Roman thinkers had for the most part maintained a cool respect towards religious tradition, regarding it as something which was to be retained but was in need of interpretation, sometimes drastic interpretation. They did not, however, regard it as a source of enlightenment. It was for them a satisfaction, at least a useful weapon in discussion and in the spreading of their tenets, to be able to read those tenets into it. But, Pythagoreans apart, they could not pretend to themselves that they were drawing from it tenets or a way of life. This now changed, not of course abruptly or completely, but yet visibly. The path of the intellect, though it had so often seemed promising, was not leading to sure results; the various keys used to unlock the secrets of the universe never quite fitted the lock; and academic suspense called for a mental austerity which was not common. Further, the rise of Rome to power set higher and higher values on practical gifts, on the administration of things as they were rather than on the interpretation of things. As the scope of philosophy narrowed till it became almost entirely ethical, it naturally tended to use religious sanctions and, though the range of its influence increased, it became less and less purely intellectual and more and more often shallow. The generality of men had of course never risen to the level of philosophic thought: the contemporaries of Socrates, though they could laugh with him at the *Birds*, could fall into a frenzy of panic over the mutilation of the statue of Hermes. What mattered now was that the salt of the earth had lost its savour, that faith in the intellect was nearly gone. Philosophy could not make windows in heaven. Could religion?

VIII

THE SUCCESS OF THESE CULTS IN THE ROMAN EMPIRE

WE have now surveyed the processes by which cults from the hellenized East made their way through the Roman world and the needs which they satisfied; and we have also noted how some of them passed into the official body of State cults in Rome itself. We must now turn to the most difficult question —the measure of success obtained by these incomers, how widely they established themselves, and how great an ascendancy they obtained over men's minds in the period in which Christianity was spreading. Our answer is of course conditioned by the limitations of our material, which is at its fullest, first, from the Antonine period to the middle of the third century A.D., and secondly, for the fourth century. Certain conclusions do, however, emerge clearly.

In the last century of the Roman Republic society fell into three classes—the ruling class, represented by the Senate and composed of those who had held public office, nobility belonging to those who could show a pedigree of such holding; the financial class of freeborn Romans who were called the Knights; and the third class which comprised the rest, including doctors, architects, poets (unless of family), and hucksters alike. The first had those prejudices which humanity usually dignifies with the name of principles; they stood for the maintenance of Roman ways and of a conservative nationalism. The feelings of the second are less well known to us, but their natural tendency was to go with the first. The third was more diverse. Many of the poets and writers who belonged to it enjoyed the patronage of members of the first and what may be called a status as temporary gentlemen: they voiced in general the attitudes which commended themselves to their patrons. Some of them, and some of the other members of their class, came from the Italian countryside and retained a feeling for its gods and rites together with a strength of national emotion which made it easy for them to embrace eagerly Roman tradition. Many members of the third class, however, were Levantine in temper. The Capitoline gods meant nothing to them, not even the patriotic emotion which they inspired in sceptical senators. They worshipped Isis and the Syrian goddess and were so lacking in any feeling of Roman propriety as to erect shrines to their favourite deities on the Capitol, which was like holding a Salvation Army meeting in the square before St. Peter's. Even they, however, would assume Roman modes of expression and fashion in religion, if they rose in society.

Literature then, as at most times till the eighteenth century, depended on patronage. This could be afforded by rich parvenus, like Epaphroditus, to whom Josephus dedicated his *Jewish Antiquities* and his work *Against Apion*, but it came in general from the ruling class and from those who had money but not standing and aped the ways and preferences of their betters. In the Empire fashion spread swiftly downward and the views of the aristocracy have dominated the literature which survives, and without doubt dominated most of the far larger literature which has perished. There were no righteous poor, no critics of society except the philosophers, and they, too, had and needed backers.

Augustus, when he became master of the world, set himself to restore the outward and visible forms of the old order and to seek for them the sympathy of all classes of society by the magnificence of the restored temples, by the appeal to the eye and to the heart of the Secular Games, and by the persuasive power of literary propaganda. He had the governing ranks behind him. This was a natural consequence of their tradition and is illustrated by the so-called Campana reliefs (plaques used in early Imperial times to adorn the ceilings and walls of houses and graves in Rome and other Italian cities) which show throughout only Greek mythological and ritual subjects, the occasional scenes from Egyptian cultus being merely curiosities, like the Egyptian landscapes in contemporary art or Chinese landscapes in the eighteenth century. Oriental religious subjects are very infrequent also in the Arretine pottery used by the poor, but it would not appear that Augustus succeeded in changing materially the attitude of the third class. Tibullus, Propertius, and Ovid all bear witness to the popularity of Isis in the demi-monde, and the incident of Paulina in A.D. 19 (p.153) shows this goddess as firmly accepted in equestrian circles, and illustrates once more the official attitude of discouraging alien cults whenever troublesome. Caligula, indeed, gave to Isis her first public temple, and under him the dramatic festival of Osiris was established in Rome, but his conduct hangs together with his notable contempt for the established tradition and did not raise the general standing of the Egyptian deities in Rome. The enlargement of the worship of Cybele under Claudius was, as we have seen, done in a Roman way.

Down to the death of Nero the old senatorial class retained its prestige. Rich freedmen like Pallas and fortunate soldiers like Sejanus had much of the effective power: but appearances were as they had been. When Claudius planned his expedition to Britain in 43 the troops were loath to leave Gaul and the world which they knew. The Imperial freedman Narcissus was sent to the camp and tried to address the troops, but they mocked at him, saying, 'Io Saturnalia,' to indicate that they regarded him as a slave, and straightway followed their commander Aulus Plautius. After 70 we see a great change.

The old senatorial nobility was now greatly reduced in numbers or financially weakened and continued to decline, the equestrian class was in many ways rising in importance, and Senate and knights alike were largely recruited from self-made men of the municipalities and the Latinized provinces. Vespasian was of this Italian stock and his régime introduced a bourgeois economy, as both Pliny the elder and Tacitus teach us. These men, though they might become more conservative than the conservatives (as, for instance, Tacitus did), were less influenced by traditional Roman aristocratic feelings of superiority to the worships of subject races. The mass of dwellers in Rome was no more cosmopolitan in the second century than in the first, in fact probably more Romanized: but the tone of society was set by the ruling class and the composition of this had changed.

It is therefore not surprising that the Flavian period saw a rise in the importance of the Egyptian gods. They remain outside the official city boundary, but appear on Roman coins in 71 and 73, and for the first time on the coins of Alexandria (which had an official character) Sarapis is called Zeus Sarapis. Domitian both rebuilt the sanctuary of Isis and Sarapis in the Campus Martius after a fire, and ordered two obelisks to be sent from Egypt to a temple of Isis built at Beneventum in the eighth year of his rule (A.D. 88). Vespasian had received help in Egypt from the priesthood: the miracles performed by him in the Sarapeum at Alexandria represent an adaptation of religious propaganda to his support, and Domitian had escaped the sack of the Capitol in the dress of an Isiac priest. The main colour of official religion is unchanged and Roman: in fact the most notable deity in Domitian's coinage is Minerva, but the alien element has now such recognition as would have seemed impossible under Augustus. Statius speaks respectfully of Isis and Cybele, and knows not merely the name of Mithras but the well-known scene of the god slaying the bull, which he mentions with the emphasis given by its being the last line of the book (*Thebaid*, i. 720).

Hadrian's accession, as we know above all from art, meant a great emphasis on Greek fashions, and these included the hellenized Egyptian cults (just as the Emperor's villa at Tibur included a Canopus). He had in his entourage an Egyptian prophet, Pachrates, and the death of his favourite Antinous was followed by a deification in Egypt which was related to the local concepts that a man could be immortalized by drowning in the Nile. Sarapis now appears on Alexandrian coins in a type which has attributes of other gods also. Again, a series of coins (possibly issued after Hadrian's death) shows the cult types, some hellenized types of Oriental deities, of the cities visited by the Emperor.

Of course, conservative feeling did not wholly disappear: it is notable that, in the age of Phlegon's collection of miracles, Suetonius describes Domitian's escape in the dress of an Isiac ministrant as 'among the petty sacrificers of a vain superstition', *interque sacrificulos uanae* (so late MSS.; earlier *uariae*) *superstitionis* (ch. 1), and Juvenal, vi. 511 ff., speaks with bitter contempt of women's superstition and tells with emphasis of their credulous submission to the representatives of Bellona, Cybele, Isis, and Judaism. It is remarkable also that the dedications of veterans leaving the *equites singulares* in Rome (a body recruited from the Rhine and Danube provinces) between A.D. 118 and 158 are directed only to the old Roman deities and to their native gods, and that among the divine names given to ships in the Roman Navy Isis is the only one of Oriental origin, and she, as protectress of the sea, could hardly be ignored. Further, Hadrian was intensely unpopular with the senatorial class. Still, there is an unmistakable rise in the importance of these cults from 70 to 134, and the Antonine age is the age of Apuleius and Aristides and that in which our taurobolic inscriptions begin and the full festival of Cybele is attested at Rome, and curious local types emerge on the coinage of Alexandria.

By the Antonine age the trend of social change has had time to bear full fruit. The governing class is now recruited from the whole Empire, East and West alike: we find men born in the province of Asia holding time-honoured priesthoods in Rome itself. The mood of the time is represented by the two works of Aelian mentioned above (p. 91): belief in the gods is in them demonstrated by miracles and not least by malignant defamation of Epicurus and Epicureans and by legends relating how heaven's hand had fallen heavily on them. Lucian and Celsus raised their voices on the other side, and uttered their contempt of mythology and foreign gods and rite and miracle, but there is in their works a very clear note of loneliness. The majority, even of philosophers, had chosen to walk by the light of unreason. Marcus Aurelius himself illustrates the transition. His fundamental attitude to the universe is the old heroic Stoic poise, and yet he thanks the gods for dream revelations which relieved him of blood-spitting and giddiness (i. 17. 20), and in obedience to an oracle from Abonutichus threw two live lions into the Danube. Whether we do or do not believe the story that at the outbreak of the war with the Marcomanni he summoned priests from all sides and performed foreign rites in Rome, there is a queer sign of the times in a coin with the legend *Relig(io) Aug(usta)* and a representation of a temple of an Egyptian deity. His successor, Commodus, was devoted to the rites of Isis and Mithras.

The next landmark is the Severan dynasty, which ruled from 193 to 235. Hitherto, although Imperial rule was in effect absolutist and in reality rested on the army, both facts were for the most part well shrouded in legal fiction. The fiction does not disappear, but it is now much less in evidence. Even earlier we have remarked on the influence exercised by an emperor's personal tastes, and that is very clear in this period. The fact of special importance is the temperament of Iulia Domna, wife of Septimius Severus, mother of Caracalla, great-aunt of Elagabalus and of Severus Alexander. She was born at Emesa, a famous religious centre in Syria, and till her death, which followed quickly on Caracalla's, occupied a dominating position in intellectual society. Philostratus claims to have received from her the memoirs of Damis on Apollonius of Tyana, and certainly enjoyed her patronage. Caracalla built a shrine for Apollonius. What Philostratus offers is a paganism interpreted by philosophy and approximating to a religious system. In this Life, and in the *Heroicus* (p. 91 above), there is a clear rise in the tension of piety: this appears again in the soldier's creed from Carvoran, to which we shall come (p. 136). Under Septimius there is no plain indication of Orientalization in official worship, and there are no clearly Oriental religious types on his coinage. He built a temple to the African Liber and Hercules in Rome, but they were the gods of his native Africa, and in 204 he celebrated Secular Games in accordance with ancient precedent. Caracalla, on the contrary, built a temple of Sarapis in the Quirinal and showed such devotion to this worship as to be called *philosarapis*, lover of Sarapis, and Elagabalus in his brief spell of power transported the black stone of Emesa (the god Elagabal) to a temple on the Palatine, transferred thither what he believed to be the palladium from the temple of Vesta, and set his fetish at the head of the Roman pantheon.

Although there is at least one reflection in military dedications of this violent policy, it does not represent Roman feeling at the time, and it was followed by a conservative reaction. Cassius Dio, whose boyhood had been spent under the very different rule of Marcus Aurelius, though no rationalist and no despiser of dreams and portents, speaks with bitter hostility of

Isis and Sarapis (40. 47. 3) and without sympathy of the temple to the African Liber and Hercules (76. 16. 3).

The economic circumstances of the time no doubt curtailed some of the old cults: the distribution of money to the Arval Brothers recorded in 241 was one-quarter of the old sum. The pendulum clearly swings back under Trajan Decius (249–51); the persecution of Christianity, probably in effect tolerated by the Severi, is accompanied by a positive revival of Roman religious feeling which continues under Diocletian and his colleagues in spite of their devotion to Mithras as patron of their rule (A.D. 307). The Decian requirement of sacrifice applied to every citizen, not only to suspected Christians: in effect it defined paganism. When in 274 Aurelian introduced the worship of Sol Invictus, the unconquered Sun, at Rome, it was a Romanized cult with a college of *pontifices*. This was, in a sense, an apogee of pagan religion, casting as it did into a traditional mould the vigorous beliefs of the hellenized Syria which found so much to share with contemporary speculation.

There, as so often, climax and end fell near one another. Apart from the small building consecrated by Maxentius in 307 to his deified son Romulus, this was the last official Roman temple to be built. Over the Western provinces dedications to Oriental deities declined greatly. The world was impoverished, there was probably less influx of merchants from the East, and Christianity was gaining. Diocletian and his colleagues did not exterminate it; their failure led inevitably to its recognition, and its recognition equally inevitably to its exclusive domination. We shall consider the Julianic reaction in Chapter X: it had not so small a chance of success as the attempt of Eugenius in 392, but it was a forlorn hope.

Religious development under the Empire falls therefore into clearly defined periods:

Augustan	*Severan*
Claudian	*Reaction of Decius*
Flavian	*and Diocletian*
Antonine	*Constantine*

This agrees remarkably with the periods into which the history of Imperial art falls.

We pass now to the question of the relative strength of Oriental religions during the central period, from about 120–260, for which we have most material. For the Western provinces Toutain has studied the evidence and drawn these conclusions: (1) the Egyptian cults spread mainly in regions which had relations with Egypt or which had foreign and, above all, military elements: the worshippers who have left records consisted on the one hand of officials high or low, on the other of freedmen and slaves, commonly Greek or Oriental, and contained hardly any un-Romanized provincials; men coming from Rome played a notable part. (2) The Syrian cults flourished mainly in regions occupied by troops, legionary and auxiliary; there is no epigraphic trace of them in the peaceful province of Africa proconsularis, and their worshippers are mainly either military—of all ranks—or of Oriental origin. No native provincials are found among them; once more Rome and Italy have played a significant part, though a certain importance belongs to troops which had been raised or quartered in Syria. (3) The

Anatolian cults found their adherents for the most part, not in the military frontier provinces, but in Africa and Gaul; above all, in ports or in towns along the great roads connecting them with Italy; the worshippers include very few soldiers and Imperial functionaries and many provincial and municipal dignitaries, only one slave and one freedman, but a number of people whose names prove their Gaulish or Spanish descent. Cybele became a really popular figure in Gaul and the *taurobolium* obtained a firm hold on the popular imagination. The cult was very much more a municipal affair than the other cults in the list, which is natural since she had early been given an outstanding part in the worship of Rome and her cult was directly under the supervision of the *quindecimuiri*. (4) Mithraism found its adherents mostly in the military frontier provinces, to some extent on the great roads and in seaports. These adherents consist of governors of provinces, high military officials—not in general till the third century,—lower ranks in the army (some Mithraea being actually built by military labour), men of the procuratorial career, that is the financial service of the Empire: there is no known case of a city or municipality building a Mithraeum and little evidence of interest shown in the cult by municipal officials or priests: there are many worshippers of Greek or Eastern extraction and very few of the native stocks of the West. The vitality of the cult is most conspicuous (*a*) under Commodus, the Severi, and the Gordians, (*b*) between 284 and 313, (*c*) in the last pagan revivals.

Toutain's conclusions relate purely to the Roman provinces of the West, not to Italy or to the rest of the Empire. For the West they are in general convincing, though we must not ignore Cumont's warning against insecure arguments from statistics and his reminder of the accidental nature of much of our information, and one or two points can now be added. The Mithraeum recently found at Dieburg was built by a man of native extraction, and there and at Königshofen statuettes of native deities have been found in the shrines.

I need hardly say that the difference which we see between Cybele's area of diffusion and those of the other Oriental deities does not point to any sort of competition. Cybele was early Romanized and did not seem exotic in anything like the same measure as these other cults with Oriental origins: further, as Toutain remarks, she suited the interests of an agricultural population. I think the paucity of adhesion among men with native names indicates that except in the neighbourhood of a temple of exceptional influence —as that of Sarapis at Alexandria—the real impulse to advance was not strong. There was at least little demonstrativeness. C. H. Moore has reckoned that in certain selected towns of Narbonese Gaul the Oriental gods have not quite 14 per cent. of extant dedications, in Bordeaux, Lyons, and Trier somewhat over 15 per cent., in Mainz, Heddernheim, Köln, and Vetera a little over 14 per cent.—and that in spite of the great popularity of Juppiter Dolichenus and Mithras at Heddernheim, where the figure is over 63 per cent., leaving under 1 per cent. for the other three towns. These proportions are probably too high rather than too low, for the worshipper of a strange god was more likely than that of an old to demonstrate his piety by a votive offering with an inscription. The restoration of temples to such deities was more likely to evoke private generosity than the restoration of temples to the old gods.

These facts from the Western provinces are interesting and significant, and a similar analysis of the position at Rome and in Italy would be very welcome. Rome is not merely the point at which all influences in religion as in other things converged: it is also the point from which ordinances and functionaries go forth. It need not invent, but it can impose. Already it is the eternal city, and, as to Lucius, the holy city. At the end of the fourth century it remains 'the temple of the whole universe' and the home of the old aristocratic circles for which paganism and the old classical culture were inseparable.

If the extension of these alien cults is hard to determine, it is much harder to form any just idea of the extent to which they affected men's religious thinking and of the proportion of adhesions which were of the nature of conversion.

Conversion implies turning from something to something else: you put earlier loyalties behind you. This was at once involved in adhesion to Christianity or in full adhesion to Judaism and in a lesser degree in the piety of the Gentiles who partly accepted the minimal demands of Judaism. It was not involved in adhesion to the cult of Isis or Mithras or their compeers. The importance of one cult, the helpfulness of one deity may be greatly stressed, and there is occasional rivalry, as when an altar set in a Mithraeum at Rome under Caracalla, who favoured Egyptian deities, was at first inscribed, *There is one Zeus Sarapis, the Sun, ruler of the world*, and *Mithras* was later substituted for *Sarapis*.

But that is all, before Christianity had attained substantial proportions and by so doing given paganism a self-consciousness. And while you can become attached to a cult without theology or hierarchy—as Nero was for a time to an image of the Dea Suria—it is hard for you to be converted to it: there is nothing to seize. The mysteries gave a revelation but not a dogma. A hierarchic organization did not exist except when Maximinus Daia in the first and Julian in the sixth decade of the fourth century created it, following Christian precedents. We shall see later that when Lucius after his Isiac initiation at Corinth came to Rome he went to the temple of Isis in the Campus Martius and felt 'a stranger to the temple but at home in the faith', but even so he was pressed to take another initiation and there is not the faintest suggestion of anything like Christian letters of introduction to a new diocese or of a holy Isiac church throughout the world. There was a will to power in the Alexandrian priesthood of Isis and Sarapis, as we see in their propaganda, but no oecumenical organization. There was a universalist point of view; Isis and Imouthes were to be praised by every tongue, but the supposed or desired piety of the world is no more than an aggregate of individual pieties. It is so with other worships of the type: there are strong centres, Ephesus for Artemis, from the fame of which she was in many places called Ephesia, the *mons Vaticanus* for Cybele at Rome (so holy that she has a cult place so called at Lyons and the kindred Virtus Bellona has one at Civitas Mattiacorum in Germany), the temple of the Dea Suria at Hierapolis, and in particular cities there are cult dignitaries, the *archigallus* for Cybele, the *pater patratus* for Mithraism: the *quindecimuiri* at Rome, as we have noted, approved the gift of the appropriate insignia to Cybele's priest at Lyons and elsewhere. But we miss any sort of general organization and feeling of unity.

There was indeed a theology which finds expression in many of these cults. To take a striking example: we possess the short creed in verse which a soldier in the third century caused to be inserted on a stone tablet found at Carvoran in Northumbria on the Roman wall.

'Opposite the Lion in the heavenly place is the Virgin, wreathed with corn ears, inventress of Justice, foundress of cities, the gifts from which it has been our fortune to know the gods. So she is at one and the same time the mother of the gods, Peace, Virtue, Ceres, the Syrian goddess, weighing life and rights in the balance. Syria brought forth a constellation seen in heaven to receive the homage of Libya. *Hence we have all learned. So* Marcus Caecilius Donatianus serving as tribune in the duty of prefect by favour of the Emperor *understood, led by thy deity.*'

Here the cult is a religion in which all humanity joins and a religion communicated of favour by revelation. The detail of this is no doubt due to the movement fostered by the Severan dynasty at Rome, but the basic idea—that the worship in question is a form (at most the best form, using the deity's favourite name) of the religion of all men—is widespread. We shall see this as an integral element in belief in Isis and Sarapis in the second century A.D. (p.150, below): we have seen it as explicit in a Clarian oracle, and in the Naassene sect (pp. 111, 115, above): we shall see it later in Maximus of Madaura (p. 260). Its popularity is shown by the common ascription to various deities of the epithet *pantheus* and by the representations of one of them with attributes of others. The latter begin in the second century B.C., but the widest extent of the development is from the end of the first century of our era. There is interesting evidence at that time of such thinking in the hymn to Apollo with which Statius ends the first book of his *Thebaid* (Apollo=Titan= Osiris=Mithras), and later in the model prose hymn to Apollo written by the rhetorician Menander at the beginning of the third century of our era. This specu- lation is drawn into the religious sphere and made dogma; but it means 'This is the significance of your earlier faith, of all men's faith': it completes and systematizes what was there, but it does not substitute things new for things old. It is a theology of unity and mutual understanding, and not of conflict. Adhe- sion to a new cult was thus made easier: it need involve no more than the devotion of Catholics to the cultus of a new saint.

IX

THE CONVERSION OF LUCIUS

Our survey of paganism has given us little reason to expect that the adhesion of any individual to a cult would involve any marked spiritual reorientation, any recoil from his moral and religious past, any idea of starting a new life. For adhesion to acquire the emotional values of conversion special personal circumstances were necessary, and we find such in the story told in the eleventh book of the *Metamorphoses* of Apuleius. This strange and beautiful work, written under Marcus Aurelius, is based upon a Greek romance telling how a young man was led by an amour into careless dabbling in magic and was as a result changed into the shape of an ass. In the original story he regained his shape thanks to the antidote (eating rose-leaves), and the ending is burlesque. Apuleius gave to it a different conclusion, in which there is more than a touch of autobiography. We must follow it closely, for it is the high-water mark of the piety which grew out of the mystery religions.

The hero, while still in the shape of an ass, awaking in the night, invokes the aid of Isis, 'being sure that the highest goddess is strong in the majesty that is all her own, and that human affairs are wholly guided by her providence, and that not only animals tame and wild but also inanimate things are given life by the divine will of her light and deity'. She appears to him in a dream, tells him of herself, the object of the worship paid by all the world to various divine names, and speaks of her festival of the morrow and says: 'At my direction a priest on the very outskirts of the procession will bear in his right hand a wreath of roses attached to a *sistrum* (rattle). So without hesitation part the crowd and haste to join the procession, relying on my favour. Come close to the priest and gently, as though you were kissing his hand, reach for the rose and rid yourself of the skin of that animal that I have so long hated. Do not fear any of my instructions as difficult, for at this same moment at which I come to you I am there also present and am enjoining on my priest in his sleep what he must do. At my bidding the closely packed throngs will make way for you. . . . You will remember absolutely and always keep stored in your heart of hearts one thing, that the remaining course of your life till you draw the last breath is made over to me. It is right that you should owe all the existence which is to be yours to her thanks to whom you have returned to humanity. But your life will be happy, nay glorious, under my protection, and when you have accomplished your span and descended to the underworld there also, even in the lower hemisphere, you will as a dweller in the Elysian fields constantly adore me whom you now see, shining in the darkness of Acheron, reigning in the recesses of Styx, and you will find me gracious toward you. And if by acts of diligent obedience, faithful devotion, and steadfast self-discipline you deserve well of my godhead, you shall know that I and I alone have the power to prolong your life beyond the bounds appointed by your fate.'

He awakened straightway and pondered over all the injunctions which he had received. The sun rose and all nature seemed to rejoice. The procession took its course and the priest in question appeared. Lucius did not like to rush forward, but crept in, the people making way. The priest, seeing all happen in accordance with the orders which he had received from Isis, stopped suddenly, put forth his right hand, and held the wreath before the lips of Lucius, and he was a man again. The throngs marvelled, the faithful paid homage to the miracle. They raised their hands to heaven and with loud harmonious voices bore witness to this manifest goodness of the goddess. We know their cry, *Great is Isis* and we know their mood; it is as at Lourdes when the word goes forth that there is a cure.

Lucius, restored to human shape, was speechless with depth of feeling. 'The priest, knowing somehow by divine admonition all my misfortunes from the beginning, although himself also profoundly stirred by this striking miracle, signed to the people to give me a linen garment to cover myself. . . . When this was done, with smiling and in truth unearthly face, in wonder at the sight of me, he spoke thus: "After bearing many and various labours, after being driven about by great tempests of Fortune and mighty storms you have at last come, Lucius, to the harbour of calm and the altar of mercy. Neither your birth nor your rank, nor the learning which adorns you availed you at all, but in the slippery time of youthful vigour you sank to the pleasures of a slave and obtained a sorry reward for your ill-starred inquisitiveness. But, however it was, the blindness of Fortune, while torturing you with the worst of perils, has with a malice which proved short-sighted brought you to this pious happiness. Let her go now and rage with her worst frenzy and seek some other object for her cruelty: for hostile chance has no power against those whose lives have been claimed as hers by the majesty of our goddess. What profit did spiteful Fortune derive from robbers or wild beasts or slavery or the hardest of journeys, bringing you back to where you started, or the daily fear of death? Now you have been taken under the protection of Fortune, yes, and a Fortune that sees, that by the splendour of her radiance gives light even to the other gods. Put on now a more cheerful countenance to match your white raiment, join with glad steps the procession of the goddess who is your deliverer. *Let the irreligious see, let them see and learn how wrong they are.* Lo, Lucius freed from his old woes by the providence of great Isis triumphs joyously over his own fortune. Yet that you may be safer and more protected, enrol in this holy soldiering, to which you were but now bidden to pledge yourself, and even now dedicate yourself to the following of our religion and take on yourself the voluntary yoke of service. For when you have begun to serve the goddess, then you will the more perceive the fruit of the liberty which is yours.'''

The priest delivered his oracle and ceased in weariness. Lucius walked on in the procession and all the people said: 'This man has this day been restored to human shape by the august will of the all-powerful goddess. Happy is he, thrice blessed is he who of a surety by the innocence and good faith of his earlier life has deserved such conspicuous help from heaven, so that having been in a way reborn he should at once be wedded to the service of holy things.' Then follows the description of the ceremony of the *Ship of Isis*, which was as it were a blessing of the waters at the beginning of the sailing season.

The friends of Lucius, who had despaired of his safety, heard of his deliverance and came in joy to welcome him and to shower gifts upon him. Then Lucius hastened back to the contemplation of the goddess and hired an abode within the temple precinct, where he lived with the priests and devoted himself to their solemn rites. There was not a night or a sleep which was not nourished by a vision and guidance from the goddess: by frequent commands she bade him now at last to be initiated in her rites, for which he had this long time been destined. But he, though willing and eager, was held back by a scrupulous fear, for he had found by careful inquiry that it was hard to observe the religion and that the keeping of the periods of abstinence was somewhat difficult. As he thought time and again on these things, he delayed for all his eager haste. On a certain night he dreamed that the chief priest presented to him his bosom full of gifts and, when asked what it meant, replied that those things had been sent to Lucius from Thessaly and that a slave of his named Candidus had also arrived thence. When he awakened, he kept turning over this vision in his mind to discover its meaning: the chief difficulty was that he was quite certain that he had never had a slave of that name. But he was assured that the gift meant some gain, whatever the sense of this omen in sleep. Accordingly, with this anxiety and awed expectation of some happy issue, he waited for the temple to open in the morning. The shining veils were drawn apart and they prayed to the adorable sight of the goddess: the priest went round the altars duly set and performed his solemn service of prayer, drew water from the inner room, and made libation with a sacred vessel. When all this was duly accomplished the religious filled the temple with their loud salutation of the new day, announcing the first hour.

Then there came to the temple his slaves from Hypata, with his white horse, too, which fulfilled his dream about the slave Candidus. Lucius treated this as an earnest of future blessings and repeatedly besought the chief priest to initiate him. 'But he, a man of high seriousness and distinguished for his strict keeping of austere religion, held back my eagerness, gently and kindly, just as parents regulate children's wishes when unsuitable to their years. By holding out the consolations of a better hope he calmed my anxious spirits. For, said he, the goddess indicates the day on which each man can be initiated and her providence chooses the priest who should perform the rite and a similar instruction fixes the expenditure necessary for the ceremonies. All this you, too, must bear with exemplary patience. You must above all beware of over-eagerness and obstinacy and avoid both faults: you must neither tarry when summoned nor hasten when not bidden. There is no one in our number so mad, so bent on self-destruction that, unless the Mistress gave him also separate instructions, he would dare to undertake a rash and sacrilegious ministry and incur the guilt of mortal sin, for the keys of Hell and the guardianship of our safety are in the hands of the goddess and the actual transmission of the mystery is celebrated in the likeness of a voluntary death and a safety given on sufferance. When the space of life is over and men are on the very threshold of darkness, and the great secrets of religion may safely be entrusted to them, then the might of the goddess is wont to choose them and by her providence to give them as it were a second birth and set them back in the paths of a new health. So therefore you, too, must await the heavenly ordinance, although the clear and manifest condescension of the great deity has shown that you are long since named and destined for her blessed service. You, too, like the other worshippers, must abstain from impure and evil foods, in order that you may the more rightly go to the hidden mysteries of the most holy worship.

'The priest finished speaking and my obedient service was not spoilt by impatience, but with my mind set on calm repose and laudable silence I was daily busied with the service of attendance on holy things. The saving goodness of the mighty goddess did not cheat me or torture me with long delays, but by clear biddings in the dark of night plainly told me that there had come the day ever desirable to me on which she would fulfil for me the greatest of wishes. She told me at what cost I should appease her with solemn rites and decided that Mithras himself, that specially dear priest of hers, was by some divine conjoining of the stars, as she said, yoked to me as the minister of the rite.' Lucius, though it was barely dawn, hastened to the priest. And as soon as the priest saw him, he said: 'O Lucius, happy are you, blest are you, whom the majestic deity honours so greatly with her gracious goodwill. Why do you now stand idly and keep yourself waiting? This is the day for which your steadfast prayers have asked, the day on which at the divine commands of Her of many names you are by these hands of mine to be led into the most holy secrets of her rites.' The priest did the morning ceremonies, produced his hieroglyphic book of ritual, and told Lucius what he must procure for the initiation.

He did as he was commanded and then was led among the band of pious to the nearest baths. There he washed as usual and the priest prayed and besprinkled him, set him before the feet of the goddess and gave certain teaching in private and also instructions in public to abstain from meat and wine and to curtail all enjoyment of food for ten days.

Lucius obeyed, and the sun sank and brought on evening. In accordance with ancient custom the faithful came together from every side, honouring him with their several gifts. All who were not holy were removed, and the priest clothed him in a linen garment and led him to the holy of holies.

'You, O zealous reader, will perhaps ask eagerly enough, what was then said and what was done. I would tell you if I might, but ear and tongue would incur the same guilt of rash inquisitiveness. Yet I will not torture you with long suspense, when you are perhaps aglow with pious yearning. So hear, yes, and believe the things which are true. I visited the bounds of death: I trod Proserpina's threshold: I passed through all the elements and returned. It was midnight, but I saw the sun radiant with bright light. I came into the very presence of the gods below and the gods above and I adored them face to face. Well, I have told you things of which though you have heard them you must not know.

'Therefore I will relate the one thing which can without sin be proclaimed to the minds of those outside. It was morning: the rites were done and I came forth consecrated in twelve robes. The dress is sacred in truth, but there is nothing which bids me to be silent concerning it, for very many were then present and saw it. As I was bidden, I stood on a wooden platform set in the very centre of the temple before the image of the goddess. I was before all eyes, in a linen garment, but one decorated with patterns of flowers. A costly cloth hung on my back from my shoulders to my heels. From whichever side you beheld me I was adorned with animals marked out in various colours: here were Indian dragons, there Hyperborean griffins, creatures of the other part of the world in the likeness of winged birds. Those who have been sanctified call this the Olympian vestment. In my right hand I bore a blazing torch; my head was duly bound with a wreath of gleaming palm, the leaves standing out like rays. So when I was arrayed in the fashion of the Sun and set there like an image the veils were suddenly drawn back, and the people streamed in to see me. Then I kept the most joyous birthday of the rite: there was a charming feast and merry banquet. The third day also was celebrated with a similar ceremonial rite: there was a solemn breakfast and legal completing of the initiation. I remained there for a few days and drew a pleasure which cannot be told from the divine image, to which I was bound by a favour for which no return of gratitude could be made. Still at length, at the bidding of the goddess, having paid humble thanks, not indeed fully, but to the best of my abilities, I at length made preparations to go home, slow in all conscience, for I found it hard to break the chains of most eager desire which held me back.'

He fell before the image of Isis, his face pressed against her feet, and poured forth his thanks and his consciousness of their insufficiency, concluding, 'But I am weak of intellect to tell thy praises, poor in resources to offer sacrifice: my abundance of words is not enough to say all that I feel concerning thy majesty, nor would a thousand mouths, a thousand tongues be enough. So I will set myself to do all that can be done by one devoted but poor: I will ever keep thy divine face and thy most holy deity in the sanctuary of my heart and picture them to myself.' He embraced the priest who had initiated him and who was now his father, and made his way home. Then in a few days at the prompting of the goddess he packed his baggage and went to Rome, reaching the holy city on 14 December. 'Nor was there anything thereafter to which I devoted myself so eagerly as daily to pray to the high power of queen Isis, who taking the name of Campensis from the place of her temple is worshipped with deepest reverence. In a word, I was a constant worshipper, a stranger to the temple, but at home in the religion.'

'And behold, the great sun had run his circle and finished the year, and again there broke in on my sleep the watchful care of the kindly deity and again it turned my thoughts to initiation and rite.' Lucius wondered what this might mean (was he not most fully initiated?) and discussed it with the holy. Then he learned that he had received the rites of Isis but was not yet illuminated with the ceremonies of unconquered Osiris, the great god and highest father of the gods; the gods were related but the initiations different. Now Osiris sought Lucius for his servant. Another dream relating to his home convinced him: once more another man (this time a *pastophorus*, a term denoting in Egypt one of a class of minor clergy and here an honorary office, like that of deacon in some denominations) had had a corresponding dream. All seemed

clear, but Lucius lacked money. The commands
continued and were urgent, and he sold his clothes to
provide what was necessary. All preparations were
made: he passed another ten days of purification,
shaved his head and was illuminated with the nightly
mysteries of the chief of the gods. Then with full
assurance he frequented divine worship and settled
down to legal practice.

'And behold after a very short time, the unexpected
and ever wonderful commands of the gods broke in
upon me again and compelled me to undergo yet
a third initiation.' Lucius was very upset and even
came to doubt the judgement of the priests who had
initiated him. He was almost beside himself with
anxiety, when the kindly vision of the deity reassured
him saying, 'There is no reason why the long chain of
rites should cause you to be frightened as though something had been omitted earlier. Rather rejoice in this
continued condescension of the deities. Enjoy your
happiness and be exultant, for that you are to be thrice
what is barely granted once to another, and from this
number of ceremonies have the surety that you will
always be happy, as you deserve. Moreover, the impending initiation is very necessary for you, as you
will see if you reflect that the cast-off garment of the
goddess which you took upon yourself in the province
remains laid in the temple and that you cannot in
Rome either pray to it, or when it is enjoined upon
you be glorified by that blessed garb. Follow then the
leading of the great gods and with a joyous heart be
again initiated in the mysteries, and may it be to your
blessing and happiness and deliverance.'

'So far the persuasive majesty of the divine dream

declared what was needed. I did not postpone the matter or cast it back into idle delay, but at once told my priest the things which I had seen and straightway submitted to the yoke of meatless abstinence and with voluntary self-restraint multiplied the ten days which the unbroken law prescribed. Then I provided what was wanted for the initiation liberally, contributing everything according to the zeal of my piety rather than the measure of my resources. I did not at all regret my toil or expenditure, for through the liberal providence of the gods I was now enriched with legal fees. Finally, after a very few days, I saw in a dream the god who is mightier than the great gods, highest of the greater gods, greatest of the highest, ruler of the great, Osiris, not transformed into the shape of any other: he honoured me by speaking to me face to face in his majesty and received me. I was bidden unhesitatingly to ply my calling as advocate with glory in the Forum and not to fear the rumours of ill-wishers which assailed the knowledge which I won by diligent study; he did not suffer me to serve his rites in the common throng but admitted me to the college of his *pastophori*, nay among the very quinquennales of the decurions (i.e. the governing body). Again, with head close shorn, I gladly went about the business of that most ancient college founded in the famous days of Sulla, neither veiling nor covering my baldness, but leaving it for every man to see.'

I have let Apuleius tell the story of Lucius. It is, as he hints, in some measure his own story. Is it trustworthy? or is it an idealized picture, bearing little relation to the mood in which the cult was normally contemplated?

The external facts are of course trustworthy: Apuleius was dealing with things which many or most of his readers would have seen. The second and third initiation have been regarded as invented by the Roman priesthood for their personal gain: the ministers of Isis lived by their religion, and were not always thought to be above considerations of profit (p. 153, later), but it is possible that these additional ceremonies were genuine and due to a tendency elsewhere observed to multiply rites. Two points particularly deserve to be checked, the theology implied and the concept of divine command.

Lucius, before his transformation, prays to the Queen of Heaven, whether she be Ceres worshipped at Eleusis or heavenly Venus worshipped at Paphos, or Diana worshipped at Ephesus or Proserpine. She appears and tells him that the Phrygians worship her as the Mother of the gods, the Athenians as Minerva, the Cypriots as celestial Venus of Paphos, the Cretans as Dictynna, the Sicilians as Proserpine, the Eleusinians as Ceres, and others as Juno or Bellona or Hecate or Nemesis, but the Ethiopians and the Egyptians with their ancient learning worship her with the ceremonies which are peculiarly her own and call her by her true name, *Queen Isis*.

We know the theory well, but what is important to notice is that theory and form alike were at home in the cult: *myrionyma* is a regular epithet for her and we find the descriptive phrase *una quae es omnia*. An Oxyrhynchus papyrus (No. 1380), assigned on grounds of script to the early second century A.D., gives us a long invocation of Isis. The initial verb of address is lost. The text opens with a list of cult names with the places at which they were used. Some of the cult names, even for places in Egypt, are Greek:

'At Aphrodites Polis in the Prosopite nome, mistress of fleets, many-shaped Aphrodite; . . . at Nithine in the Gynaecopolite nome, Aphrodite; at Pephremis, Isis, queen, Hestia, mistress of every country; . . . in the Saite nome, Victorious Athena, nymph (*or*, bride); . . . in Sais, Hera, queen, full grown; in Iseum, Isis; in Sebennytos, intelligence, ruler, Hera, holy; in Hermopolis, Aphrodite, queen, holy; . . . in Apis, wisdom; in Leuke Akte, Aphrodite, Mouchis, Eseremphis; at Cynospolis in the Busirite nome, Praxidike; at Busiris, Good Fortune; . . . at Tanis, gracious in form, Hera.'

But the list proceeds to include many places outside Egypt and to give for each an epithet or the name of a local deity equated with Isis.

'In Arabia, great goddess; in Syria, Leto; at Myra in Lycia, trusty, Eleuthera; in Crete, Dictynnis; at Chalcedon, Themis; in Rome, Warlike (?); at Pathmos [*sic*], young; . . . at Paphos, holy; . . . at Chios, marching; at Salamis, watcher; in Cyprus, bountiful; in Chalcidice, holy; in Pieria, blooming; in Asia, she of the cross roads; at Petra, saviour; at Hypsele, greatest; in Samos, holy; in Hellespont, initiate; in Myndus, divine; in Bithynia, Helen; in Tenedos, the eye of the Sun; in Caria, Hecate.'

The list includes places in Syria and Phoenicia, and also the Amazons, and Indians and Persians, and Magi, and Italy. It agrees with Apuleius in mentioning not merely Hecate and Hera, but also the more recondite Dictynnis.

Now this papyrus list is not, as it stands, an original composition: so much is shown by a number of superficial corruptions and by the fact that various places

are mentioned out of the geographic sequence. In the
list of Cypriot cities Chios suddenly appears, in that
of Syrian cities Sinope and Delphi, and further Syrian
names come after another interval. It is of interest also
that no distinction is made between genuine epithets
holy, mightiest, undefiled, and the names of other deities
identified with Isis. That is to say, the identifications
are regarded as complete and the local names of other
goddesses so equated as pure epithets of Isis.

After this long invocation in the accusative follows
further descriptive matter, giving general aspects of
Isis; and then comes a direct hymnological description
in the second person.

> 'Thou willest that women in health cast anchor with
> men, all the old sacrifice in [   ], all the maidens at
> Heracleopolis praise thee and speed to thee and have dedi-
> cated the land to thee. *Those who invoke thee in their trust in
> thee see thee*. . . . The grace of thy two commands is gentle
> and easily won.'

There follows a description in this style of the benefits
conferred by Isis on mankind, very like the description
in the first person ascribed to Isis in the *Praises of Isis
and Osiris* discussed earlier. We may note in particular
l. 202, 'Thou didst found Isea in cities for all time and
to all give ordinances and a perfect year . . . in every
place thou didst show, that all men might know, that
the heaven was stablished by thee.'

In this universalist scheme, therefore, Apuleius is
following the tradition of the cult as well as the tendency of his time. It is so likewise with the idea of
command and vocation. At every point from his first
appeal to Isis his conduct is prescribed by visions and
such prescription counts as a special grace. We have

seen commands of Sarapis earlier, given to Zoilus and
to the priest on Delos (pp. 49, 51). Pausanias tells that
the temple of Isis at Tithorea was the holiest of all the
sanctuaries made by Greeks for the Egyptian goddess
(x. 32. 13):

> 'For the Tithoreans deem it not lawful to dwell round
> about and there is no admission to the shrine except for
> those whom Isis herself has favoured with an invitation in
> a dream. The same thing is done also by the underworld
> gods in the cities on the Maeander: they send visions in
> dreams to whomsoever they wish to enter their shrines.'

Their commands could be special and specific.
Josephus (*Jewish Antiquities*, xviii. 65 ff.) tells how in
the year A.D. 19 a Roman knight, Decius Mundus, had
tried in vain to seduce one Paulina. A freedwoman of
his, seeing his distress and knowing that Paulina was
greatly devoted to Isis, bribed the priests of the goddess,
and the oldest of them went to Paulina and said Anubis
was in love with her and bade her come to him. She
came gladly with her husband's consent, having boasted
to her friends of the honour done to her. Next day she
told her husband of the god's epiphany and gloried in
it. Her women friends were sceptical and Mundus
told her the truth: her husband told Tiberius, who
crucified the freedwoman and the priests, destroyed the
temple, had the image of Isis thrown into the Tiber, and
banished Mundus. The story may contain invention,
and it certainly sounds like Dr. Achilli's revelations
on the inner conduct of the Catholic Church, but
the persecution is certain. Again, the *katochoi* in the
temples of Sarapis appear to have resided there until
the god indicated that they might go, and they received
numerous prophetic dreams.

Now the idea of divine commands given by oracles or dreams is known in earlier Greece, especially in connexion with Asclepius and his activity as a healer (where again a dream is something which needs to be interpreted by the priesthood). Divine commands are mainly associated with the direct official pronouncements of an oracle, but Dionysus, when playing the part of one of his ministers in the *Bacchae*, answers the question 'Whence did you bring these rites to Greece?' by saying 'Dionysus the son of Zeus set me in them', and Pentheus asks (469) *Did he compel thee by night or in thy sight?* The reply is *He saw me and I saw him and he gave me the mysteries.* Here it is assumed that the god's chosen vessel was impressed by him into his service, and when the Bacchanalia were put down provision was made for those who said it was *necessary* for them to have such worship (p. 73 above). Socrates says (Plato, *Apology*, p. 33 c) of his habit of questioning people: 'The command to do this has been given me by the god through oracles and dreams and every other medium by which any divine destiny ever ordered a man to do anything.' Greece and Rome knew well dreams conveying commands. Greece knew also the idea of the vocation of particular individuals, priests and seers (above all the founders of or members of families carrying on the concern), and poets, and Stoicism emphasized the duty of individual vocation. But the idea of commands to individuals and that of vocation are far more emphasized in Graeco-Oriental cults, which had in their background the Oriental conception of god as autocrat, master, and patron, and of man as subject, slave, favourite. Dedications 'in accordance with the command of the god' are very common and we read of 'those whom Juppiter Optimus Maximus Dolichenus has chosen to serve him'.

There is, therefore, a certain change of atmosphere. In classical Greece some men, as for instance Pindar, had a special devotion to a particular deity, but the normal ideal was that of the man who performed all due observances punctually and well without seeking particular light and leading.

We have reason to trust Apuleius. The picture which he draws us is very remarkable. It is like that of a man received into the Catholic Church, spending a season in retreat in a monastic house: for a time, like some in the early centuries, putting off baptism because of the obligations which it imposed: then eager to push ahead (as it might be to try his vocation in the religious life) and held back, and finally becoming a member of the Third Order of St. Francis and living in the world but not as of the world. The priest who gives the first initiation is a kind but firm spiritual director. The ideal expressed is one of submission and faith and joy fortified by contemplation of the image of the goddess, by dream revelations of her will, and by the daily round of the Divine Office. Lucius is not forbidden to take part in other cults, and formal public observances he would no doubt make, but any other worship must to him appear tame and inferior. His devotion is the devotion of a man delivered from evil straits: it is an outpouring of love and gratitude. It cannot be supposed that his is a normal level of pagan religious emotion, but it should certainly be remembered that it is a level which it could and did reach.

X

THE LAST PHASE

THE strength of paganism is seen in the power of resistance it displayed in face of the growing influence of Christianity. Its tenacity strengthened as it lost ground. In its last phase we find conversions back to paganism, not merely people lapsing in times of persecution. There had always been defections from Christianity. Pliny tells in his famous letter of converts who said that they had abandoned Christianity before there was any inquiry, some many years before. The first fine careless rapture could disappear in face of the ever-present loss of social amenities, club life, and festivals: or the Christian might have sinned and been excluded from communion by a conservative church which did not hold with penance and reconciliation. So Lucian speaks of Peregrinus as put out of the body. Even in Paul and Acts *endurance* is a characteristic term of Christians being constant, and the word was in the first century A.D. used in the south Russian records of manumitted slaves who were made completely free except for the obligation of respect for the synagogue and faithful attendance. It was a question not only of resisting social pressure and occasional persecution but of holding out against boredom, a state as well known in antiquity as to-day. From this point of view the strife against gnostic views and the early Christological controversies were probably very valuable: they gave men continued objects of love and hate.

Down to the middle of the third century men relapsed into paganism: we do not hear of their embracing it.

Now we find Porphyry, according to a tradition which need not be doubted, a Christian for a time, only to return to the faith of his fathers and to attack Christianity with the enthusiasm of a convert from it.

The best known of these conversions is that of Julian. Here we are fairly well informed on the details of the process. Julian himself speaks of the way in which the sun's rays and light fascinated him from childhood, and tells us of the library of George of Cappadocia, to which he had access during his life at Macellum: it contained 'all kinds of philosophers, many commentators and not least plenty of writings of every kind of the Galilaeans'. Then came the contacts at Nicomedia with Libanius, which deepened if they did not actually inspire his passion for hellenism as a cultural force. Libanius, a sympathizer who was a notable rhetorician, says in a speech delivered at Antioch to welcome him (*Oratio* xiii. 11): 'There was in concealment here (at Nicomedia) a spark of the prophetic art which had with difficulty escaped the hands of the impious. This first enabled thee to pursue the truth, and under the softening influence of the prophecies thou didst check thy violent hatred against the gods.' This is most important, for it shows us Julian as an eager Christian, and his writings reveal him as throughout saturated with Christian thought. A prophecy moved him, no doubt an oracle reminding him of the devotion of his ancestors to the Sun, perhaps substantially like the words of the Sun to the young man in his myth, 'We wish to purify thy ancestral house out of respect for thy ancestors. So remember that thy soul is immortal and descended from us, and that if thou followest us thou wilt be a god and wilt

with us see our father.' Somehow Julian heard of the
surviving Neoplatonists who still practised theurgy,
and went to Aedesius, Eusebius, and Chrysanthius at
Pergamon, and then to Maximus at Ephesus. Maximus
initiated him in the Neoplatonic mysteries based on
the *Chaldaic Oracles* mentioned earlier. Other factors
may have entered in; dislike of Constantius, the excite-
ment of the rising of Magnentius and his temporary
restoration of full rights to paganism in Rome, but in
the main Julian's conversion is due to a cultural ideal
quickened by the sense of a personal and at the same
time hereditary mission; this feeling came as a result
of religious experience. It was an emotional and not
an intellectual quest: it was therein different from that
of St. Augustine, although they resemble one another
in that each ends in a return to something which has
all the time been in the background.

To the passionate nature of Julian the issues between
Christianity and the new paganism was an *Entweder-
oder*: between the two rivals there was a great gulf
fixed, and it was not to be passed except by psychological crisis. It would be wrong to generalize from
him or to suppose that the enthusiastic support which
he received in various parts of the Empire (above all
Syria, where a deep-rooted local feeling centred around
the great temples) represents piety of his type and
earnestness, and a desire to convert humanity: men
felt joy at the abolition of interference with good old
customs. Even Julian had been content to yield external conformity, like Bishop Pegasius. It was now
possible to enter the Church without any profound
changes of mental furniture and spiritual orientation,
and, if Julian or Eugenius was in power, to leave the

Church with equal ease; possible again, having entered it, to come later to view the misfortunes of the Empire as due to its defection from the Roman gods. St. Augustine's *City of God* may well be directed against regretful Christians rather than recalcitrant pagans.

The two opposing forces had drawn near one another. Paganism had moved largely towards a sort of monotheism, and Julian's revival depended on the giving to it of those features which had in Christianity been most effective, theological and moral dogma, hierarchic organization, and systematic works of charity and benevolence. Julian purposed, we are told, to adorn pagan temples with the equipment and order of Christian piety, with seats according to dignity, with teachers and readers of pagan dogmas and exhortations, with establishments for men and women who had decided to be philosophers, with hostelries for strangers and beggars and general benefaction to those in need, with penance and letters of introduction like those given by Christian bishops. Augustine, who was eight years old when Julian died, remembers this attempt at religious teaching, which no doubt outlasted the Emperor's death. 'Only the other day we heard such healthful interpretations being recited in the temples to the assembled people'; he is speaking of allegorical interpretations of myth, freeing it from objectionable elements.

But a return might always be passionate, and there is another instance to add to that of Julian. A poem wrongly ascribed to Cyprian and probably belonging to the fourth century is addressed *To a senator who had turned from the Christian religion to be the slave of idols*. It complains of his return to the service of Cybele with her eunuch priests and of Isis, in whose honour (like Lucius) he has shaved his head and wears the dog mask of Anubis. 'It is common talk which has reached our ears that you have actually said, "*O goddess, I have sinned: forgive me. I have returned*".' Later the poet says, 'You pretend you are a philosopher in your change of opinion. For if the people's anger stirs your wrath you will turn Jew and you are deemed altogether lacking in stable purpose.' Later at Rome itself paganism, revived for a moment, hangs together closely with the old culture: the last pagans are known to us as students and editors of the Latin classics.

At the same time, the suppression of paganism took the form of the prohibition of cultus and seasonal observances, the destruction or appropriation of temples and the exclusion of recalcitrants from office and the army. There is no persecution in the Decian or Diocletianic sense: there was nothing to persecute in that way: and there are no pagan martyrs.

We have from this point of view surveyed a long development. We have seen the incoming of a series of alien cults into a world of different traditions: we have seen some of them establish themselves and consolidate their position in the culture which they found. Yet the surprising thing is the slightness of the change which they effected in the fundamental temper of the people among whom they took root. Our way of thinking is throughout coloured by the nature of Christianity. We conceive of religion as 'all or nothing'. To us it involves above all a view of the world and of the soul: sacrament and rite may bulk very large, but they do so because of their relation to this view, and to doctrines of redemption and original sin and grace. To the ancients the essence of religion was the rite, which was thought of as a process for securing and maintaining correct relations with the world of uncharted forces around man, and the myth, which gave the traditional reason for the rite and the traditional (but changing) view of those forces.

Everything made for the conservation of custom. We are used to a certain recoiling by one generation from the views of its predecessor: the son of a church-goer often becomes a freethinker, and the son of a freethinker often embraces a dogmatic religion. As the father of a musician who is a friend of mine said to him, 'We were brought up on Bach and have come to love Gilbert and Sullivan: you were brought up on Gilbert and Sullivan and have come to love Bach.' At one point in the history of Greece this was so—in the fifth century B.C., when the younger men were fascinated by the new thought then in the air and destructive criticism was fashionable among them. This was exceptional and short-lived. The humanistic education of Isocrates and of his successors, the philosophical tendency of Plato and his, both made for fixity, and the Cynic protest was something on which the average man looked as till recently he looked on the individual doubts and doctrines of Bernard Shaw. The tendency to conservatism was greatly strengthened by the rise of Rome, which glorified parental authority, the wisdom of age, and the value of ancestral custom, and had a horror of innovation. Innovation might involve a menace to the established order. Above all, the governing classes, which set the tone of society, must not indulge in it. Tacitus tells how Agricola when young showed an interest in philosophy: his mother anxiously saw to it that he should not pursue it too far. Of course, anything like conversion would be a breach of etiquette: it would mean *superstitio*, unreasonable enthusiasm characteristic of the lower orders.

Men become angry and excited when their material needs and desires are not satisfied. If these are, and sometimes even if they are not, men become angry and excited about other matters, and commonly then not about things in themselves but about their ideas concerning things. They love and fear not realities as such but realities as transformed by their imaginations, by the power of suggestion which their surroundings exercise, by these very emotions of love and fear when once called into play. Abstractions interest them just in so far as they can take a shape around which emotion can be kindled. They desire heaven for themselves: they are of Paul or Cephas or Apollos or Newman. The abstraction has to fulfil their desires or to justify their prejudices.

What did the ancients love? They loved local traditions and other traditions which, while alien in origin, had become naturalized; they loved the worships of the household and of the State; they loved the reverent practices which had grown up around the dead. What did they fear? The possible loss of the benefits thought to be derived by State and individual from these inherited ways. What did they desire? Civic well-being: all the temporal blessings of this life: and the intangible things of which we have spoken— immortality sometimes, freedom from the ban of fate sometimes, knowledge sometimes, a dignified status in the universe often. These fears and loves and desires were associated with worship, which was one of the facts of life. Worship had no key to life's meaning: that was offered by philosophy: but precisely because worship rested on emotion and not on conscious theory and thinking it had deeper roots in their natures, and was not easily refuted by reason.

So long as you did not try to take from these men anything which they had in religion, they could not as a rule object to new methods and new processes. So long as the priest and the silent Vestal climbed the Capitol, Balbus might build his Mithraeum, with the feeling that the established order was secured and that he was getting something additional for himself, something perhaps for the community also. And so the fact of Balbus and his like frequenting the Mithraeum did not usually involve conversion. But ask of him that he should consent to the ending of the Capitoline cult, and he would be shocked or even frightened: and if you were to win him you had to convince him, to convert him: at least you had to do this until the time came when the law made paganism a thing the profession of which required moral courage such as was formerly needed for the profession of Christianity.

XI

CONVERSION TO PHILOSOPHY

THE place which Greek philosophy occupied in the
life of the ancient world does in the last instance
arise from the special nature of Greek religion. India,
Babylon, and Egypt had centralized societies with
priestly classes: learning was the property of those
classes, and served practical ends, calendar regulation,
observation of the stars for portents, land measurement,
and the like. Greece had no such class: Delphi
answered questions, but only the questions which were
put to it. Zoroastrianism, Judaism, and Christianity
have put forward as part of revealed religion a view
of the origin of the world and of man; and of necessity
Christianity has given further doctrine on man's nature
as equally part of revealed religion. Any religion of
salvation must give some such explanation of its postulates. But official piety in Greece and Rome was not
such a religion: Orphism was, but Orphism did not
capture the established Church—in fact, as we have
seen, there was not an established Church to capture.
Local cults went their ways with some reference to
Delphi, and, while local cults preserved and cherished
their legends, the systematization of those legends
was the work of the poets, who, though often thought
to be inspired, were secular persons. There was
not a priestly class as such, but only priestly families
with functions in individual shrines. The legends as
systematized were admittedly in detail man-made,
and subject to further modification. The instinct for
legend-making naturally included cosmogony in its

range, and we have in Hesiod crude tales spun around imperfectly personified figures.

Speculative interest became really powerful about the beginning of the sixth century: its early manifestations in the Ionian philosophers show at every turn a close similarity to mythological thinking. Such speculation was thoroughly unfettered. It should not be forgotten that even on the traditional scheme, freely held as it was, the universe is prior to the gods actually worshipped. The natural powers, vaguely personified, who figure in Hesiod are not in the main recipients of cultus: the Olympians are, like the Greeks, new-comers who control a fabric which they found there. The gods of popular religion had nothing to lose. A man who speculated along these lines need not offend the conservative: he was filling a gap. He could even take a prophetic tone like Heraclitus or Empedocles. Religion and philosophy were very close in the Greek settlements of south Italy at the end of the sixth century. The followers of Pythagoras formed societies entered after preliminary discipline, with ascetic doctrine and practices, an intense group-consciousness, and a Pythagorean life prized by its followers and ridiculed by others: the affinity to Orphism is clear.

The philosophic movement in the main, as it proceeded in the fifth century, became more radical and through the dissemination of its ideas aroused popular antipathy at Athens, but it remained a professorial movement, ready to communicate its conclusions to disciples but not fired with any desire to free humanity from error or to lead it into truth. The activity of Socrates marks a turning-point. His sense of a mission which led him finally to martyrdom, his preoccupation with personality and with the quest for a basis for right conduct, his power of attracting and influencing disciples, all these things through the impress which they made on his disciples set a standard for *lovers of wisdom* and the *love of wisdom*, philosophers and philosophy: it is now that the words acquire popularity and definite meaning. Adhesion to Socrates somehow meant giving your soul to him. We have in the opening of Plato's *Banquet* the perfect picture of the fanatical disciple, Apollodorus.

> 'Now in a general way, whenever either I am talking about philosophy or I hear others so doing, I receive very great pleasure in addition to the sense of having good done to me, but whenever I hear other talk, and especially that of you rich commercial people, I am vexed by it and I feel sorry for you who are with me, since you think you are attaining something though you are attaining nothing. Possibly you in your turn think me a poor fool, and I suppose your opinion is right, but as far as you are concerned I do not think it but I know it full well.'

The interlocutor replies: 'You are always the same, Apollodorus: you always revile yourself and others alike, and I do in fact think that you consider that except for Socrates every one (yourself included) is wretched.' Near the end of the dialogue Alcibiades pays his tribute to this fascination. Socrates thus created an atmosphere of personal influence and discussion. Plato's foundation of the Academy gave to this tradition a permanent *locus standi*. Like the Pythagoreans his group had a sense of solidarity, and like the Pythagoreans it was fundamentally religious, and its religion was a reverent and living feeling for the glory and unity of the universe growing out of its scientific investigation, something essentially akin to the attitude of Einstein to-day, but its solidarity was not the solidarity of dogma. In so far as the world at large was outside it was because it lacked the preliminary training which alone made it possible to join in the pursuit of truth. Yet though the world could not participate, the Dialogues were written largely in order to give to wider circles some idea of the direction in which truth lay, to stimulate thought, and to enable the individual here and there who had a call to philosophy to realize his vocation. This dual aspect of philosophic activity was crystallized by Aristotle, and abides.

Why did these schools hold so dominant a place in the spiritual history of the succeeding centuries? Firstly, they offered intelligible explanations of phenomena. The Greek was naturally inquisitive, and the intellectual and political ferment of the fifth century had left many open questions. Secondly—and this is a point of cardinal importance—the schools offered a life with a scheme. One of the terms for a school of philosophy, whatever its kind, is *agoge*, which means way of teaching and way of living. The contrast of the life of virtue and industry with that of sloth and vice we know in Hesiod, and the fable of Heracles at the cross-roads, choosing between the two paths (ascribed to Prodicus), is a vigorous metaphor, but it was left for philosophy to give a *raison d'être* for the disciplined life. There was the Pythagorean life, like the Orphic life, with a religious theory of asceticism: that was for those who had deliberately chosen it, had deliberately renounced their former way of living, and such men there were not merely in south Italy throughout the fifth and fourth centuries, but also at Athens in the fourth (where they excited the derision of writers of comedy), at Rome and elsewhere in greater force in the first century B.C. and the first century A.D. We know a little of this revival, which had private religious rites (that queer stories arose about them need not be said), its own way of burial and the old theory of the soul and its relation to the harmony of the universe. It had a prominent representative at Rome in Nigidius Figulus, a sympathizer in Varro: it affected the school of Sextus and Sotion and through them Seneca, who writes (*Epistles*, 108.17), 'Since I have begun to set forth to you with how much greater zeal I betook me to philosophy when young than I proceed with it when old, I shall not be ashamed to admit what a passion Pythagoras inspired in me,' and proceeds to tell the reasons assigned to him for Pythagoras' abstinence from meat and how he himself so abstained for a year, desisting thereafter at his father's advice. At that time, in the early years of the principate of Tiberius, foreign religions were persecuted (p. 153 above), and abstinence from certain meats was a ground for suspicion; but his father's motive was not fear but a dislike of philosophy. It is likely that the underground basilica found in 1917 near the Porta Maggiore in Rome was meant to serve for the meetings of a sodality of Pythagoreans. Here was a life with a scheme and a brotherhood and religion. Also it had its saints, a point to which we return. This body finally disappears, doubtless through being merged in the Platonic revival of the second century A.D.

Again, there was the Cynic life of detachment and freedom. The Cynic school, founded by Antisthenes, put into practice ideas earlier advanced on the worthlessness of conventional standards and taught men to cut clear of the trammels of social life. The anecdotes told of the founder and of the even more famous Diogenes testify to the enormous impression made by this movement on society. Adhesion to such ideas meant something like conversion. We have the story of the rich Hipparchia, who, loving the Cynic Crates, left her wealth and lived with him the Cynic life: we have in the third century B.C. the causeries of Teles—called diatribes—a genre invented by Bion, and poems of Cercidas (a man who played a part in public life) expressing these ideas with apt simple illustrations and stories.

The wandering Cynic talking to those who would hear was a familiar figure later under the Empire, begging his bread, haranguing, and at times showing the free speech and utter indifference (dare we say rudeness?) of a Christian martyr. Dio of Prusa, who had a sincere admiration for Diogenes himself and uses him as the lay figure of six of his discourses, delivered a speech at Alexandria (probably early in the second century A.D.), in which after mentioning philosophers of the professional type he says (xxxii. 10):

'There is no small number of those who are called Cynics in the city: in fact there is a crop of this as of anything else. It is, however, a spurious and ignoble tribe of men who know hardly anything, but need food. They beg at cross-roads, in alleys, in the porticoes of temples and cheat slaves and sailors and the masses of that type; stringing together jests and much chatter and the well-known cheap repartees. Accordingly they do no good but rather the greatest harm, for they accustom the foolish to mock at philosophers: it is as though one were to accustom children to laugh at their teachers.'

We know the frequency of the type from references in Lucian, who gives us in his *Demonax* a picture of the ideal Cynic: well into the fourth century we find Julian polemizing *Against an unlearned Cynic*. Now any of these preachers might be seeking to effect some sort of change of life—and the embracing of the profession meant in itself some sort of sense of vocation.

'He must know', Epictetus (iii. 22. 23) says of the true Cynic, 'that he has been sent by Zeus to men as a messenger (*angelos*), in order to show them that in questions of good and evil they have gone astray and are seeking the true nature of good and evil where it is not, while never noticing where it is. The Cynic is a scout meant to spy out what things are friendly to men and what hostile.'

This is in a picture drawn for the benefit of an intending Cynic and drawn by a Stoic who says (iii. 21. 18) of the teaching profession that one needs to have been advised by God to take it up 'as God counselled Socrates to take the task of confuting men's opinions, Diogenes that of rebuking men in a kingly manner, Zeno that of instructing men and laying down doctrines'.

Stoicism also, throughout its development, supplied a motive for the life of discipline and for the taming of the passions in its doctrine of natural law and of man's conformity thereunto, in its emphasis on the writing of the law in man's reason, on the ideal standards of its paradoxes concerning the Wise Man, and (in its later form) on an active doing of good, and throughout, on the acceptance of the world-order in a ready obedience. This reaches a climax in the prayer which Seneca says he heard from the Cynic Demetrius (*Dial.* i. 5. 5):

'The only complaint which I can make concerning you, O immortals, is that you did not first make your will known to me: if you had, I should have taken the initiative in coming to where I am now at your call. Would you take my children? It was for you that I reared them. Or some part of my body? Take it: it is not much that I promise, for I shall soon leave the whole. Or my life-breath? Of course I will not hinder your receiving back that which you have given. Whatever you seek, you will have from me with my consent. What is it then? I would rather have given it than surrendered it. What need was there to take it? You could have it as a gift: even as it is, you do not take it away, for only the man who holds on to a thing is deprived of it.'

The doctrine of moral progress in later Stoicism gave to the individual a way of self-improvement of which theoretically there had been no hope when the orthodox view left nothing between the complete wisdom of the sage and the complete madness of all others. But above all it made the universe intelligible: in Edwyn Bevan's phrase, 'it made man at home in the universe'. And in Posidonius it created the idea of a lofty detached piety— something very like the speech put in St. Paul's mouth in Acts xvii, if we subtract therefrom the references to Jesus and to the Resurrection.

So again Epicureanism gave to its ideal of the calm life the driving force of a joy rooted in deliverance from fears of capricious divine action and of supernatural terrors, the joy we may say of a great simplification of life which others must be enabled to share. We may recall the outburst of Lucretius iii. 1053 ff. on the futility and boredom of his contemporaries: it would not be so, he cries, if they knew the causes of their emotions.

'Often a man grows weary of being at home and goes forth from his stately halls and suddenly returns, since he

perceives that it is not a whit better outside. He speeds his
ponies and rushes to his villa as though he were in hot haste
to take help to a blazing house, and as soon as he has
reached the threshold he at once yawns, or sinks heavily
to sleep and seeks forgetfulness, or even hurries to the city
again. In this way each one flees from himself—and the
self he cannot escape clings to him against his will—and
hates himself, since in his sickness he does not know the
cause of the complaint. Each one if he saw this well, would
abandon affairs and seek first to know the nature of the
universe, since the issue at stake is the condition of all time,
not of one hour, all the existence waiting and to be expected
after death.'

The real note of Epicurus and of his followers is
a simple evangelical fervour. Nothing illustrates this
more strikingly than the confession of faith which one
Diogenes of Oenoanda caused to be inscribed in a
portico about the end of the second century A.D.:

'Being now through age at the setting of life and all but
on the point of leaving it with a fair hymn of praise for the
fullness of all pleasant things, I have wished to give help
now to all men of parts, lest death should come on me first.
As I have said before, most men suffer alike from false
opinions, just as if it were in a plague, and the number of
sufferers increases (for through imitation they catch the
disease from one another like sheep). Now it is right to
give help to future generations (for they are ours, even if
they are yet unborn). Therefore, having regard also to the
love of mankind and to the duty of giving help to strangers
who are at hand, I have decided to use this colonnade and
to set forth in it the means of safety for all to see, for the
benefits conferred by the written word are spread abroad.'

Elsewhere he says: 'Now what it is which neither wealth
can give nor civic reputation nor monarchy nor fine

living and a luxurious table nor the refinements of sexual pleasure, but philosophy can alone secure, this I shall set forth later.' *Epicuri de grege porcus?*

Philosophy at this time appeared as in a sense a unity, as to Juvenal xiii. 19 ff. and to the lexicographer Pollux, who a little later (iv. 39 f.) defines the philosopher as the man able to relieve humanity of this and that failing, and his functions as reproaching and exhorting and teaching. Any philosophy of the time set up a standard of values different from those of the world outside and could serve as a stimulus to a stern life, and therefore to something like conversion when it came to a man living carelessly. It is said that Polemo when drunk and garlanded went into Xenocrates's lecture-room, was moved to abandon his earlier ways, and devoted himself so eagerly to philosophy that he became next head of the school. Again, in one of Lucian's *Dialogues of Courtesans* (x), we read how a teacher of philosophy has forbidden Drose's lover to come to her, promising that his pupil would after training in hardship be happy and virtuous.

Dio of Prusa had been in the early years of the Flavian period a rhetorician, a man of means and position, and a foe of philosophy, against which he wrote. Under Domitian, probably in 82, a powerful friend of his fell, and Dio himself was banished. He began, he tells us, to ask himself whether exile, poverty, old age, sickness, and other such things were not heavy to some and light to others, according to their strength and purpose, and went to the Delphic oracle. The oracle told him to go on with what he was doing and to pursue his purpose to the end of the world. So he put on humble raiment and set about wandering everywhere. Some called him a tramp, some a beggar, and some a philosopher, and with no intention or pride on his part the last name stuck to him and people used to come and consult him. He saw their need of guidance and followed the example of Socrates. This is a very notable story. Dio did not suddenly feel the attraction of a philosophic teacher or school. External events shattered his world and imperceptibly he gravitated towards the only way of finding a scheme of values which would make life tolerable and give it meaning.

The ascetic life, without a positive complement, can attract for a time a man who is disgusted with himself : declamation against luxury formed a staple feature of the mime, and Seneca (*Epistles*, 108. 9) tells us that lines condemning avarice were applauded in the theatre, but asceticism requires a positive complement. In Cynicism and in not a little popular Hellenistic philosophy this complement was the sense of freedom. You had simplified your life: you were secure in the arsenal of your self-sufficiency: and Fortune could not hurt you. At worst, you would have had the satisfaction of playing well the role dealt to you on this queer stage, and this, as we shall see later (p. 194), was no mere conventional metaphor. Commonly the complement for the deeper student of philosophy was the joy of the life of contemplation. There is mystic contemplation— as when we hear in Plato's *Banquet*, p. 220, of Socrates on the campaign of Potidaea standing wrapt in thought all day and night and then at dawn saying a prayer to the sun and going his way. But more prominent is the steady concentration on knowledge as the worthiest occupation for a rational being. 'Blessed is he', says Euripides, 'who has won the learning of knowledge, who does not rush to harm citizens or to do unjust actions but contemplates the unaging order of immortal nature, where and how and whence it came to be: to such an one intentions of evil never occur.' His great scientific contemporary Democritus says that he would rather find the explanation for one thing than become king of the Persians. Plato in his *Theaetetus* gives two striking pictures, one of the philosopher absorbed in eternal verities, the other of the worldling. But the classic formulation of the idea was given by Aristotle. One of his early works, the *Protrepticus* or *Exhortation to Philosophy* (addressed to a Cypriot prince Themison), is a passionate plea for the supreme value of this life of contemplation. Much later, at the end of the *Nicomachean Ethics* he says (p. 1177 b. 26 ff.), 'Such a life would be better than a man's life: for he who lives so will live not by virtue of his humanity, but by virtue of the divinity in him. . . . If mind is in comparison with man divine, so also is such a life in comparison with man's life'; in the *Metaphysics* contemplation is the sole activity of God. This enthusiasm runs through subsequent antiquity. We have to think of its echoes not merely in the serious Virgil, but in the frivolous Propertius and Ovid: we have to think of the influence exerted on the young Augustine by Cicero's following of Aristotle in his *Hortensius*.

Thirdly, philosophy produced some of the most striking ideal types, the saints of antiquity. Around all the prominent figures who founded or developed schools there grew not only anecdotes but also haloes. Plato received cultus almost immediately after death and soon could be spoken of as Apollo's son; Pythagoras acquired a legend which grew continually;

Epicurus is to Lucretius a god; Diogenes is to Cercidas, a century after his death, 'the heavenly dog'. Apollonius of Tyana soon becomes superhuman, Epictetus a pagan saint. Celsus suggests Orpheus, Anaxarchus, and Epictetus as men really worthy of veneration. Popular story is full of philosophic martyrs who died rather than flatter cruel tyrants, as for instance, Theodorus, or the Stoics in Tacitus, and there was a 'death-bed' literature. The literature which grew up around philosophers, particularly Pythagoras, appears to have had no small influence on early Christian hagiographic legend, above all ascetic legend. The philosopher was in popular imagination superhuman and liable to be thaumaturgic. Celsus speaks of his being unassailable by magic. Porphyry, *ad Marcellam*, 11, of his being given the power of a god by God. This heroization was, of course, in the first place the product of the impression made by philosophy, but it was cumulative and had a considerable effect on the popular imagination.

Fourthly, there was the philosopher in person to hear, like the Cynics mentioned earlier, or like the professional philosophers lecturing to students or (as Dion of Prusa) to general audiences or (as Maximus of Tyre) to fashionable audiences, or again the philosopher companion, as we find him in so many great Roman households. In education philosophy had very great prestige. The development of speculative thought in the fifth century B.C. had coincided with a widespread demand for higher education: in the fourth we know the rivalry between Plato's training by philosophy preceded by suitable preliminary studies and the purely literary training of Isocrates. This antithesis faded during the Hellenistic period, philosophy taking an interest in the theory of style and rhetoric in the discussion of general abstract issues; from the beginning of the first century B.C. till late in the Empire few doubted that philosophy was the natural crown of education: after the rudimentary stage came the grammarian's teaching, then the rhetorical school, from which those who could proceeded to philosophy. It corresponded to going to the university. Only a limited number could go to Athens or one of the other famous centres: but a great many heard some philosophy, for there were many private teachers scattered over their world and it is known that some of them were men of standing in their cities: further, we are told that there were not a few impostors in the profession, a fact which suggests that the demand was considerable: in the later Empire the profession waned, but in the first century of our era it was at its height. Nor was a man's chance of acquiring some tinge of philosophy limited to youth. We hear of famous persons dropping in at the lectures of Posidonius; Maximus of Tyre seems to have had audiences comparable in social quality with some of M. Bergson's; and Lucian in his *Hermotimus* has drawn for all ages the pathetic person who starts late to study the Stoic system and is always painfully hopeful of mastering it.

A lecture might have on any of these men the effect which it had on Polemo: we must recall the prominence in popular philosophic teaching and writing of declamation against luxury and vice. A man who heard Musonius Rufus or Epictetus at Rome was doing the thing most nearly equivalent to hearing a Christian sermon later: the technique was in fact inherited.

Epictetus remarks, iii. 23. 37, in criticizing those who read and discuss for the purpose of display, 'Or tell me, who, when hearing you reading a work or discoursing, felt in great distress about himself, or turned to look into his soul, or having gone out said, *The Philosopher touches me to the quick*: I must no longer act thus?' (cf. Seneca, *Epistles*, 108. 3). His discourse (iii. 21) against people who light-heartedly take up sophistic lecturing is equally instructive for his conception of the responsibilities and possibilities of the position. To him the philosopher's lecture-room was a 'hospital for sick souls'.

Again, a striking feature of the early Empire is the presence in rich households of philosophers, commonly, no doubt, freedmen. We know previously the calling in of philosophers as tutors for kings' sons (as Philip sent for Aristotle) or as advisers and companions (as Euphraeus was sent by Plato to Perdiccas III, Dionysius sent for Plato, and Alexander took Callisthenes East, Callisthenes actually coming as a writer: Antigonus Gonatas invited Zeno to Pella and secured Persaeus). The rise of Rome brought many Greek philosophers into Roman households either as slaves who received their freedom or as free men who were impoverished.

Such Greeks might come either as tutors, who would stay on in the household, or as companions useful for various purposes in view of their versatility. These men were, as has been remarked, the equivalent of domestic chaplains: we find them at death-beds, as for instance Demetrius the Cynic at Thrasea's (Tacitus, *Annals*, xvi. 34). A philosopher who was mainly a writer or a professional teacher might also have similar close relations with individuals: we need only think of the works addressed by Seneca to particular friends, or of the intimacy of Cornutus with Persius. And a philosopher in the flesh could receive something of the homage paid to the philosopher saints of the past, as Epicurus did from Metrodorus: Seneca tells us (*Epistles*, 108. 13) how when he heard Attalus denouncing sin he regarded him as exalted and raised above the summit of humanity.

Again, philosophical literature exercised no small influence. In this respect Plato above all put philosophy on the map: the supreme stylistic value of his writings gave them a public which they might otherwise have lacked. At Oxyrhynchus, where little other philosophy has been found, there is some Plato and a fragment of Aristotle's *Protrepticus*: at Memphis there was a real philosophical library. It is particularly important that a large literature of elementary introductions and summaries grew up and was widely used. The Christian apologists found the concepts which they employed not merely ready made but predigested.

We can here use the word conversion for the turning from luxury and self-indulgence and superstition (another frequent object of philosophic criticism) to a life of discipline and sometimes to a life of contemplation, scientific or mystic. Plato spoke of the object of education as a 'turning around of the soul' (*Republic*, 518 D ff.): the word *epistrophe*, later used by Christians of conversion, is applied to the effects of philosophy, meaning thereby an orientation or focusing of the soul, the turning of men from carelessness to true piety, for which *conuersio* is used by Cicero (*On the Nature of the Gods*, i. 77). General exhortations to humanity include the instruction to sober up. We find *metanoeo*, the verbal correlative of *metanoia*, repentance, in the Poimandres tract (p. 4 above), and the noun itself in a curious popular work, the *Picture* of Cebes, ascribed on internal grounds to the first century A.D. The term implies an intellectual value judgement, and commonly a momentary realization rather than the entry on a state: it is also a word used by general rather than by philosophical writers.

Cebes wrote a moral dialogue supposed to be inspired by an allegorical painting in a temple of Kronos. It describes the good life and the bad life: the only deliverance from the bad life is given by Metanoia. The man who chooses the good life is safe (ch. 26). 'He will never be disturbed by pain or grief or incontinence or avarice or poverty or any other evil thing. For he is the master of all things and is superior to all that formerly distressed him, as those who exhibit snakes (are to their snakes). Nothing distresses him any more because he has a remedy.' Earlier Cebes says (ch. 3): 'If a man comes to know, folly disappears and he is saved: he becomes blessed and happy throughout his whole life.'

The goal is a deliverance; *sozesthai* occurs eight times in this short treatise, *diasozesthai* once: both imply being put out of reach of certain dangers. The ultimate authority lies in the commands given by the Daimonion to each man when entering on life. This deliverance must be sought by men with all their energy: they must not suffer themselves to be distracted by trivialities such as the liberal arts; so says Cebes, and so says Seneca. Other philosophers took a less rigid view, but all expected that devotion to philosophy would make a difference to their hearers.

Further, this idea was not thought of as a matter of purely intellectual conviction. The philosopher commonly said *not* 'Follow my arguments one by one: check and control them to the best of your ability: truth should be dearer than Plato to you', but 'Look at this picture which I paint, and can you resist its attractions? Can you refuse a hearing to the legitimate rhetoric which I address to you in the name of virtue?' Even Epicurus says in an argument, 'Do not be deceived, men, or led astray: do not fall. There is no natural fellowship between reasonable beings. *Believe me*, those who express the other view deceive you and argue you out of what is right.' Epictetus, ii. 19. 34, also employs the same appeal, *Believe me*, and counters opponents by arguments which appeal to the heart and not to the head. Inside the schools, at least inside the Academic school, there was an atmosphere of hard thinking, of which something survives in the various commentaries on Aristotle. Yet even in the schools this was overcast by tradition and loyalty. Thus, while Plotinus was an independent genius, the subsequent development of Neoplatonism is a building of thinking upon earlier thinking which has become dogma. Even technical philosophy was scholastic in the less complimentary sense of that epithet. In the last struggle Christian dogma was in conflict not with the free Greek spirit, but with other dogma and with fossilized tradition. The philosophy which addressed itself to the world at large was a dogmatic philosophy seeking to save souls.

What response did the appeal of philosophy evoke?

It is noteworthy how often philosophers use the metaphor of initiation or of a series of initiations to describe the apprehension of philosophical truth: its attainment is an *epopteia*, a seeing. To take one example, Seneca (*Epistles*, 90. 28) thus describes the function of philosophy:

> 'She shows which things are evil, which only seem evil; she frees the mind of idle nonsense; she gives solid greatness, while checking swollen greatness which takes airs without justification; she does not allow the difference between the great and the inflated to be missed; she gives a knowledge of all nature and of her own. She sets forth what the gods are and what their nature is, what are the powers of the underworld, what are *lares* and *genii*, what are souls given a permanent existence in the second shape of deities, where they are, what they do, what are their powers and desires. These are her initiatory rites; they open not some local shrine but the vast temple of all the gods, the universe itself, whose true images and true likenesses she has brought within the mind's eye.'

The change produced is fundamental. In an earlier letter (6. 1) Seneca writes:

> 'I understand, Lucilius, that I am not only being improved but that I am being transformed. I do not already promise or hope that nothing is left in me that needs change. . . . The very fact that the soul sees failings in itself which it previously ignored is a proof of its change to a better state. . . . I want to pour everything over into you, and I rejoice in learning that I may teach.'

With these no doubt sincere professions we may compare those of a young contemporary, the poet Persius. His fifth satire, addressed to his teacher Cornutus, tells incidentally how, as soon as he came to years of manhood, he put himself under Cornutus (36 ff.), who received his tender years in a Socratic bosom. Hereupon the poet's soul felt the weight of reason and was eager to be overcome by it, and took new features. He warns others, young and old, to follow his example (64 f.). Most of his small book of satires is in this vein: the formal inspiration is from Horace or Lucilius, but the content is largely Stoic preaching. The second satire is in effect a diatribe on prayer with criticisms of popular superstition. The third is perhaps a veiled *Confiteor*: and here again he turns to humanity at large (l. 66):

'O poor wretches, learn, and come to know the causes of things, what we are, for what life we are born, what the assigned order is, where the turning-point of the course is to be rounded gently, what limit to set to money, for what it is right to pray, what is the use of hard cash, how much you ought to spend on your country and on those near and dear to you, what kind of man God ordered you to be and where as a man you are placed.'

The objections of the Philistine, here a centurion, are mentioned, and a vivid imaginary dialogue of a patient with a doctor gives the answer by inference—'you are much worse than you will let yourself realize. Let philosophy diagnose your case.' Persius would have accepted the phrase of Epictetus, iii. 23. 30, 'the lecture-room of a philosopher is a hospital'.

In theory, at least, this conversion could be instantaneous. Plutarch says in the treatise which bears the title *A summary view of the fact that the Stoics make more Paradoxical Assertions than the Poets* (4):

'The man who is in the eyes of the Stoics worst at morning is, if it happens, best at evening. He may fall asleep mad (*or*, capricious) and ignorant and unjust and unchaste, yes, and a slave forsooth and poor and needy, and rise up on the same day having become a king and rich and prosperous, and temperate and just and firm and free from idle opinions. He has not grown a beard or the signs of manhood on a young and tender body: instead, on top of a weak, soft, unmanly, vacillating soul he has acquired a perfect mind, supreme intelligence, a godlike disposition, a knowledge set above idle opinions, and a temper free from change, and that although his wickedness never abated before. On a sudden he has become almost a hero or a daimon or a god where he was a beast and the worst of beasts.'

So much for the direct contact with the philosophers. There is one famous instance of conversion by a book. St. Augustine (*Confessions*, iii. 4) says:

'Among these people, being not yet in manhood's strength, I was learning books of eloquence, in which I wished to shine with a purpose flighty and to be condemned, in the joy of human vanity. In the usual order of studies I had come to a book of a certain Cicero, whose speech is admired by almost all though his heart is not. But that book contains his exhortation unto philosophy and is called *Hortensius*. Now that book changed my affections and turned my prayers to Thee thyself, O Lord, and made my wishes and desires quite other. Suddenly all vain hopes grew cheap in my eyes and I yearned for the immortality of wisdom with a burning zeal which passes belief and I began to rise that I might return unto Thee.'

He was eighteen at the time.

Again we may recall the words of Porphyry in his *Letter to Marcella*, his wife (5):

'Philoctetes suffered his wound from a deadly snake, you in full knowledge of what a fall, how great a fall it is which our souls have had into the world of becoming, while the gods have not neglected us, as the sons of Atreus did him, but proved our saviours and not forgotten us. I invite you, who have had to struggle and contend with many things that were painful, now above all to hold to the moorings of philosophy—the only safe moorings—and not to give way more than you should to the distresses resulting from my absence, and not in your longing for the teaching which I can give to lose what has already been given.'

He speaks of her as thinking that in leaving him she would leave the way of salvation and the guide along with it (8). Here, as elsewhere, philosophy is an initiation and actions are the proofs of each man's opinions; '*he who has believed must so live, in order that he may himself to his hearers be a witness to what he says*'; the whole tone is religious.

In the previous chapter we have seen sporadic indications of conversion to religion in antiquity. Against them we can set a far greater body of evidence for conversion to philosophy. A mystery evoked a strong emotional response and touched the soul deeply for a time, but philosophy was able both to turn men from evil and to hold before them a good, perhaps never to be attained, but presenting a permanent object of desire to which one seemed to draw gradually nearer. Further, in spite of differences of ideas, philosophy in the Hellenistic age and under the Empire was an entity and philosophers were a class falling under a specific rubric; there was a general antithesis of philosophic and common ethic and values.

When Julian initiated his attempt to revive paganism he used the one thing which could conceivably have given to it the power to hold its own, and that was the way of philosophy. His friend Sallustius, after a general survey of belief, says (ch. 13), 'Of the gods and of the universe and of human affairs this account will suffice for those who neither can be steeped in philosophy nor are incurably diseased in soul.' On the other side, Christianity did not disregard these values, and Ambrose could use his Cicero, just as, earlier, Philo and the Apologists, while regarding pagan religion as unworthy and untrue, were eager to reconcile pagan philosophy and their own teaching.

XII

THE SPREAD OF CHRISTIANITY AS A SOCIAL PHENOMENON

THE frame of mind in which a man interested in Christianity approached it was in the first place determined largely by the impressions of it generally current in society as a whole. We must here endeavour to form some idea of the nature of these impressions and to see Christianity not as Irenaeus or Eusebius saw it but as the John Doe and Richard Roe of the second century did. First, however, we must briefly review the early evolution of the Church. The Christian movement started as a ferment within Judaism and was at Jerusalem so placed as to be able to influence other Jews who came up for festivals and visiting Jews from the Dispersion in all its extent. Such personal contacts and carryings explain the presence of disciples of John the Baptist at Ephesus, and the origin of the Christian communities at Rome and Alexandria. There was much coming and going; a rescript of Claudius in 41 refers to the fact that the Alexandrian Jews were in the habit of bringing in their brethren from Syria or Egypt and forbids the practice.

It is not likely that the Apostles in Jerusalem had a missionary aim in the full sense. Difficult as it is to disentangle the threads of our tradition, such sayings as Matt. x. 5–6, '*Go not into the way of the Gentiles, and into any city of the Samaritans: but go rather to the lost sheep of the house of Israel*'; x. 23, '*Ye shall not have gone over the cities of Israel, till the Son of Man be come*'; and xv. 24, '*I am not sent but unto the lost sheep of the house of Israel*', ring true as indications of the character of this first period. The task of the followers of Jesus was ideally to prepare the chosen people for the impending coming of the kingdom and the end of the present world-order; in fact, to prepare as large a proportion as they could. They did this not by an attempt primarily at persuasiveness but by a statement of certain facts which Israel ought to know: *kerygma*, heralding, implies an activity like that of the town-crier. Like the town-crier they made known the resurrection of Jesus as proving his divine mission, the duty of repentance, and the future coming of the Kingdom and the Judgement of God. From their point of view they were a movement within Judaism destined by God to proclaim to it God's summons to fulfil its vocation. This purpose was radical, but in a sense comparable with that of the Pharisees in their beginning, and with that of the people of the New Covenant at Damascus, known to us from the so-called Zadokite work (in which, be it remembered, the official caste at Jerusalem is stigmatized very much as in the Synoptic Gospels). Of necessity the failure of the main body of Jews to respond to their announcement made them, like the Covenanters of Damascus or the Wesleyans in the Church of England, into a community within the community. Their interest in the reception of foreign proselytes was probably no greater than that of normal Judaism: perhaps it was less, for they had a special and pressing duty with their own folk.

There was, however, in this movement, even from the earliest stage, an element which had in it the seeds of development in a further direction. It was the belief that the Spirit of God had been poured out upon the community. It is not necessary here to discuss the precise origins of that belief: what is relevant is that we should observe that the Jewish prophets ascribed this possession to the future Messiah and (later) to the people of Israel, that a general outpouring of Spirit was expected to come in the days of the Messiah, that the belief is very firmly fixed in our tradition, and that this fixation is manifested by the variety of concepts current both as to the possession itself and as to the way in which it was communicated to each individual who adhered to the movement. The consciousness of spirit-possession carried with it the consciousness of authority. The Synoptic Gospels give us an uncertain answer on the nature of this Spirit experience: but in effect the truth is that John the Baptist had appeared in the guise of a prophet and had opened the long-closed flood-gates of the tide of prophecy, and Jesus had thrown them wide. The Synoptists ascribe this consciousness of authority to Jesus personally and represent him as giving it to the Twelve and to the Seventy. This means that individual Jews of the larger world with a wider perspective and freer views would be liable to feel empowered to take a bolder line. Acts preserves the memory of the emergence of such men in its account (ch. vi), of the appointment of the Seven, all men with Greek names and one a proselyte of Antioch: their appointment is expressly described as resulting from complaints of the 'Hellenists', Greek-speaking disciples, against the Jews in the Christian community.

One of the Seven, Stephen, incurred a charge of blasphemy and was put to death after uttering a passionate protest against the behaviour of official Judaism. This incident quickened the pace of events. It made the movement as a whole suspect to Jewish conservatism, which did not shrink from coercive measures: there was a dispersion.

> 'Those who were scattered after the tribulation in Stephen's time went as far as Phoenicia and Cyprus and Antioch, speaking to none save Jews alone. Now there were some of them from Cyprus and Cyrenaica who came to Antioch and talked to Greeks also, preaching the Lord Jesus. And the hand of the Lord was with them and a large number believed and turned to the Lord. And word concerning them reached the ears of the Church in Jerusalem, and they sent Barnabas to Antioch.' (Acts xi. 19–22.)

There first the disciples were called Christians.

This means that in the life of that city, where Greek and Semitic elements blended freely, and where there were many Gentiles who had been drawn to Judaism, there grew up a full self-consciousness in the new movement. While there may be an accentuated conservatism in a group living under these conditions, the inward pressure of Jewish loyalty on reformers was weaker here. To break with tradition in Jerusalem was a hard thing; it was like starting the Protestant Reformation in Rome. In Antioch Judaism and this new sect within it had their being in a community the external culture of which was pagan, in spite of the presence of many Jews.

This community was joined by Paul, who had earlier attached himself to the Christian movement under circumstances which gave him a new attitude. The Twelve in Jerusalem, and no doubt most of their early adherents, had found in the Gospel of Jesus and the Gospel which took shape around Jesus the integration and completion of the religious traditions in which they had always lived. For them he came to fulfil, and not to destroy. Paul, on the other hand, had regarded them and theirs as apostates and had thrown himself heart and soul into the struggle to suppress them. For him to become a Christian meant in the first instance a complete change of face. It is the first conversion to Christianity of which we have knowledge. He brought to it not merely a fresh enthusiasm but also an imperious inner need to discover an interpretation and reconciliation of the old and the new in his religious life.

From Antioch Paul and Barnabas set out to Cyprus, no doubt because it was Barnabas's home: there they operated in synagogues. What induced Paul and Barnabas to go farther afield, whether for instance the puzzling story of the encounter with Elymas before Sergius Paulus covers some real success in the wider world, we do not know. Movements go ahead on their impetus and belief in the Spirit gave an authoritative if disciplined sanction to the sudden impulses of the mind.

According to Acts, this missionary journey and those which succeeded it observed the principle that the message must be preached first in synagogues. It reached in this way the public of Hellenistic Jews, proselytes, sympathizers who would not go the whole way, and others who were drawn to the synagogue by the rumour that an interesting visitor was in the city: gossip travelled fast in an ancient town. From the point of view of the last class the coming of Paul was of the order of the arrival of Dion of Prusa or any other wandering sophist. He talked also to individuals in the market-place at Athens and by special invitation before the Areopagus, but normally he used the synagogue until that was made impossible for him, as at Corinth.

where he taught for eighteen months in the house of Justus (xviii. 7), and at Ephesus, where he used the lecture hall of Tyrannus (xix. 9); even so at the next town he went to the synagogue; at Rome of necessity he taught in his own quarters (xxviii. 16 ff.). At Lystra he spoke perforce to the multitude (xiv. 15 ff.), but otherwise he did not, like a wandering Cynic, address popular audiences at random.

This is no doubt characteristic of the early spread of the movement. The world as a whole did not know much of Christians as distinct from Jews till the fire of Rome in 64, when Nero seized on them as scapegoats to satisfy popular resentment and made the admission of Christianity proof of guilt. Thereafter they were in the public mind, rather than in the public eye, as the object of the general odium directed against the Jews for being an anti-social and highly cohesive body, and of the special odium incurred by their reputation as incendiaries, revolutionaries, and generally abominable. But they were not conspicuous. The works directed against Christianity do not allude to out-of-door preaching. In the second century literary works were written in defence of the new faith, but there is no indication that they were read by any save Christians or men on the way to be such or professed students of the movement such as Celsus. There was a school of religious education at Alexandria at the end of the second century, but it did not advertise its existence, and presumably people were brought to it or came to it as a result of incidental knowledge of it. There were no visible out-of-door ceremonials, no temples recognizable as such till much later, and no priesthood displaying its character by its dress or its tonsure, or (in the early stages) its abstinence from secular employments. I mean that the man in the street did not know this as a type like the priests of Cybele or Isis. The magistrate did, as we see from the singling out of Ignatius for punishment. The one Christian type known to the populace was that of the martyr.

We must seek to make clear to ourselves what a martyr was from a non-Christian point of view. Law has been defined as the interference of the State in the actions and passions of humanity. The martyr is the man who resists this interference, who claims that his resistance is based on other and higher sanctions, and who will not concede a point even if compliance would save him from the consequences of his previous disobedience. Often he welcomes the opportunity of bearing witness to the faith which is in him. For the Christian there was no doubt how he must act. 'Whosoever therefore shall confess me before men, him will I confess also before my Father which is in heaven. But whosoever shall deny me before men, him will I also deny before my Father which is in heaven' (Matt. x. 32–3). To fail at this point was the supreme betrayal and damnation; to succeed, the supreme proof of love and assurance of Heaven. Herein Christianity follows a Jewish tradition which crystallized in the time of the Maccabees and appeared again under Caligula: to die rather than break the law was the ideal way of hallowing God's name.

We have to see this as did pagan spectators. They knew similar situations. Dionysus in the *Bacchae*, appearing as one of his priests and standing before Pentheus, is a perfect type: he cannot yield to the king, having received his commission from the god in person and he knows that the god will deliver him when he wills. Four centuries later this scene comes into Horace's mind as an illustration of the front which the wise man can present to hostile circumstances (*Epistles*, i. 16.73). Socrates again, in Plato's *Apology*, p. 29 c, makes the explicit statement :

> 'If you should say to me, *O Socrates, at the moment we will not hearken to Anytus, but we release you on this condition, that you no longer abide in this inquiry or practise philosophy—and if you are caught still doing this, you will be put to death*, if then you would release me on these conditions, I should say to you, *You have my thanks and affection, men of Athens, but I will obey the god rather than you and, while I have breath and power, I will not desist from practising philosophy.*'

Further, in *Crito* we are taught that he respected the laws of the city and would not run away. For him safety was not enough: he had to witness, not indeed to a dogma (for he had none) but to the imperious validity of his vocation.

The blood of martyrs is the seed of the Church: the death of Socrates created the type of wisdom and virtue standing in heroic opposition to a world which can kill but which does not have the last word. We have seen that philosophic martyrs were not lacking later. Epictetus, in a discourse *On Firmness*, thus sets forth the lesson that we must fulfil the duties to which we are called (i. 29. 45). If a man is told to lay aside his purple-striped robe and go forth in rags, how will he do it? As a witness called by God. '*Come and bear witness to me: for you are worthy to be brought forward as a witness by me.*' Elsewhere he remarks (iii. 24. 112):

> 'Zeus wished to make me obtain from myself the proof of this and himself to know whether he has in me such a

soldier, such a citizen as he should and to produce me before the rest of men as a witness to what things are unworthy of choice. Behold, all of you, your fears are false, your desires are vain. . . . Zeus shows me to men in poverty, out of office, in sickness: he sends me to Gyara, he carries me off to prison, not in hatred nor in neglect . . . but by way of training me and using me as a witness to others.'

Again Epictetus tells of the answer which Helvidius gave to Vespasian's message forbidding him to attend the meeting of the Senate (i. 2. 19):

'It is in your power to forbid me to be a senator: but while I am I must attend.' 'Well, but when you attend keep silence.' 'Do not ask my opinion and I will be silent.' 'But I must ask it.' 'And I must say what seems right to me.' 'If you do I will put you to death.' 'Well, did I say to you that I was immortal? You will do your part and I mine. It is your part to put me to death, mine to die without a quiver, yours to send me into exile, mine to go without repining.'

So in a passage from Porphyry's *Letter to Marcella* quoted earlier (p. 185) the word *martys* is used of the constant witnessing to one's tenets by one's actions. Of course the word *martys* is not a title; it is a predicate describing the role of individuals who by their conduct testify to the goodness of the scheme of the universe; so Seneca says of the Cynic Demetrius, 'He is not a teacher of the truth but a witness to it' (*Epistles*, 20. 9).

We have spoken earlier of the life of Apollonius by Philostratus. It tells how Apollonius was brought before Tigellinus (iv. 44); there was a miracle, and Apollonius expressed his utter indifference. 'The God who allows him to be terrifying allows me to be unterrified.' The judge feared that he might be fighting against God. Later, Domitian was said to desire him to stand his trial for treason. Apollonius went voluntarily to Rome, holding on the way at Cicero's villa a discourse in which he maintained that the wise man ought to lay down his life for his tenets (vii. 14): 'he will cleave to all he knows no less than to the sacred rites in which he was initiated.' When summoned before Domitian he was ready to trust the inspiration of the moment (vii. 30): in prison he lifted his leg out of the fetters and put it back again (vii. 38). He looked forward to his trial as a dialectical discussion rather than as a race to be run for his life (viii. 2). The final charges were (1) Apollonius's peculiar dress, (2) his being called a god, (3) his prophecy of the plague at Ephesus, (4) the sacrifice of a boy. Domitian acquitted him in the open court, which was attended by all the notables, but kept him for private discussion. Apollonius uttered a few words and vanished from sight. This type of the philosopher martyr is very notable; in stories of persecution, Christians are represented as referring to the condemnation of Socrates as typical of the evil things done by paganism.

The Neronian persecution may well have suggested to the onlooker no such analogy. It is not clear that recantation availed then as it did later: the victims were socially inferior to the class whose sufferings were glorified; the charge was in substance incendiarism; and the proceedings (like the measures against magicians and astrologers at various times, or Jews and Isiac worshippers under Tiberius, or Jews under Claudius after tumults) were police measures to secure public order. Trajan wrote very pertinently to Pliny: 'We cannot establish any universal ordinance which should have, so to speak, a fixed form' (x. 97). Some popular emotion of sympathy might of course be aroused (Tacitus says it was, *Annals*, xv. 44), such as occurred in A.D. 61 when it was proposed to put to death the whole household of Pedanius Secundus, who had been murdered by one of his slaves: the execution had to be carried out under strong military protection. But from the time of Domitian probably, Trajan certainly, it was clear that 'obstinacy' was punished and that a Christian on trial for being such could save his life by recantation. To a calm person like Pliny this seemed a blameworthy quality: 'I did not doubt that, whatever it was they admitted, their pertinacity and unbending obstinacy ought to be punished'; and in like manner Marcus Aurelius says (xi. 3):

> 'What a fine thing is the soul which is ready if it must here and now be freed from the body and either extinguished or scattered or survive. But let this readiness come from a personal judgement and not out of a mere spirit of opposition, like that of the Christians; let it be in a reasoned and grave temper, capable of convincing another, and without theatricality.'

Now this word *theatricality* deserves careful consideration, for there was a certain fascination about self-chosen death. We see this not only in the Stoic cult of suicide in the first century of our era (it is then the Stoic form of martyrdom *par excellence*), but also in the constantly recurrent literary commonplace of the Gymnosophistae (Brahmins) who threw themselves into the fire and thereby made a demonstration against Alexander, and again in the frequent tendency of Christians in times of persecutions to force themselves on the notice of the magistrates by tearing down images or by other demonstrations, with which we may compare the offer of Rusticus Arulenus to veto the decree of the Senate against Thrasea. Clement of Alexandria says:

> 'We ourselves blame those who have leapt on death: for there are some who are not really ours but share only the name, who are eager to deliver themselves over in hatred against the Creator, poor wretches, passionate for death. We say that these men commit suicide and are not martyrs, even if they are officially executed.'

This popular attitude has various causes—a sort of fascination of death, the aura surrounding voluntary death in legend and life, a desire for theatrical prominence, the very widespread idea of the body as a prison for the soul, and pessimism. In Christianity there is the special conviction that it was the way to life, as in Ignatius, who begs the Roman community not to make interest to save him. *Amor mortis conturbat me.*

We must linger a little longer on these considerations, for they bear materially on our understanding of the ethos of the time. The Hellenistic period saw the birth of the novel. The earliest complete specimen, that of Chariton, is not later than the second century of our era, and the genre is certainly earlier. It is an imaginary narrative based on romantic history: the specimens preserved have plots which conform closely to a type. A young married couple (in later forms a pair of lovers) are separated by circumstances, pass through a series of tragic and violent misfortunes, and are finally reunited. The misfortunes generally include some very close approximation to death, often something which to the one member of the pair appears to be in truth the other's death, and generally the flogging of one or both parties, sometimes other tortures. Throughout there is an accent of theatrical pose. One incident may suffice. In the romance of Achilles Tatius (vi. 20–1) Thersandros has in his power the heroine Leucippe. She refuses to accept his advances and he begins to threaten. Leucippe says: 'If you wish to exercise tyranny, then I wish to suffer it, only you shall not take my virtue.' And she looks at Sosthenes and says: 'Bear witness how I face evil treatment: for you wronged me even more.' Sosthenes is ashamed at having been caught out and says: 'She should be scourged with whips, master, and subjected to countless tortures, that she may learn not to despise her master.' 'Do as Sosthenes bids,' says Leucippe, 'for he gives excellent advice. Produce your tortures. Bring a wheel: here are my hands, let him stretch them. Bring whips: here is my back, let him beat it. Bring fire: here is my body, let him burn it. Bring a sword: here is my neck, let him cut it. Behold a novel contest: one woman contends against all tortures and conquers everything. . . . Tell me, are you not afraid of your Artemis, but do you force a maiden in the Maiden's city? O Mistress, where is thy bow?' A little later she says, 'Arm yourself therefore: now take against me your whips, wheel, fire, sword: let your counsellor Sosthenes enter battle with you. I naked, alone, a woman, have one weapon, freedom, which is neither crushed by blows nor cut by the sword nor burnt by fire.' Earlier (v. 18) she writes to her lover Clitopho: 'For you have I left my mother and entered on wanderings. For you I have suffered shipwreck and robbers, for you I have become a victim and scapegoat and died twice already, for you I have been sold and bound with iron and carried a hoe and dug the earth and been scourged; and all that I may be to another man what you have been to another woman? Heaven forbid!' Such episodes are recurrent in these novels.

This is popular writing of a type hardly mentioned by superior persons—except by the Emperor Julian, when in his account of what pagan priests should read he says, 'It would be suitable for us to handle histories composed about real events: but we must avoid all the fictions written of old in the style of history, love subjects and everything in fact of that type.' The Greek novel bears witness to the fascination exercised by the thought of invincible chastity and beautiful young persons facing pain with reckless readiness, features which we find again in hagiographic romance. Leucippe's utterance is the popular equivalent of Seneca's: 'Here is a contest worthy of God, a wise man at grip with Fortune.' The same attitude appears in the school exercises in declamation of the period, for instance in one speech in the collection passing under Quintilian's name (*Declamationes maiores*, vii) in which a poor man offers to be tortured, taunts his rich adversary with fears as to what he might then say, and enlarges on the sufferings which he is prepared to face.

Lucan's epic on the civil war is written in this tone: one episode which may be mentioned is that of the cutting off of a detachment of Caesar's men under Vulteius in the Adriatic. Before the last conflict against overwhelming odds Vulteius says to his men (iv. 492): 'The gods have set us on a boat which allies and foes can both see: the waters, the land, the island with its soaring rocks will all give witnesses; the two opposing forces will watch from different shores. You, Fortune, are preparing some great and memorable example by what happens to us.' That is it: they have the spotlight on them, and they will go into the *examples*, the collections of instances of valour and other virtues compiled

> To point a moral or adorn a tale.

In all this there is a certain stridency of self-expression. Man struts his hour upon the stage: he must not fail to make an impression on the audience of the present and future. He will in any event die, but let him, like a Homeric hero, die 'having done something great to come to the ears of those who are to be'. To most of us it is obvious that our portion after death will very soon be oblivion. The men of the ancient world lived in more limited circles, which clung to memories and preserved them. The prospect of being forgotten was to them very terrible, and to avoid that a man would do and suffer much.

It is some distance from words to deeds, but Lucian gives us an extraordinary story of how a Cynic Peregrinus, who had been a Christian, burnt himself to death on a pyre at Olympia as a way of apotheosis. Cassius Dio (liv. 9. 10), in commenting on the self-immolation of an Indian at Athens in 20 B.C., says:

> 'Wishing to die either because he was of the caste of sophists (i.e. Brahmins) and was therefore moved by ambition, or because of old age, in accordance with ancestral custom, *or because he wished to make a display for the benefit of Augustus (who had come there) and of the Athenians*, he was initiated into the mysteries of the goddess . . . and cast himself alive into the fire.

It is important to realize that the common metaphor

of life as a stage on which Fortune casts us for different roles is no superficial metaphor.

To return to methods: the definite rejection of the new ideas by conservative Judaism and the withering of Jewish Christianity after the disaster of 70 and its sequel in 135 cut the connexion with the synagogue, though its members and the fringe of interested Gentiles remained a source of individual converts. Christianity had by now its own unobtrusive places of meeting. Pliny's Christians met before dawn, but the place is unspecified although, as Pliny tells us, the numbers involved were considerable. Celsus taunts them with privately doing and teaching the things which seem good to them, and speaks of Christian rites as performed in cobblers' shops or fullers' shops.

We do not hear of open-air preaching to large audiences. For one thing, the early movement probably included few people of sufficient rhetorical skill to be an attraction; for another, at any time from the Flavian period onwards, even when there was no direct persecution, there was the possibility: it was wiser not to be provocative, except perhaps in Anatolia, where the numerical strength of the movement early became considerable. We find mass conversion in Pontus in the third century. There Gregory the Thaumaturge, when he came, was a man far superior in culture to the *milieu* in which he preached.

It has been remarked earlier that Christianity had no outdoor ceremonies capable of catching the eye. Their own private worship was not likely to excite interest. Those on the way to baptism were excluded from the Eucharist proper; so were outsiders. The group which met for these purposes in any place would be composed of people who knew one another, and while there would be visitors from other communities they would have letters of introduction. Of course in the larger bodies, as for instance at Rome, it would no doubt have been possible for an inquisitive person to find his way in, as Burton did to Mecca. If he did, he was probably very disappointed. He saw no orgies, and he saw little which would suggest to him worship as he knew it. He certainly witnessed nothing so moving as the rite described by Walter Pater in *Marius the Epicurean*. He heard scriptural readings, a little wearisome, perhaps, by reason of their length, an exhortation like those of the synagogue, and his impression here also may well have been that this was of the nature of a philosophical school. If he was able to stay for the central ceremony, he would have difficulty in recognizing it as cultus in any ordinary sense. The officiants did not use a fixed form of words, followed as in Roman prayers through fear that the supernatural powers invoked would not give what was desired if one syllable or gesture was varied.

The impression made on an educated pagan would probably be that this was of the nature of superstition, that is ungentlemanly popular religion. It might seem to him as extemporary prayer in public worship does to a man brought up in the tradition of the Roman liturgy. The prayer was unusual also in its absence of careful invocation by name—except for the prayers which in certain churches were probably addressed to Jesus—and with reference to favourite seats of worship. The culminating point was but the distribution of bread and wine with a formula, after a long recital of God's mercies. In pagan worship of a mystery type what theology there was grew out of the rite; in this the rite was till the fourth century a very simple expression of a theology, with no deeper sense that would be apparent unless you were in the know. Even in the fourth century, when the Eucharist acquired a dignity of ceremonial appropriate to the solemn worship of the now dominant church, it is not to me clear either that there was a deliberate copying of the ceremonial of the mystery dramas or that any special appeal was made by the ritual to the new mass of converts. It is surely not without significance that at Antioch, where there had indeed been substantial Jewish influence in the Christian community, there was a tendency in the fourth century for churchmen to attend merely that part of the service which was concerned with the reading of scripture and not to join in the prayers and assist in the celebration of the Eucharist proper. The elaboration of ceremonial would appear to be in fact due to the new standing of Christianity and to the influence of Old Testament ritual, and perhaps in some measure of the Apocalypse and its account of the worship performed in Heaven, certainly to the idea of the union of human and angelic worship. The one piece of straight copying is the screen, or *iconostasis*, and that came from the theatre and not from cultus.

The *True Word* of Celsus which we know from Origen's refutation and the liberal excerpts therein contained gives the view taken by a highly educated pagan of the movement in the latter part of the second century of our era. To him, as to other onlookers, Christianity has or is a new rite: to him, writing as he did from a detached speculative standpoint and maintaining the distinction of superstition and piety (formulated in the Academy and maintained in different ways by Epicureans and Stoics but involving throughout a cultural distinction), in so far as Christianity is or offers a rite it may be compared with other Oriental or popular forms of worship.

'The Christians act like folk who put an illogical faith in those who collect alms for the Great Mother and in examiners of portents, and in figures like Mithras and Sabadios or whoever it is on whom a man has chanced, or in visions of Hecate or of some other daemon or daemones. Just as there wicked men often impose on the simplicity of the gullible and lead them where they will, so it is among the Christians. Some will not give or hear reason about their faith, but stick to *Ask no question but believe* and *Thy faith shall save thee* and *The wisdom in the world is a bad thing and the foolishness a good.*'

Later he compares Christianity with Egyptian religion, with its combination of brilliant temples and animal-worship, remarking that the Christians mock at Egyptian piety (which suggests that Celsus has read some of the Christian apologetic writings: in them, as in earlier Jewish apologia, attacks on Egyptian animal-worship are *de rigueur*) although that piety has a symbolic meaning. Again, before describing Christian hole-and-corner preaching, he says, 'We see those in the market-places who make the most infamous demonstrations and beg (i.e. the priests of Dea Suria or Cybele or Isis) would never come into a concourse of men of intelligence or dare to show their tricks there, but are sought after and glorified wherever they see striplings or a crowd of slaves and fools'. He says later,

'They do these things to excite the admiration of the ignorant like those who in Bacchic rites bring forward visions and terrors'. Further, he compares the Mithraic ladder as a symbol of the soul's passage through the spheres with the diagram of a Christian sect (the Ophites) and draws a parallel between Christian thaumaturgy with its foreign names and the names of power in Egyptian magical books.

From the standpoint of morality Celsus makes a contrast between Christianity and its rivals:

'Those who invite people to other *teletai* make these preliminary announcements: *Whosoever is pure of hand and wise of tongue*—or again others, *Whosoever is pure from every defilement and has no evil on his conscience and has lived well and justly.* These are the preliminary announcements made by those who provide means of cleaning away sin. But let us hear whom these people invite: *Whosoever*, they say, *is a sinner, whosoever is unwise, whosoever is foolish*—in a word, *whosoever is a wretch*—*he will be received into the Kingdom of God.*'

He again draws a parallel between Christianity and other religions of salvation when he asks:

'If they introduce this one (Christ), and others another, and all have the common formula ready to hand, *Believe if you would be saved, or go away*, what will be done by those who really wish to be saved? Will they cast dice and so get an omen for the path which they are to take and the people whom they are to join?'

Celsus thus far puts Christianity on a level with popular mysteries and immigrant Oriental cults in general. He is not a rationalist and his theism is not purely theoretical. But like most serious thinkers of antiquity he objects to what he regards as the piety of the ignorant and gullible, and he has a genuine moral indignation against ideas which seem incompatible with his high concept of the supernatural.

Yet to Celsus there is a vital distinction between Christianity and these parallel phenomena. To him and to his like Christianity is primarily a mass movement of falling away from tradition, as earlier Suetonius says of the Neronian persecution, which he reckons among the acts of Nero which were not blameworthy (*Nero*, 16. 2), 'There were punished the Christians, a race (*or*, kind; *genus*) of men characterized by a novel and maleficent superstition.' Both the Christians and their opponents came to think of themselves as a new people: and it is clear in the work of Celsus that his real aim was to persuade the Christians not to forget loyalty to the State in their devotion to this new state within the State. Other Oriental incomers were to Celsus mildly contemptible: this was a social phenomenon fraught with danger. It is to be noted that, though the test before Pliny was invocation of the gods in a form prescribed by him, the offering of incense and wine to the Emperor's image and cursing Christ, Trajan's reply indicates that 'prayer to our gods' would be a sufficient indication of conformity to give immunity, and in the serious persecution of Decius only a document recording past piety, the performance of sacrifice and libation, and tasting of the victims in the presence of a commissioner was required. That is to say, there was no formal and explicit abjuration of Christian cultus.

The average man in antiquity has left little record of his thoughts. We know his epitaphs, his dedications, his proverbs, but ancient literature is aristocratic and little interested in the ordinary citizen except as a foil

or as the material for a *genre* study. So far as we can
infer his attitude to Christianity, it was not altogether
unlike that of Celsus. To him, as we saw, it was at
first something indistinguishable from Judaism, and
then a subdivision which bore the odium of the fire
in Rome and under Domitian was perhaps particularly
liable to incur the official wrath with which Jewish
proselytism was then visited. In time it became apparent that this was a separate movement of godlessness, with peculiar cohesion and special charities.

He might turn in passionate hatred against this
anti-social organization. Persecution was in many
cases forced on the magistrates by the crowds, who
clamoured, *The Christians to the lions.* We have a very
interesting petition from the people of Lycia and
Pamphylia to Maximinus in 311–12 (in an inscription at Arycanda) asking him 'that the Christians,
who have long been mad, and still continue in their
diseased state, be made to stop and not by any foolish
new worship to transgress against that which is due
to the gods'. The petition is probably inspired and
due to men who knew that the Emperor desired to be
thus entreated, but it crystallizes a popular attitude.

There was much in ancient feeling to explain this:
notably the idea that the welfare of the Roman State
hung together with the due performance of the traditional Roman rites (we find an emphasis on the cult
of Vesta at the very time of the Decian persecution);
the belief in Jonahs—I mean the belief that the
misfortunes of the Empire might be due to this widespread apostasy; a general willingness to accept additional rites which made the Christian refusal seem
cantankerous and unreasonable; and also a wide-

spread readiness to believe the strange stories of sexual excesses and ritual murder and cannibalism which always attach themselves to a sect which is under the ban of social disapproval. All this was powerful and gave strength to the resistance of paganism. Our concern in the remaining chapters is with the analysis of the attitude of those who heard the word gladly.

Pure curiosity and casual contacts, sometimes due to a wife, might bring a man within its periphery. If he had Judaizing tastes he came naturally; here were the merits of that which had attracted him and he was not treated as one of the lesser breeds without the law. Again, if people died rather than perform a sacrifice which could be as much a matter of convention as standing for a national anthem, the divine name on which they relied might have its effectiveness, and the use of this same name of Jesus in exorcisms and cures by the Christians had its effect. At least it was worth adding to the Egyptian, Babylonian, and Greek names used in magic: 'I adjure you by the god of the Hebrews, Jesus' occurs in the great Paris magical papyrus. But a man's curiosity might lead him further and cause him to hear the preaching. What would he know of it from the outside? Certainly that it would mean his forsaking polytheism: that he must believe in a certain Jesus who had died for man's sins and risen, fulfilling thereby ancient Jewish prophecies; that he must repent and obtain forgiveness of sins and rebirth by a sacrament; that he must live by an ethic of love in a society of like-minded men. The sacrament of rebirth would not bother him: he knew of such, if he had not used them (they were, as we have seen, expensive), and, if he had, there was no objection to one more; in any case the new content ascribed to rebirth was attractive (p. 220 below). So much (with the possible exception of baptism) he would know: what more he might know, and what he would learn in the community when being prepared for baptism we shall consider next. Before we pass to this, one word of caution is perhaps necessary.

We are sometimes told that the unique attractiveness of the central figure of Christianity as presented in the Synoptic Gospels was a primary factor in the success of Christianity. I believe this idea to be a product of nineteenth-century idealism and humanitarianism. In early Christian literature those aspects of the Gospel picture which are now most prominent in homiletic writing are not stressed, and all the emphasis is on the superhuman qualities of Jesus, as foreshadowed by prophecy and shown by miracle and Resurrection and teaching, and not on his winning humanity. He is a saviour rather than a pattern, and the Christian way of life is something made possible by Christ the Lord through the community rather than something arising from the imitation of Jesus. The central idea is that of divinity brought into humanity to complete the plan of salvation, not that of perfect humanity manifested as an inspiration; it is *Deus de deo* rather than *Ecce homo*. The personal attractiveness of Jesus had done much to gather the first disciples, though even then the impression of power was probably more important than the impression of love: thereafter the only human qualities which proved effective were those of individual Christian teachers and disciples.

The success of Christianity is the success of an institution which united the sacramentalism and the philosophy of the time. It satisfied the inquiring turn of mind, the desire for escape from Fate, the desire for security in the hereafter; like Stoicism, it gave a way of life and made man at home in the universe, but unlike Stoicism it did this for the ignorant as well as for the lettered. It satisfied also social needs and it secured men against loneliness. Its way was not easy; it made uncompromising demands on those who would enter and would continue to live in the brotherhood, but to those who did not fail it offered an equally uncompromising assurance.

XIII

THE TEACHINGS OF CHRISTIANITY AS VIEWED BY A PAGAN

WE have seen that in the expansion of Christianity in its first two centuries within the Roman Empire there was little, if any, direct preaching to the masses. A pagan came in contact with the movement in a number of casual ways. He had become friendly with a member. He had seen or heard of an exorcism. He had been present when a martyr suffered in a curious and unreasonable way for an idea, tortured to deny and not to admit: he had gone away and puzzled over the matter. Or again he had heard talk of the Christian body as a dangerous organization of subversive tendencies and immoral practices. Now that which is socially condemned very often exercises a certain power of fascination, and subterranean movements have an intrinsic attraction. We saw this in the numerical strength attained at Rome by the Bacchanalian cult. Further, the small man in antiquity suffered from a marked feeling of inferiority and from a pathetic desire for self-assertion, of which the epitaphs supply abundant illustration. By adhesion to a society like the Church he acquired a sense of importance; 'Quartus, a brother' could have his place in Paul's greeting to the community at Rome.

In some such spirit a man who did not at once recoil in conservative hostility might come into relations with a Christian body. We have seen some of the inner desires which might be in his soul; a vague helpless speculative instinct, fostered by the vivid if shallow lectures of philosophers who talked at street corners, seeking the contentment of being made at home in the universe and not wholly satisfied; a resentment against the pitiless fixity of Fate's decrees; a desire, if not for assurance of survival, at any rate for assurance that any continuance of consciousness after death would not be cold and comfortless or even painful.

He came in some such spirit. He was then informed of certain beliefs and was told that if he accepted them and promised to live by them he would be admitted to baptism and thereafter to the communal meal. This idea of something from which he was excluded pending the fulfilment of conditions might then act as a further stimulus. We all desire to enter grounds marked *Private*, especially if there goes through them a foot-path which is said to lead to the New Jerusalem. We do not always inquire too closely into the trustworthi-ness of the directions given by the signpost.

What were the requirements? They appear in a phrase of Justin Martyr (*Apologia*, i. 61. 2), 'Those who are persuaded and believe that the things which we teach and say are true, and promise that they can live in this manner'. The picture which emerges thence is confirmed by other sources which set forth the condi-tions imposed for baptism. They may be summed up as repentance and faith; repentance involved the promise of good conduct in the future and the renuncia-tion of idols; faith involved personal belief in the central propositions of Christian theology—the unique power and position of God the Father, the redemptive work of Jesus, the life-giving activity of the Spirit. The Egyptian Church Order, which probably preserves the *Apostolic Teaching* of Hippolytus, who was active at

Rome in the first quarter of the third century of our era, lays down that 'when the day draws near on which they shall be baptized, the bishop binds every one of them by oath that he may know if they are pure'. The details of the renunciation and of the declaration of faith are known to us from later texts, but it is likely that they had taken shape early and certain that creeds are in their origin baptismal creeds. With their developed forms we are not concerned, for the chief factor in elaboration was the desire to provide against views which had arisen within the movement and had been rejected.

Theoretically the creed was not in later times given to the intending Christian till the time of his baptism and, by a practice which goes back to early times, he was excluded from the Eucharist. But this discipline of keeping a secret was at all times a sort of agreed legal fiction which preserved a due atmosphere of solemnity and after the end of persecution gave to entry into the Church a note of seriousness like that associated with pagan mysteries. Such a proceeding had not been necessary and did not obtain in the times of trial. Writings of Justin Martyr and Tertullian, which were intended for the public at large, whether they reached it or not, show no signs of reticence, and in fact afford quite full accounts of Christian teaching and worship. In any case, no man accepts initiation without knowing at least in outline the promises as well as the requirements implied. It was so with the pagan mysteries. Secrecy did not there belong to the prospects held out, or even to the main lines of the rite, for Justin Martyr says of the cult of Mithras (i. 66. 4) 'that bread and a cup of water are set among the ceremonies of the man

being initiated you know or can learn'; it belonged
to the pass-words, which gave admission to private
ceremonies, and again to certain important details of
the rite.

Let us therefore consider the requirements and tenets
of Christianity from the point of view of the pagan who
had not quite made up his mind. We may start with
the moral demands, as they are presented by Justin
Martyr in a treatise addressed to Antoninus Pius and his
associates in the intention of proving the unreasonable-
ness of persecution. He speaks of the change produced
in the lives of Christians (i. 14):

> 'We who formerly rejoiced in uncleanness of life and now
> love only chastity; we who also used magic arts and have
> now dedicated ourselves to the good and unbegotten God;
> we who loved resources of money and possessions more
> than anything, and now actually share what we have and
> give to every one who is in need; we who hated one another
> and killed one another and would not eat with those of
> other race, and now since the manifestation of Christ have
> a common life and pray for our enemies and try to win
> over those who hate us without just cause.'

He then gives an anthology of precepts from the
Gospels: first on sexual purity, then on love, generosity,
mercy, and freedom of thought for the morrow, then
on bearing ill and helping all without anger, then on
avoiding oaths and telling the truth, then on reverencing
God and God only. In all these ways moral reformation has, he says, been secured by those who have
entered the body.

These ideals would of course be at variance with the
habits of society as a whole at that time, as at any other.
Yet they are not widely different from the ideals then

held up by philosophic teachers of the popular type. We have spoken earlier of the sermons given by such men. We may recall how Musonius insisted that even in wedlock there should be no intercourse except for the procreation of children, and that the owner of a slave girl should not have relations with her; we may recall the passionate outburst of Dion of Prusa against prostitution, or the polemic in frivolous poets such as Ovid and Martial against abortion and self-abuse, or the frequency in mimes, a form of entertainment corresponding in vogue to the revue to-day, of declamations against luxury. We must not forget the gradual penetration of the Roman law by ethical and humanitarian considerations, which appear in the provision made against castration, cruelty to slaves, and the like.

When we turn to contemporary religion, we find that purity was required of those who would enter a temple. True, it was ritual more than moral purity. If abortion necessitated a quarantine of forty days, contact with a corpse meant ten; if intercourse with any person other than husband or wife meant two days, lawful intercourse meant one. What was required was disinfection and a lapse of time sufficient for your unholiness to wear off. Yet even in this realm there was a tendency to make demands of a more far-reaching kind. We have seen how the priest commanded Lucius not to return to the sinful pleasures of his youth. In various ways religious sanction was given to the idea that right conduct was indispensable for happiness here and hereafter. The ordinances of a private shrine built in honour of Agdistis at Philadelphia in Lydia about the conclusion of the second century B.C., or at latest at the beginning of the first, are almost as rigorous as Justin himself could have desired.

'Let men and women, slave and free, when coming into this shrine swear by all the gods that they will not deliberately plan any evil guile, or baneful poison against any man or woman; that they will neither know nor use harmful spells; that they will neither turn to nor recommend to others nor have a hand in love-charms, abortives, contraceptives, or doing robbery or murder; that they will steal nothing but will be well-disposed to this house, and if any man does or purposes any of these things they will not keep silence but will reveal it and avenge. A man is not to have relations with the wife of another, whether a free woman or a married slave, or with a boy, or with a virgin, or to counsel this to another. . . . Let not woman or man who do the aforementioned acts come into this shrine; for in it are enthroned mighty deities, and they observe such offences, and will not tolerate those who transgress their commands. . . . These commands were set up by the rule of Agdistis, the most holy guardian and mistress of this shrine. May she put good intentions in men and women, free and slave alike, that they may abide by what is here inscribed; and may all men and women who are confident of their uprightness touch this writing, which gives the commandments of the god, at the monthly and at the annual (?) sacrifices in order that it may be clear who abides by them and who does not. O Saviour Zeus, hear our words, and give us a good requital, health, deliverance, peace, safety on land and sea.'

Accordingly, while the Christian requirements were severe, they were not marked by an unheard-of severity, and the analogies to them were not confined to the most cultivated circles in society. The Greek words for conscience are words of common speech, little used in formal philosophic language. It is in any case a grave error to think of the ordinary man in the Roman Empire as a depraved and cruel fiend, dividing his hours between the brothel and intoxication, torturing a slave from time to time when he felt bored, and indifferent to the suffering and poverty of others. Cruelty and pleasure in exercising and witnessing cruelty existed in the amphitheatre and in the household, but we have seen earlier some curious indications of tender-heartedness even in what is commonly thought of as the brutal Roman mob (p. 197 above). As for luxury, the few had it, but not after Nero's death in anything like the measure of which we have knowledge in the first half-century of our era. Further, as Gilbert Murray has said, 'There was not more objective luxury in any period of ancient history than there is now; there was never anything like so much. But there does seem to have been more subjective abandonment to physical pleasure and concomitantly a stronger protest against it.' To most serious-minded men the good life seemed to involve a certain deliberate self-denial. Seneca had two hundred citron tables, but he lived on something like a hermit's fare. As for social services, the age of the Antonines set a standard which has only recently been again attained.

The real novelty in Christianity was the motive which it supplied for good conduct and the abhorrence of past bad conduct which it demanded. Of course, philosophy gave its motives. Stoicism, which is of preeminent importance in this, emphasized the idea of obedience to the law of nature and found room for an emotional warmth of devotion to that god behind phenomena whom you could call Zeus. Yet in Stoicism,

as in society as a whole, the real driving force was a
consciousness of your dignity as a human being. It was
a business, as in Galsworthy's story, of keeping form,
a morality of rulers;

> Their shoulders held the sky suspended.

For some Epicureanism supplied its motive—the avoid-
ance of all those excessive emotions which endangered
the true happiness to be sought and found in untroubled
calm. Again, the religious cults of the time also gave
motives—the desire to come in cleanness before a deity,
to comport yourself in such a way as would lead to
happiness hereafter.

None of these circles demanded sorrow for past sins.
Christianity demanded such sorrow and supplied more
effective motives—fear of God, as in Judaism, devotion
to Jesus who had suffered in order that sinlessness
might be within man's reach, and love for your fellow
Christians, who had like you been delivered by him
from death and sin. This important element of affection for your brethren had analogies in contemporary
thought. It was a marked feature of popular philosophy, as we see in Seneca's arguments for kindness to
slaves and in Dio's case against prostitution. Within
the religious sphere we may recall the way in which the
faithful of Isis welcomed Lucius as one of them, the
phrase in the soldier's confession of faith at Carvoran,
'thence we have all learned'—in which humanity is for
a moment one great family in worship (p. 136 above)
—and the use of 'dearly beloved brethren' for a group
of worshippers of Juppiter Dolichenus. But there is
no doubt that this love of the brethren was altogether
more lively and more far-reaching in Christianity.

Few things are more impressive than Lucian's account of the period in the life of Peregrinus during which that wandering soul became a Christian, and a Christian of prominence, and was put in prison for his faith. He tells with interest, if with contempt, of the attention of the community. And, for our present purpose, be it noticed also, that he relates that when the Christians found Peregrinus to be guilty of immoral conduct they removed him from their midst.

Christianity did not only give a motive. It claimed to give power to satisfy its requirements. It claimed that the baptized Christian received grace which, if he made reasonable effort, would enable him to live as he should. This is a point of cardinal importance. While some, but perhaps not many, intending converts would be of the type which James calls the sick soul, anxious about a supposed guilt, there would be very many who had moral ideals not unlike those of Christianity and found themselves unable to live up to them. To such there was a great attraction in this promise and in the examples of its fulfilment shown to them. While it must be admitted that there does not appear to be direct evidence for this precise attitude, there is no doubt of the impression made by Christian holiness, and literature shows the popularity of the motif of the converted sinner. Much of the pathos and of the power of Christianity in the past has lain in Guinevere's parting words to Launcelot: 'Therefore, Sir Launcelot, wit thou well I am set in such a plight to get my soul heal, and yet I trust through God's grace that after my death to have a sight of the blessed face of Christ and at Domesday to sit on his right side, for as sinful as ever I was are saints in heaven.'

Stoicism had taught that there was in man a particle of the divine spirit as a thing inherently bound to be present in his nature. But this was in a sense something up to which he must live rather than something by which he must live. In any case, it was supposed to be present in all men. It may have been better psychology than the Christian view of the special gift of the Spirit, but it was less effective psychology.

We pass to the renunciation of idolatry. The intending Christian was required to give up all worship of pagan deities: a command to sacrifice to them was used by the State authorities as a test, and compliance was regarded as satisfactory evidence of freedom from Christian errors. Two views might be held of pagan deities. First, that they were figments of the imagination, or at least not existing supernatural beings; second, that they were in fact supernatural beings but evil *daimones* or *daimonia*. The first view was taken by some Christian thinkers and derived considerable support from those ancient writers who held that the gods commonly worshipped fell into two classes, one composed of dead men to whom as to dead kings or to dead emperors divine honours had been accorded by the gratitude or servility of humanity, the other of personifications of the elements and heavenly bodies and natural forces, which were in fact only parts or aspects of creation. This view drew its material from Greek speculation, which was the source of the frequent Jewish and Christian criticisms of the immorality of Greek myth and the crudity of Greek cult. The second view is developed with great elaboration by Justin. All sins and delusions are due to the activity of these demons: the similarities of pagan and Christian rites are due to imitation by them, and, as far as baptism is concerned, to imitation of the rite as foretold by the prophets. This elaboration of the idea, copied by Athenagoras and Tertullian, was no doubt peculiar to speculative thinkers, but it is certain that the majority of converts regarded the old objects of their worship as existent, worsted indeed by Christ but still active and not wholly to be deprived of their activity till the coming of the kingdom of God. For the Apologists as a group and for Tertullian in his apologetic work the redemptive operation of Christ lay in deliverance from demons rather than in deliverance from sin.

How would an intending convert receive what he was told? and what would the description of his gods as daimones mean to him? *Daimon* is a word used from Homer onwards, at first to denote a supernatural force in a vaguer way than *theos*, to express that less sharply anthropomorphic way of thinking which is in Homer characteristic of the speeches of his figures as contrasted with his own narrative, and which crops up continually and was probably a feature of ordinary life as opposed to literature. *Daimon* and, for the matter of that, *theos*, *theoi*, *to theion* are constantly used to denote the incalculable non-human element in phenomena. *Daimon* is again in Hesiod used of the men of the past who have after death retained vigour and power and are now supernatural beings able to give blessings. It commonly denotes also the protecting spirit of a family or individual, and acquires the meaning of an angel guardian and almost of an astral self. The first definite theory of *daimones* appears in the *Banquet* of Plato. Here they are a special class with distinct functions. Diotima says (203 E), 'Through this race goes the whole science of divination, the art of the priests and of all concerned with sacrifices and initiations and spells and all divining and magic. God has no intercourse with men: it is through this race that all intercourse happens between gods and men.' This theory was developed by Xeno-crates and others later; so in Plutarch's treatise *On the Failure of Oracles* it is suggested that *daimones* are respon-sible for oracles and that the failure of these may be due to the fact that, though long lived, *daimones* are not immortal, which is illustrated by the story of the death of Great Pan. It is again the view set forth by Apuleius *On the God of Socrates* and by Celsus and others who are concerned to safeguard the doctrine of divine activity in the universe and the value of prayer and sacrifice without weakening divine transcendence.

In all this the term *daimon* has no evil colour at all: it is neutral. We hear of the toast to Agathos Daimon —which means 'Here's luck!'—and of the cult of the Good Daimon. There were also avenging *daimones*, but they were not in themselves evil; you could speak of a person's 'other *daimon*' or evil daimon as we might say unlucky genius, but this is clearly personal and *ad hunc*. However, the word acquires a more definite connotation. This may be due in part to the appear-ance of a book of Ostanes, supposedly translated from the Persian and full of angelology and dualism, but results in the main rather from an increasing trend to monotheism among thoughtful men, an aversion, less widespread but noticeable, from ordinary cult, and a very common reluctance to accept myth at its face value. Such men could not bring themselves to deny the reality of the beings ordinarily worshipped; but they could and did lower the place of gods, or some of them at least, in the hierarchy of the universe. For them *daimon* was a convenient word as vague and in a way inferior to *theos*, and the whole scheme harmonized the conservative instinct with the desire to think of the Divine as wholly good and transcendental. They might take a more or less favourable view of the *daimones* and of their activity. The *daimones* were ordinarily thought of as subject to God, and their worship appeared to be in a sense inferior but right. Celsus, Porphyry, and other writers tell us that *daimones* induce us to believe that bloody sacrifices and incense offerings are necessary, their motive being a selfish desire to feed on them. By this means they make us corporeal and like themselves and distract us from the service of higher powers. Again, a tractate in the *Corpus Hermeticum* states that *daimones* drive the evil to fresh sins (xvi. 10 ff.). For all these men the ideal is the sacrifice by reason. One and all they are interested in the encouragement of a pure philosophical piety divested of all the coarseness of popular worship. One and all they mistrust and hate its atmosphere, and wish to educate men in the direction of something better. One and all if challenged by a magistrate would have performed the ordinary sacrifices as a thing without inherent value but to them indifferent.

It is important that we should do justice to this widespread attitude of thoughtful men, to the contempt, again, which the practical Ammianus Marcellinus feels for the hecatombs of his hero Julian. At the same time we must remember two things. First, this is a learned and not a popular attitude. The man in the street retained his faith in bloody sacrifices even if he could not often afford to offer them, and meats offered to

idols were a regular feature of everyday life. Secondly,
it is a theoretical attitude. None of these men, if lifted
to the throne by a sudden turn of fortune, would have
prohibited sacrifice and many of them probably felt
that, irresistible as seemed the chain of reasoning
which had led them to their conclusions, it was nevertheless not quite safe to discontinue the offerings cus-
tomarily made by the magistrates and priests of the
State or by the head of the household. They could say
with Paul, 'Is what is offered to an idol of any force?
or is an idol of any force? No,' but unlike him they
would shrink from acting on their conclusions. After
all, though this actual theory is new, a certain cold-
ness towards ordinary cult had been common among
thinking men since the early days of Greek philosophy.
We have seen something of this earlier (p. 120). The
views of the Roman antiquarian Varro are the more
striking in that they stood in the introductory book of
his work on *Divine Antiquities*, the most comprehensive
storehouse of facts on the cults and legends of a people
made in Greece or Rome. He said that if he were
founding Rome anew he would have consecrated the
gods and their names in accordance with the scheme
of nature. But as it was, the State being long established, he wrote with the purpose that the masses might
be willing to worship the gods rather than to despise
them. He regretted image-worship: for over 170 years
Rome did without it and, if things had so continued,
the gods would be worshipped with greater purity.
Sacrifice was not wanted by the real gods. Yet there
were many things which the masses should not know,
many delusions that were useful: that was why the
Greeks walled off the mysteries in silence.

So the position of Christian apologetic was in agreement with much contemporary Greek thought, from which it drew so freely. The man in the street cannot have been altogether easy to convince. Against Christianity was set the whole force of tradition and ancestral custom. It was all very well to argue like this: but suppose a plague came? or a famine? or an inroad of the Goths? shall we not

> Take hands and dance there, a fantastic ring,
> Round the ancient idol, on his base again,—
> The grand Perhaps!

So it was that after the establishment of Christianity as the State religion it was necessary to provide new rural processions to take the place of the old. Worship was not just the expression of love and praise and fear. It was the averting of the possible wrath of the supernatural forces around men; it was their placating; it was the expression of gratitude in forms which would encourage these forces to render in the future services like those which they were thought to have rendered in the past; and—above all to a Roman—it was the strengthening of them for those services, the giving to them of power to satisfy the needs of their worshippers. Just how important this last aspect was we see from the length of the polemic which Arnobius directs against it in the seventh book of his work *Against the Nations*. Sacrifice and other rites were of the nature of *actio*, as this term was later used of the Eucharist. Just how this idea took shape we do not know; but it was natural, as we see from the way in which in Vedic India sacrifice came to be regarded as an indispensable factor in the cosmic process.

It was a wrench to give up all this, and to give up the veneration paid to idols and in particular to old shapeless survivals from earlier times: in the eyes of the common man they were charged with force, and could even be regarded as the gods themselves. A strong emotional conviction fortified by the common doctrine of the Christians that immorality and paganism belonged together would, however, enable even the little educated to make the necessary clear cut. It should be borne in mind that the majority of the early converts were town dwellers and therefore not particularly interested in agrarian rites (*pagani* means backwoodsmen), and again came from a social stratum which had not old and dear traditions. The issue was very much one of tradition. So in the fourth century we find the antithesis of the pagan aristocracy of Rome and the Christian bourgeoisie of Milan.

The intending convert had to renounce the official worships of the State and of the municipality. He had therefore to renounce the public cult of the Emperor. He could not swear by the Emperor's genius, the life-spirit of his family; he could not take part in the celebrations of the days of his birth and of his accession; he could not as a soldier or as a municipal magistrate take part in those acts of worship in which either would participate: he could not hold a municipal or provincial priesthood of the cult, although his wealth and social standing might make such a position appropriate for him or incumbent on him. In all these things his attitude was the same as a Jew's. The Jew's conscientious objection was recognized and allowed—in spite of the passing megalomania of Caligula and occasional outbreaks of Jew-baiting in Alexandria and elsewhere in which the mob attempted to compel the chosen people to contravene their principles. Christians did not enjoy such privileges. Had the movement remained a sect within Judaism it obviously would have, as we have seen. Christian, however, came to have the same sort of connotation as heretic in the Middle Ages and as Communist in America and western Europe to-day. The fear of political danger was not a red herring drawn across this particular trail. The Romans had a genuine dread of the stirring up of sedition under the cloak of religion: they were deeply concerned with the regulating of associations. Christianity gave special cause for fear because of its teaching on the kingdom of God. Justin Martyr says (i. 11), 'You, having heard that we expect a kingdom, have formed the uncritical impression that we mean a kingdom in the human sense.' Such an idea would always arouse suspicion, and after Bar-Cochba's revolt in 135 the world must be kept safe from Messianism. With these facts in view we can see that no concession could be expected by the Christians. The Jewish reluctance to worship the Emperor seemed queer, but the Christian dangerous. Hence the emphasis in Christian apologetic on their loyalty and their prayers for the Emperor.

Two further remarks may here be made. First, there was ordinarily no obligation on the private citizen to take part in the actual worship. An oath he could hardly avoid, but that was the most that was normally incumbent on him. When Pliny bade the Christians sacrifice to the Emperor, he was imposing a test and not making an ordinary requirement. Secondly, the ideals of the Christians and the position into which they were forced by events caused them to ascribe to ruler-worship more content than it possessed. By the time of Claudius it was an outward sign of loyalty which involved little sentiment. This is further illustrated by the number of its outward manifestations which passed into the customs of the Byzantine and ultimately of the Papal Court. In our own time a case has been made by Catholic theologians for permitting Japanese converts to take part in traditional observances to the Mikado, because of the purely formal and patriotic character of the proceedings and because of the Byzantine precedent.

The convert must forswear also the use of astrology and of magic. On both topics the Apologists enlarge, and on both their attitude was fully in agreement with the official policy of the Empire. The arguments which they advance against astrology are drawn mainly from the old objections of the Academic school: magic was for them naturally another of the delusions imposed upon humanity by the *daimones*. On both heads they were fighting ideas which were popular with the classes among which Christianity won its first successes. Yet even here their stand would command a certain measure of sympathy, for, as we have seen, there was a widespread desire to escape from Fate, and while there was not a popular fear of demons there clearly was a fear of witchcraft, which shows itself in epidemics of cruel punishment in the fourth century of our era, possibly, of course, complicated by political considerations. In the long run astrology and magic proved superior to faith, law, and argument.

We may now come to the positive teachings of the Christians. Their doctrine about God the Father was

easily acceptable. In its origin it is Jewish, but there
is development: for while there is no doubt that the
Jews believed as intensely as the Christians in the
Fatherhood, goodness, and accessibility of God, it is
nevertheless to be remarked that the Christians never
had the Jewish scruple against using his name, and
that the Fatherhood of God was by them more
emphatically thought of as a relation to the individual
rather than as a relation to the nation. This teaching
was not foreign to a Greek. As early as Homer Zeus
is father to all men, Greeks and Ethiopians alike: as
early as Hesiod he is the god of Justice, concerned with
its maintenance even in the details of life. He is not
in the mythology the maker of the universe, not even
its shaper, but in speculative thought, above all in
Stoicism, his name was the name most used for the
fiery breath which was held to be the formative and
animating principle of all things.

This view tended towards a doctrine of Zeus as
immanent in phenomena—as when Cato in Lucan (ix.
580) is made to say 'Jupiter is whatever you see and
whatever motion you experience'. But a personal
colour could be retained and commonly was. We
cannot forget the outburst of Epictetus (i. 16, 20):

> 'What else can I do, an old man and lame, but praise
> God? If I were a nightingale, I would do the part of a
> nightingale; if I were a swan, the part of a swan. But, as it
> is, I am a being of reason: I must praise God. This is my
> work: I do it and I will not leave this post as long as it is
> given to me, and I exhort you to the same hymn.'

Or the saying of Marcus Aurelius (iv. 23): 'A famous
one says, Dear city of Cecrops, and wilt not thou say,
Dear city of Zeus?' His teaching involves immediate

relations of men to God as creator, commander, and leader.

These views are in origin philosophic products of the study, but in time they worked their way down to the masses. They were helped by the fact that the popular mind, although it saw the gods through the presentation of them in literature and art, did not in fact hold such sharply anthropomorphic views, and by the other circumstance, that mythology was always to a certain extent in flux. The allegorization of myth which rendered possible these schemes was very well known indeed. Ancient writers on rhetoric, that is to say the art of fine writing and fine speaking, supply us with an admirable way of finding what ideas had become the common coin of the day. One of them, Alexander, whose father wrote under Hadrian, begins his treatment of the topic *On how many heads one should praise a god*, by referring to the philosophic view that god is unbegotten and not susceptible of destruction. Another, Aristides, in his prose hymn to Zeus, shows the influence of Stoic concepts. He speaks of Zeus as having made all things, he emphasizes the etymology of Zeus from *zoe* (life), of Dia, the accusative of the name, from *dia* (the preposition 'through'), and the fact that the functions of all other deities are derivative. For him Zeus is a cosmic figure and the Homeric presentation of the god a thing to be deprecated. The most remarkable evidence for the influence which such speculation exercised within religious circles is an oracle claiming, probably as to its substance rightly, to come from the shrine of Apollo of Claros. In it the inquirer is told that there is one god, Eternity (Aion), and that the other gods are angels and a small part of him. It was widely held that the gods of paganism were emanations of virtues or at most subordinates of the Supreme Being.

When God was spoken of as maker of heaven and earth, difficulty would be caused for men of philosophic education, for they commonly held that matter was pre-existent; but they could in practice interpret this as 'shaper of matter into heaven and earth'.

The doctrine about Jesus was not wholly repellent. The idea that a god could have a son was a commonplace of ancient mythology, as of all mythologies; in fact Justin Martyr has to guard against a physical interpretation of the begetting of Jesus. Origen denies emphatically that any holy man ever celebrated his birthday, and Arnobius, vii. 32, mocks at the birthday of *Tellus* (Mother Earth); there is no indication of a Christmas festival before the beginning of the fourth century. Further, for the popular imagination, this divine habit of parenthood was not confined to the past. According to a story which grew up soon after Plato's death his supposed father was warned in a dream not to approach his wife until she had given birth to the child which she had just conceived, for it was by Apollo. A similar tale was attached to Augustus. In the intrigues connected with Lysander's attempt to introduce changes at Sparta a son of Apollo was produced as the heaven-sent man to secure occult oracles, advantageous to Lysander (Plut. *Lys.* 26). Again, there could be a curious belief that a man had at one and the same time a divine and a human father. No one questioned that Alexander was the son of Philip and Olympias, and yet the oracle of Ammon in Libya hailed him as the god's son. So various Greek heroes had a human and a divine father, Heracles for instance having Zeus and Amphictyon. An Egyptian Pharaoh was born in the same way as any other man and yet in the eyes of faith he was begotten by a god and suckled by a goddess. It was so also with early rulers in Mesopotamia. So in the fourth *Eclogue* of Virgil it is prophesied that a child shall be born, whose growth will synchronize with the gradual return of the world order to its old goodness. The child is obviously human, and its mother's pain and weariness in pregnancy are treated with tender sympathy. And yet the child is 'dear offspring of the gods, great descendant of Jove'.

Life, like myth, has its allegorical meaning. As myth when interpreted comes down into the sphere of ordinary things, so life when interpreted rises into that sphere. This is an important aspect of ancient thought. It underlies the great importance attached to mythological parallels. In Pindar's *Odes* the victor in an athletic event is set in the heroic context of the legendary ancestor of his line or the legendary founder of the games; so are the countless dead men on whose funerary monuments heroic scenes are represented. The Greek was more interested in a generalized truth living behind individual facts than in those facts. This is what underlies Aristotle's remark that poetry is more philosophical than history, forasmuch as history handles particular things, as for instance what Alcibiades did, whereas poetry handles general things. In point of fact this way of looking at things is not foreign to our days. People think of themselves and of others in terms of types; they act or think of others as acting in borrowed roles.

To resume: a son of a god could die. Asclepius, the son of Apollo, was killed by the lightning of Zeus for raising a dead man to life; later he was restored and active as the deity of medicine. Heracles died on the pyre of Oeta and, having purged away his mortality in its flames, lived thereafter on Olympus. A god could have a passion and resurrection—Zagreus, Attis, Adonis, Osiris. With the last three it came to be thought of as something which happened each year and only secondarily as something which had happened once definitively. Sallustius says, in an interpretation which is philosophic and yet true to the spirit of ancient belief (4), 'All this did not happen at any one time but always is: the mind sees the whole process at once, words tell of part first, part second.' These ideas were in time applied to Christianity. The Eucharist, a meal and thanksgiving linked to the symbolic act by which Jesus made his disciples willing partners in his death, became the re-enacting of that death. Medieval piety developed the drama of Holy Week with increasing realism and in the domain of the Greek Church the popular attitude is still that at every Eastertide Christ rises, and that if he did not rise the crops would not grow.

It was of course peculiar to the Christian creed that Jesus had suffered voluntarily and had suffered for men, and that this suffering was itself the basis of deliverance. It was peculiar also that these soteriological events were pinned down to a precise moment in history. This no doubt represents both the intense interest felt by the Church in its scheme of history and also a measure of protection against mythological speculation. It was not wholly strange. Most cults in antiquity had the story of their institution, real or legendary, not as a rule tied to a precise date but cherished as important. In Mithraism, indeed, the sacred story was definitely fixed at the beginning of the world-order; and Mithras, unlike other gods, had a complex *Vita*, shown in a sequence of scenes in art and corresponding to the Gospel story; but Mithras did not die.

There is another aspect of belief about Jesus which must be emphasized as a factor making for its easy naturalization in the world around. We have seen the wide dissemination of an idea of a single god behind phenomena, the supreme cause and even the supreme benevolence. With it existed also the notion that our prayers and offerings should not normally be addressed to the Supreme Being direct. Celsus, for all his theoretical monotheism, upbraids the Jews for thinking God worthy of adoration, but denying this to the moon and stars and His other parts, 'the truly heavenly angels'. An intermediary hypostasis was a necessity to much philosophy for the reason already noted as making for demonology: it is notably emphasized in the Hermetic literature, in which we read for instance that no sacrifice is to be offered to the Supreme Being. Astronomical thought combined with such theology to put him out of reach. Further, this thought corresponded in a way to the facts of worship. In a Mithraeum there was sometimes a representation of the Sky-god or Eternity, but effective worship was addressed to Mithras, who stood between man and 'the eternal silence of these infinite spaces'. Sarapis could by an identification with Zeus be regarded as the Supreme Being; so in mythical circles could Dionysus, but commonly Zeus stood over him. Attis, Adonis, Osiris could not be thought of as supreme: they were all figures with whom the law of the universe had had its will. There was therefore something very intelligible in the Christian idea of an approach to the Father through Jesus and of an activity of the Father mediated by Jesus as the Word.

There was, however, one difficulty in Christian teaching to which our attention is directed by the *Catechetical Oration* (a discourse on how those seeking baptism should be instructed) of Gregory of Nyssa (dated about 383). After discussing arguments against polytheism, atheism, and the concept that the Divine nature is imperfect (the last a view which is not, he says, to be expected), he devotes himself at length to the doctrine of the Logos. 'Perhaps the pagan', he says (ch. 5), 'by reason of general ideas, the Jew by reason of scriptural arguments will not dispute the existence of a Word and Spirit of God. But each of them alike will reject the plan of God's Word (*or*, God the Word) in relation to man as improbable and unsuited to God.' The argument shows that there was a substantial objection to any idea of incarnation—of God or a power of him taking human flesh and passing through birth and death, both seeming undignified. This may seem strange in view of Attis and Adonis, both of whom were in some legends born of human mothers, both of whom in the general story died. Yet their births were placed in the mythical period and both were in the world at large the expression of natural processes: neither was an aspect of the Supreme Being. Both, like Mithras, had divine and not human cycles of life. This was not a belief in incarnation. The existence of these gods began at their birth: they had no pre-existent glory to leave for us men and for our salvation. It is sometimes said that the ancient rulers were supposed to be avatars of deities; but, except for the theoretical and theological identification with divinity of the king in Egypt and a poetic fancy about Augustus, this is not so. Further, if Augustus was, as Horace suggests, Mercury in human shape, this was an epiphany in a shape assumed for the moment—such as the men of Lystra ascribed to Paul and Barnabas. It was like the appearance of Athena to Telemachus in the guise of an old friend, and unlike the coming of a Bodhisattva. It was easy enough for an ancient to think of this mortality putting on immortality, Heracles being the most familiar instance, and the mysteries implying the idea: but the reverse process was not envisaged. 'None of the heavenly gods will leave the bounds of heaven and come down on earth,' says the writer of *Corpus Hermeticum* x. 25, and he expresses the general view of antiquity. Humanity, in its essential nature and quality, was regarded as a liability rather than as an asset.

Most churchgoing people have in the creed recited 'according to the Scriptures' as a phrase which has now little interest and meaning other than those which cling to a survival. It is a commonplace that the passages in the Old Testament which were thought to foretell the coming and death and rising of Christ can bear no such sense, that they refer to imminent or past events of an earlier time. Yet, in considering the impact of Christianity on the world of the time, we must for a moment think away all these things. To the Apologists the prophetic writings seemed their strongest argument for the truth of Christianity. Justin gives a long collection of selected proof texts, prefacing it with the words (*Apol.* i. 30),

> 'Now in order that no one may in opposition to us ask, What prevents him whom we call Christ, a man born of man, from having by magic skill done the miracles which we describe and from having therefore seemed to men to be the Son of God, we will give the proof, not trusting to those who recorded the events, but believing as we must those who before they took place prophesied them. We do this because with our own eyes we see these things having happened and happening as was prophesied. In our opinion this will appear to you the greatest and truest proof.'

Athenagoras speaks (7) of the diversity of opinions among poets and philosophers 'moved each by his own soul to seek, in accordance with a sympathy existing between it and the breath from God . . . expecting to learn about God not from God but from their individual selves', and says in contrast:

> 'But we have as witnesses to our ideas and beliefs the prophets who by divine spirit have spoken out concerning God and the things of God. Those of you who excel others in reverence for the divine could tell how unreasonable it is to refuse to believe the Spirit from God, that has touched the prophets' mouths like musical instruments, and to pay heed rather to human opinions.'

This was not merely an apologetic device; the same argument is developed in a similar way by Irenaeus in his *Demonstration of Apostolic Preaching*, a plain statement of doctrine addressed to a fellow Christian, Marcianus.

Such a view of inspiration was familiar, and we have seen how much importance was attached by men at large to the guidance of inspired personages. When Justin says of the prophets (*Dial.* 7. 2), 'They did not rest their speeches on proofs, for they were trustworthy witnesses to truth standing above all proof', very many of his contemporaries would have sympathized and would have disregarded the small recalcitrant minority of intellectuals. We have seen the astonishing success of Alexander of Abonutichus.

This value set on prophecy was not confined to the living voice of the inspired man, but belonged also to books recording prophecies, very many of which were in circulation. Particular weight attached to the supposed utterances of such persons from a mythical past. This was so throughout antiquity. In Greece there were the prophecies of Bacis and Musaeus and the various Sibyls. The use of the books of the Sibyl of Cumae runs like a thread through the religious history of Rome, where any emergency called for their consultation and any ritual innovation was justified by the finding or fabricating of a passage in justification. The value set on such books rests both on the belief in inspiration, that is to say the belief that a human being can in ecstasy serve as the mouthpiece of a deity, and on the belief in the wisdom of the past, which has been discussed earlier (p. 113). This belief in the wisdom of the past was particularly strong in relation to the past of non-Greek nations. It was a conviction based on a recognition of the far longer continuity of culture, and above all priestly culture, in Egypt and Babylon. Hence arose the idea that the early Greek philosophers, and for the matter of that Plato, had learned their wisdom on voyages to the East. So, when Philo or Clement or any other Jewish or Christian apologist claimed that Greek writers had borrowed from Jewish writers, they were following a theory which was in other forms widely held. The argument from the Jewish prophecies was reinforced by arguments based on supposedly genuine and relevant pagan prophecies.

The fulfilment of a forecast is a thing which has always fascinated men. We all notice the striking and successful coincidences which occur: 'and so it proved' is one of the favourite turns of speech in popular narrative, and ancient history is full of the significant verification of lucky guesses. Further, it should be noticed that it was normally expected that a great man would be heralded by signs and prophecies. We may recall the rival prophecies which Cleon and the Sausage-seller in the *Knights* of Aristophanes utter as foreshadowing their activities. For Augustus there were portents before his birth, at his birth, and throughout his life, indicating the greatness of the part which he was to play on the stage of the world and his destiny to live with the gods thereafter. There was a series of portents marking out Vespasian as destined to rule: even of Galba it was related that Augustus had said to him, 'Thou too, Galba, shalt have a taste of Empire'.

The men to whom these arguments were addressed would certainly never have seen a copy of the Septuagint. We have seen earlier how little knowledge of its contents had reached the outer world (p. 79); Posidonius in his treatment of primitive prophets did not mention the Jewish prophets. At most the name of Moses and scraps of Genesis became known—a fact which is particularly intelligible when we remember how markedly Philo's interest in the Old Testament is confined to the Pentateuch. When the convert came into a Christian assembly he heard readings from the prophets as well as from the writings of the Apostles (Justin, *Apol.* i. 67. 3). In any case, his natural instinct would be to take what he was told as true. Throughout the Imperial period one of the conspicuous features of intellectual life is a readiness to accept statements because they were in books, or even because they were said to be in books. It was hard to unroll a papyrus, but how many even of the worst of modern scholars would have written in Alexandria as Didymus does of the so-called eleventh Philippic, 'It might be not unreasonably conjectured that this small speech is a cento put together from some compositions of Demosthenes. Some say that this exhortatory oration is by Anaximenes of Lampsacus, and that it is now to be found almost word for word in the seventh book of the History of Philip,' and left it there? If it was so with the expert, how was it with the layman?

On the doctrine of the Spirit something has been said. We need here only recall that the Stoics held that in all men there was a divine *pneuma* and that most people believed that prophetic inspiration was the product of what inspiration literally means, breathing in. It remains that we should speak of the Church and of the expectation of the resurrection of the flesh and of the life of the world to come.

The Church of the second century thought of itself as the new people of God, the spiritual Israel which had entered into the enjoyment of those promises which the Israel after the flesh had lost by blindness of heart, Both to themselves and to outsiders they appeared as a people rather than as an organization. In any case they were unique. The priestly system and organization of the Jews were confined to Palestine: there were *episkopoi* who collected dues from the synagogues of the Dispersion, but these synagogues were all independent entities. They had a standard of faith in the Law, but their application of it rested with the rulers of the individual congregation. We have seen how little cohesion there was in any contemporary pagan cults. The Christians had something new—the letters of introduction given to a member of one community about to visit another, the relations and mutual assistance of one congregation to another (as for instance of Rome to Corinth), the formulation of agreed tenets and of an agreed view of their own history. Apart from times of persecution, a poor man must have gained a great sense of security from the organization. He knew that care would be taken of him in and after life, and that he would not be wholly left to his own resources.

Our convert could thus without difficulty acquire devotion to the Catholic Church. But when he came to Christian teaching about the last things he was on strange territory. Acts xvii represents Paul as delivering at Athens a speech nearly all of which could have been spoken by a Greek philosopher of the time and as leaving this common ground by saying that repentance is now necessary, for that God has appointed a day to judge the world by Jesus whom He has raised from the dead. At this point the audience interrupted, some mocking. Here was the disturbing element in Christian doctrine. And yet it was fundamental. The central fact in the teaching of Jesus was not a novel doctrine of God or man but the heralding of the kingdom. It was not new: it had been in many Jewish minds for a century and more: it had been urged with compelling force by John the Baptist. Yet it was taught with a new vigour and power. The business of those who heard the message was to labour to prepare Israel for the Day of the Lord, for the end of the present age and for the world assize which would usher in the new age. Israel in general was unwilling to be prepared and the New Israel took its place. But, even so, and even when the expectation of the final act of the cosmic drama became fainter, the Church was in the last analysis not an organization for the sanctification of souls in the present so much as a nursery of the people of the future. The things seen were temporary. Other men held that. Sallustius says (ch. 3), 'The universe itself can be called a myth, since bodies and material objects are apparent in it, while souls and intellects are concealed.' But these philosophers thought that the things that were seen followed the types of a permanent and unchanging reality that was not seen, and that the time process was like a straight line. To the Christian the visible world and its order were not so much a type of the eternal as a passing phase, a stain on its radiance which was to fade and pass.

Something like the Christian idea, in fact its ultimate source, was known to the ancients. I mean the Zoroastrian scheme. In its first form, as put forward by Zarathustra, it had been very like the teaching of Jesus. The triumph of the good was imminent, and in that triumph the righteous would all share and those of them who had died would rise again and have their part, receiving material and spiritual recompense. Zarathustra tells how he asked of his god, Ahura Mazda, a question very like Peter's 'Lo we have left all things and followed thee: what shall our reward be?' Will he receive ten mares and a stallion and a camel? Here as in Christianity the brightness of the vision faded and there grew up a doctrine of periods, corresponding to those which we find in Jewish and Christian apocalyptic but more symmetrical. For 3,000 years Good was triumphant, for 3,000 Evil, for 3,000 they would contend, and then the time of happiness was to begin.

A doctrine of periods became an integral part of Stoicism. According to this school, the present structure of the universe is at regular intervals dissolved by fire and water, the interval being the number of years which it takes for a particular conjuncture of all the heavenly bodies to repeat itself (the so-called Great Year). After this destruction comes a fresh identical creation, passing through the same sequence of phases. So all life would for ever repeat itself. Ideas of this kind were very widespread. In Virgil's fourth *Eclogue* a new order is heralded. This comes without any cosmic catastrophe and the ages return upon themselves. We do not start again at the beginning but work backwards. There is another difference. A man of this age can hope to live into the new and better day: at least the poet prays that he may. Such a living into the new era is thought of in an ordinary way: the poet will die in due course, whether he lives into the good days or not, and the dead will not rise. There will be a new Achilles and a new Tiphys, as figures in the time preceding a new Golden Age.

Such an age was often in the minds of ancient writers. It was a time of peace and goodwill between man and man and between man and animals, a time when there was neither toil nor seafaring nor war nor sickness. It was commonly thought of as something which had been once in the springtime of humanity and had for ever passed away through a fatal process of degeneration. We know this in Hesiod: it is like the many stories told by primitive peoples of the days when there was no death, days which by some mistake or misunderstanding have gone from the earth. The Golden Age has been: its ways might be thought of as continuing in some supposed islands just off the map, the Islands of the Blest or the City of the Sun as imagined by Iambulus. But they would not come again—or only as part of a new cycle which would reproduce this one mechanically without continuity and without memory of this, which would be as though it never had been. So men ordinarily thought. There are occasional exceptions: the fourth *Eclogue* and a Greek prophecy which is perhaps contemporary, and another from Ptolemaic Egypt of the second century before Christ. From this last we may quote one phrase: 'The times will be so good that the dead might wish to come alive again.' But they were not to, not in any of these dreams begotten of dismay and despair and the incurable feeling that happiness must be round the corner:

> The living are the living,
> And the dead the dead must lie.

How strong the idea of cycles was can be seen from the way in which Persian ideas were transformed in the Graeco-Roman world. In Mithraism it is clear that the concept of a sequence of ages, world-destructions and world-renewals, took the place of the Zoroastrian concept of a unique series of events, and that the idea of the resurrection of the dead disappeared or was at least thrust into the background in favour of the Greek idea of the liberation of the soul from the trammels of the body.

The concrete expectations of the Christians had no doubt an attraction for many who found life heavy and unjust and who looked for conditions under which its inequalities would be set right. The century which preceded the remaking of the Roman world by Augustus had seen several abortive attempts to initiate a social revolution. The firm government which followed did much to humanize life and certainly left to such movements no chance of success: we see very few signs of anything of the sort before the fourth century of our era, when the Circumcelliani in North Africa showed levelling ambitions like those of the Mazdakites in Persia a century later. The men who might have been expected to make uprisings did in fact display rather a sullen resignation like that of the Egyptian fellahin in all ages. Their outlook appears in the epitaph so often found over the remains of slaves and gladiators, 'I was not. I was. I shall not be. I do not care.'

None of these men, unless they had fallen under Christian influence, expected divine intervention to change things. If they acquired any general theory of the probable course of events it would be that common among educated men—that history was composed of unconnected cycles and that they were at the time living in one of the down-swings. The world was growing grey and old and feeble; it seemed that virtue had gone out of man and earth alike. Yet we must not think of this as disturbing people, any more than we are disturbed by astronomical predictions that the universe will in some millions of years perish. Men desired that their memories might remain for ever, but they meant by that that they might remain for as long as the imagination could grasp. Nor must we suppose that this picture of cycles was felt to be a weary round from which men wished to be emancipated or that the Christian scheme was necessarily felt to be a liberation from this point of view. The suggestion deserves a moment's consideration. Lucretius does indeed say everything is always the same, *eadem sunt omnia semper* (iii. 945), but he puts it in the mouth of a personification of Nature which is made to reprove man for complaining of the advent of death. Nature says: there is nothing new that I can invent or devise for you if you were to live on indefinitely. This is no complaint against the cycle theory. This is no feeling such as we find against the theory of Fate, in regard to which Epicurus said that it was worse to be its slave than to follow the myth of the gods. The explanation is simple. Fate affected man in his individual interests and desires, and this he minded: just as he would wish to escape from the cycle of transmigration and reincarnation if he believed in it.

Nevertheless a man could be argued out of this theory without any deep offence to his feelings. It was otherwise with the doctrine of resurrection of the body. This was a denial of the dearest hope of many. To quote Sallustius once more (21), 'Souls that have lived in accordance with virtue have as the crown of their happiness that, being freed from the unreasonable element and purified from all body, they are in union with the gods and share with them the government of

I

the whole universe.' We have seen earlier (p. 26) the origin of this idea in the Orphic conception that man has an immortal element prisoned in the tomb of the body. The mythology on which this was based had long ceased to matter; but the fundamental view had become a very widespread conviction. Man felt himself to be, as Marcus Aurelius says, 'a small soul carrying a dead body'. The popularity of this rests on a fact of experience, common enough in all conscience, the struggle between noble aspirations and physical leanings, between the tenets of philosophy and the law in one's limbs. It is, says Epictetus, no equal struggle between a young man beginning philosophy and a fair young girl (iii. 12. 12). The body wins time after time and the man feels each time a little less his own master. Discipline can do something, but the only true liberation will come with freedom from the flesh; so they thought. Christian theology did not deny the value of these ideas. The glorified body of the risen man is in the higher theology, as in Paul, quite distinct from the earthly body and would have no tendencies to evil, no sensual cravings; in the resurrection they would neither marry nor give in marriage; and the present body of man needed mortification and ascetic control. But Christian theology did find itself in radical opposition to the philosophic notion of the soul as a thing essentially divine and essentially immortal and of an immeasurable superiority to the body, needing only purification and freedom from carnal contacts to enjoy God for ever. Such ideas made any belief in redemption unnecessary and any belief in the resurrection of the body unpalatable.

This deep cleavage explains the warmth of Tertullian's arguments for the soul's fallibility and its dependence on the body. Paganism stood for the deliverance of the real self, aided by sacrament and system, but having in the last resort within itself the means of salvation and struggling for immortality in bliss as a prize to be won by those who had wished to live in accordance with virtue and succeeded. Christianity stood for the redemption and resurrection of the whole as an entity containing higher elements, helpless in itself, but capable by divine favour of receiving salvation and destined at the end to become a glorified unity. The issue is after all the doctrine of grace. The genius of Christianity lies on the side of Augustine, the genius of paganism on the side of Pelagius. The one built on a consciousness of sin and on revelation, the other on a consciousness of goodness and on common sense. On this issue we must all take sides.

We have reviewed the central ideas of Christianity as they would present themselves to an ordinary man from the world around. We have seen that they were in general quite intelligible to him: there were difficulties, but these difficulties existed mainly for those of superior education who found the new thing foolishness. Such men were relatively rare in the first century and a half. Clement of Alexandria is the first of whom we have knowledge: his teacher Pantaenus was no doubt of the same calibre.

This intelligibility of the teaching did not rest on any particular psychological skill in presentation. It does not mean that men, being in one intellectual and spiritual position, succeeded in putting themselves in another and in getting under the other man's skin.

Such sympathetic understanding we know in the work of Mencius and of other early Jesuit missionaries in China; but they were exceptional. Religious propaganda generally operates on the basis of a common cultural background or, as in modern missions, on superiority of culture.

The effectiveness of early Christian propaganda as we know it turns largely on two further points. First, the apologists were without exception men who were not the sons of Christians but had been converted to Christianity themselves. The *apologia* of each of them was therefore in a measure an *apologia pro vita sua*. Secondly, they all represented Christianity as something which had come not to destroy but to fulfil. They maintained that its essential principles were what humanity at its best had always held or sought. They went back to their Jewish sources, but they claimed that Plato drew from these same sources. For them the whole wisdom of the past was in support of their position, even if few went as far as Justin and held that all who had lived with reason (logos) were Christians, a development of the idea expressed in the prologue to the fourth Gospel.

This was a valuable point of view. It squared with the general belief in the wisdom of the past of which we have spoken (p. 113). Others who had views to commend to the world at large used the same technique. The Stoics interpreted Homer as Philo interpreted the Pentateuch; just as he found Platonism in that, so they found their philosophy in Homer and Hesiod and the Orphic writings; so later the Neoplatonists found their philosophy in Homer as well as in Plato. An ancient canonical book was an authority,

so much so that it was worth interpolating or invent-
ing suitable proof-texts to supplement the artful aid
of exegesis. We have Orphic fragments which teach
Stoic pantheism: we have others which teach Jewish
monotheism; we have Hermetic fragments and Greek
oracles which support Christianity; Justin and his
fellows rest much of their case on the Jewish prophets,
but they quote also the prophecy of the supposed
Persian Hystaspes, and Lactantius in particular makes
extensive use of the prophetic literature which passed
under the name of Sibylline oracles, apparently without realizing that it had been created largely by Jews
and partly by Christians with an apologetic intention.
The Sibyl became an important figure in yet later
Christian apologetic. The appeal to antiquity was an
effective thing. It was an answer to what was at the
time a most damaging criticism of Christianity—
namely, that it was a new thing followed in contraven-
tion of good old customs. The Jewish writer said in
weariness of spirit, 'There is nothing new under the
sun'. Most thinking citizens of the Empire would have
resented this suggestion that there could be.

Lastly, we must emphasize that thinking men expected that the ultimate explanation of the universe
should be straightforward. Nothing is more striking
than the way in which philosophical reasoning constantly assumed that you could base valid arguments
on analogy and on the hypothesis that the universe is symmetrical and neat, that bodies which
move in straight lines are naturally different from
bodies which move in circles. Ancient conceptions of
the character of motion, for instance, rest on popular
maxims, accepted by philosophy from common sense

without scrutiny—that like attracts like, that like
nourishes like, and that like affects like.

From this point of view Christianity was satisfactory.
So was Manichaeism, of which we shall have more to
say in the next chapter. It made a strong appeal to
the intellectuals of the time. Had it taken shape earlier
it might have been a very serious rival. As it was, it
did not appear on the scene until Christianity had
consolidated a body of adherents who were in their
compactness much more influential even than their
numbers would suggest, and it had less appeal to non-
intellectual circles. The comparison of the relative
success of the two movements, the original and the
derivative, is instructive. Manichaeism was very much
more of a synthesis of the thought of the time than was
Christianity. It was very much more outspokenly an
attempt to answer the problems raised by the universe.
And yet, while it proved to have a great power of life,
it failed. One cause may be suggested, in addition to
the fact just mentioned, that it came into the field
second. Manichaeism held out a standard of perfection
which was for the few. Christianity, indeed, early
developed the idea of a special sanctity which was for
the men who could renounce the world wholly. Nevertheless, at the same time, it held to the belief that a life
which was quite adequate for full enjoyment of the
privileges of religion was at the disposal of all who
followed it while living in the world and submitting to
a tolerable measure of self-discipline. Christianity did
indeed go a long way with those in whose eyes sexual
life was unclean; it gave satisfaction to the many who
were fascinated by asceticism, but it repressed those
elements within itself which overstressed that point of

view, and it never set its face against the compatibility of normal life with the full practice of religion. It valued a hot-house atmosphere, but it did not insist on it.

This is in a measure typical of the Catholic Christianity which prevailed, as opposed to Manichaeism and to gnostic and other sects which maintained a more consistent point of view. The central body shows constantly a greater grasp on actual life, a wider vision of things and men as they are. Its teachings commended themselves as fitting the needs of the age better than did doctrines which were more deliberately assimilated to thought around, much as many old buildings constructed without any knowledge of technical principles of audibility are in fact better for hearing than their modern rivals. The Christian householder brought forth from his store things old and new: the old was not obsolete and the new was not incomprehensible.

XIV

THREE TYPES OF CONVERSION
JUSTIN, ARNOBIUS, AUGUSTINE

THE book of Acts describes various types of conversion. We start with the witnesses of the manifestations of the Spirit at Pentecost in Jerusalem, who were moved by what they saw and by Peter's argument from prophecy. We pass to those who were impressed by the miracles done by the Apostles, to the Ethiopian eunuch reading Isaiah and learning from Philip what it meant, to Cornelius the Roman whose heart was set towards Judaism and who met Peter after they had both had visions, to those who heard the preaching of the little band from Jerusalem scattered and exiled after the death of Stephen. We come to the Pauline mission, the conversion, thanks to miracle, of Sergius Paulus and the jailer at Thessalonica and some at Ephesus, the conversion of Jews and proselytes and others present as a result of sermons in synagogues in which the argument from prophecy bulked large, the conversion of a few Athenians as a result of a lecture before the Areopagus. There can be no doubt that the account as a whole gives us a faithful picture of the way in which things happened. It is clear that the two most important factors were prophecy and miracle: it also appears that the latter sometimes (as in ch. xxviii) had no such effect—partly, perhaps, because in the view of the common man there were so many miracles and wonders that no special inferences need follow from another.

We pass to three later converts, all of whom have

told us just what it was which moved them to embrace the new faith. Even here we need not take their accounts as representing the literal truth—at least not the whole truth, for a process of conversion as looked at afterwards by the man himself commonly assumes a new colour. Few of us are capable of entirely faithful autobiography. Yet the main lines are clear and significant.

Justin, writing in the middle of the second century, came from Nablus in Samaria. He calls himself a Samaritan by birth, but tells us that he was uncircumcised, and was certainly brought up in a pagan way. He says of his conversion in *Apol*. ii. 12, 'I myself used to rejoice in the teachings of Plato and to hear evil spoken of Christians. But, as I saw that they showed no fear in face of death and of all other things which inspire terror, I reflected that they could not be vicious and pleasure-loving.' Finding the common charges untrue he turned to the movement. In his *Dialogue with Trypho*, a more elaborate defence of Christianity against Jewish attacks, he tells us more of his experiences. The Jew has asked him what are his views on God and what is his philosophy. Philosophy is, he says, the most precious of possessions and most honourable in God's sight. It has split into various schools through men's enthusiastic following of particular teachers. Justin had begun by attaching himself to a Stoic. But he learned nothing about God from the Stoic, and his teacher did not regard this branch of knowledge as necessary. So Justin turned to a Peripatetic: he left him in disgust when the philosopher invited him to name a fee. This, to Justin, proved him no philosopher. The next move was to a Pythagorean.

He insisted that a mastery of music, astronomy, and geometry was an indispensable preliminary, in order that the soul might be removed from objects of sense and made suitable for objects of the intellect. Justin left him, this time in sorrow, for the Pythagorean appeared to have some understanding of the matter. In despair he decided to give Platonism a trial, for it had a considerable reputation. In this he found no small satisfaction: the contemplation of the Ideas fired his imagination and he hoped that he should see God. So he thought fit to have a long solitude and retired to a lonely spot near the sea. There he was met by an old man who engaged him in converse, proved to him that the philosophers could not have knowledge of God, and having reduced him to a condition of argumentative helplessness introduced him to the prophets and to Christ.

According to this account Justin came to Christianity at the end of a chapter of a disappointed intellectual search. The similarities between this story and others of like quality have been discussed earlier (pp. 107 ff.). There is undoubtedly a certain element of literary commonplace in the narrative, and yet it seems to correspond to the attitude of the time. Lucian has in his *Hermotimus* described an attempt on the part of a man of just such limited intelligence to master a philosophy, with the same buoyant optimism and the same helplessness in the face of destructive criticism. It was no doubt the way things happened, for philosophic ideas had become so widespread and accessible that many a man without training could be fascinated and perplexed by them. He could again be in a queer way satisfied that he was getting somewhere, that, as Hermotimus says, after about twenty years' application, he still hoped in not over twenty years more to understand the system fully; but this satisfaction would be no match for even elementary dialectical skill.

Arnobius wrote in Africa at the end of the third century. He tells us (i. 39):

'But the other day I venerated images just brought from the furnace, gods made on the anvil and with hammers, elephants' bones (i.e. images of ivory), paintings, fillets hanging on rotting trees. Whenever I saw a stone anointed and fouled with olive-oil, just as though there were in it a power ready to aid, I flattered it and spoke to it and prayed for blessings from the trunk that had no perceptions, and those very gods of whose existence I had persuaded myself I insulted grievously, believing them to be wood or stones or bones or to live in such objects. Now having been led into the ways of truth by the great teacher I know what all these things are; I hold worthy opinions apportioned to the merits of their objects; I insult no divine name and I give to each person or individuality its due without confusion of rank and authority. Are we not then to regard Christ as a god or to give to him the greatest worship paid to divinity which we can devise, when we have long received these great blessings from him and await yet fuller blessings when the day comes?'

He has been saved from error, and the acknowledgement of the deity of Jesus is natural gratitude. This is a genuine Graeco-Roman point of view: it reflects the mood which originally prompted many honours to rulers. One instance may be quoted: it is the decree passed by Mytilene about the year 27 before Christ conferring various privileges on Augustus and providing for possible future additions, 'so that he may be deified as much as possible'. It is equally pertinent to recall the way in which both Metrodorus and Lucretius used the language of worship to express their gratitude to Epicurus.

The substance of the book which Arnobius wrote shows proportions very different from those of earlier apologists. The weight is thrown on an exposure of the errors of paganism, of its unworthy views of the gods, its futile and unseemly modes of worship, its exaggerated faith in the unaided powers of the human soul, its unjustified demand for an answer to all the riddles of the universe which are of no importance for the art of right living, its illogical belief in tradition and in antiquity, its idolatry and anthropomorphism. Arnobius is not greatly concerned with the argument from prophecy: he is interested in a way of escape from mortality and fate. We should not perhaps take his autobiographical statement literally, for the reason that his account of his former attitude agrees almost verbally with the common ancient descriptions of the type of the superstitious man. But it is clear that Christianity was for him a deliverance from what had been burdensome and stupid and unworthy. The significance of his work is threefold. First, it reminds us of the very substantial hold which traditional paganism still had on men's minds, in spite of some decay in ritual observances, which was partly due to economic stringency. We have seen earlier how much space he devotes to refuting the characteristically Roman idea that man by his offerings strengthens the gods to help him. Secondly, Arnobius shows the popularity of certain interpretations of paganism by allegory and philosophy. Thirdly, he makes it clear that an interest in the hereafter was widespread.

The earlier apologists had been concerned to show that Christianity was ethically and intellectually respectable, and that it was in line with the best thought of the pagan past. Arnobius wishes rather to show its difference from the normal pagan present. He refers in passing to the earlier apologetic works (iii. 1). He can now spend his energies in making paganism intellectually disreputable. We note in the discussion, time after time, ironical concessions to the other side: 'for the sake of argument, let us suppose that there is a god Aesculapius'. Christianity is now on the offensive and, while knowing that it has a long way to go, is beginning to be quite confident of ultimate success.

Our third figure, Augustine, comes from the time when that success has been won. In his boyhood the face of society as a whole was becoming Christian, but the process was far from complete. Manichees sought converts and were not under any effective restraint by law. Before a poetic competition a soothsayer came to Augustine and asked him what fee he would pay for success, that is to say, for sacrifices which would guarantee it (iv. 2). Astrologers plied their trade busily. Further, while the Christian hierarchy on the one hand and the pagan aristocracy of Rome on the other maintained intransigent and opposing positions, there was a fairly wide no-man's land in religion. Augustine's father was a pagan who lived in harmony with a Christian wife and did not prevent his son from being marked with the sign of the Cross or veto the idea of his being baptized in a serious illness (i. 11).

In time he became a catechumen (ii. 3). The paganism
of educated men was largely philosophical and mono-
theistical in character. Pagan worship was for it a way
of approach to the central mystery of the universe, not
the only way but the time-honoured way. As Symmachus had said in his speech on behalf of retaining the
Altar of Victory in the Senate-house, 'There cannot
be only one way to so great a secret'. For many
who shrank from becoming Christians the deities of
paganism had ceased to matter as individual and
personal figures. An exchange of letters between
Augustine when bishop and one Maximus, a scholar
of Madaura, shows the weakening of the antithesis.
Maximus says, 'Which of us is so mad or mentally blind
as to deny that it is most sure that there is one supreme
God without beginning or physical offspring, a great
and magnificent Father? We invoke by many titles his
virtues, which are spread throughout the universe,
because we do not know his own name. For *God* is
a name which all religions share', much in the tone
in which a liberal theologian engaged in controversy
with a scientist might assure him that he had heard
of Darwin and of the *Origin of Species*.

To such a man monotheism was obvious. He would,
of course, feel not much need for redemption and
sacraments, certainly not for new sacraments. At the
same time he might allow that baptism was perhaps
useful as an additional safeguard after death, but at
the same time perilous: when it was past, sins could not
be washed away once and for all by a single sacramental act. We see the two sides of the matter when
we remember that Augustine's mother, the pious
Monnica, did not wish him to be baptized as a boy,

on the ground that he must needs fall into sin (i. 11), and that, on the other hand, a friend of his who had been brought up as a Christian, but led by him into Manichaeism, was baptized when unconscious in a severe illness (iv. 4): Augustine hoped to win him back on his recovery, but failed. For many baptism was invested with a character of finality, such as now goes with entry on the monastic life or with a solemn profession of faith on a death-bed. At Rome, in fact, a public declaration of faith was made by the neophyte (viii. 2).

Augustine thus grew up

> Between two worlds, one dead,
> The other powerless to be born.

He has told us his story with a wealth of introspective self-analysis. We see first the pious atmosphere of his childhood, the carelessness of adolescence, the impression made by the *Hortensius* of Cicero, which inspired him with a yearning after higher things (p. 184 above), the discouraging nature of his first reading of the Bible, the adhesion to Manichaeism. It is clear that paganism was at no time a possible alternative to Christianity for him: it was something of the past to which certain circles clung and to the claims of which he replies in formal fashion in his *City of God*, but which had for him no message or meaning. So, in his treatise *On the Catechizing of those who are Unversed*, he explains how the Christian scheme of faith should be set forth. It is all done on the values of the thing in itself. There is no emphasis on the renunciation of heathen beliefs and practices. They come in merely as dangers against which the neophyte must be warned. After the brief statement of what needs to be taught, Augustine says (ch. 7):

> 'Then indeed man's weakness needs to be equipped and encouraged to face temptations and stumbling-blocks, those within the church and those without; by those without I mean Gentiles or Jews or heretics, by those within I mean the chaff of the Lord's threshing-floor. I do not say that we should argue against each class of misguided men and discuss and refute formally their monstrous opinions, but, since we have not too much time, we should show that this was so foretold, that trials afford useful lessons for the faithful, and that there is a remedy in the example set by the patience of God, who has determined to permit these things to continue until the end.'

Thereafter he refers to wearers of charms and soothsayers and astrologers and diviners, along with the drunken and covetous and extortionate, as sinners rather than as heathen.

From early manhood Augustine sought to find an adequate theistic scheme of the universe. This quest fascinated him, and he could not escape from it. The various things which interested him—Manichaeism, Neoplatonism, Christianity—did so in so far as they contributed to this problem. Ethical considerations were secondary: the question so far as they are concerned was, Could he live in the manner rendered logically necessary by his solution of the theological problem? He judged matters of conduct as one might the baggage which can or cannot be taken over a particular frontier. Throughout, Christianity was at the back of his mind. He moved from it or towards it, with as it were a subconscious conviction that he would end in it if and when he could find it intellectually adequate.

He moved towards Manichaeism in the revulsion of feeling produced by the unfavourable impression made on him by the Christian Scriptures, which offended him, as others, by their style (iii. 5). He made the acquaintance of members of the movement and was intoxicated by their scheme of the supernatural, their doctrine of the source of evil, their criticism of what they represented as the anthropomorphism of Christianity, and their doctrine of universal and particular justice. At the same time he continued to consult astrologers, till a friend convinced him of the falsity of the theory underlying their practice (iv. 3). There was a fascination in the religion of Mani, with its bold comprehensive view of phenomena, with the picture which it claimed to give of the inner workings of the universe, and with the claim to inspiration which its teachers made. Augustine felt all this, and his account of his emotions helps us understand the long history and wide success of these ideas. At the same time he had difficulties. For nine years he waited till an opportunity came of laying them before the Manichee bishop Faustus. The meeting was a disappointment. Faustus was agreeable in himself and in his style, but he had no deep knowledge and could not answer Augustine. All the same the latter remained alienated from Christianity and attached to its rival. In an illness at Rome he did not seek baptism and he continued to be in union with the Manichees who were there. And now doubts arose in his mind. Might not an Academic attitude of suspension of judgement be the wisest course? Several positive considerations held him away from Christianity. It still seemed to him to be tainted by an anthropomorphic view of God: the doctrine of

the incarnation involved for him some defilement of
the divine essence: and he retained his belief in the
existence of positive evil.

He now moved to Milan. This meant life in an
atmosphere where paganism had not the same cultural and social pre-eminence as in Rome. At Milan
Ambrose was the strongest figure from the point of
view of intellect as well as of character. It was natural
that Augustine should fall under his influence. He
went to his sermons at first to study Ambrose's skill of
speech, which was his professional interest: Ambrose
was the greatest speaker there. The result was something unexpected, or at least not consciously expected.
Augustine found himself becoming deeply interested
in the content of what he heard. He came to the
conclusion that Christianity could be intellectually
respectable. The allegorical interpretation of the Old
Testament which Ambrose employed opened new
possibilities. It removed certain obstacles to belief;
it obviated the ascription to God of conduct inaccept-
able.to a philosopher but clearly asserted on a literal
exegesis. The set of Augustine's mind was largely
determined by this. He had difficulties, the crucial
problem at this point arising out of his inability to
conceive of a spiritual substance. As a consequence he
remained sceptical, but decided to become a catechumen 'until some sure goal to which I might direct my
steps should become clear'. His mother joined him at
Milan, and he was under the influence of her life and
faith as well as of Ambrose's sermons.

He became assured of the providence of God and of
the dignity of truth veiled in allegory (vi. 5). Then
with a group of friends he entered on a communal life

in retreat. His mind moved away from Manichaeism. He was certain of the changelessness and of the incorruptibility of God, but was not clear about the cause of evil (vii. 2 f.). Then he happened on some Platonist literature which clarified his mind. He was still uncertain as to the exact position to be taken about Christ, but he turned to Paul and other inspired writings and did not now find in them inconsistencies with the Old Testament.

At this point the influence of Simplicianus, a priest, came into his life. Augustine was fired by the story of the conversion and public profession of faith of Victorinus, one of the band of scholarly defenders of paganism in Rome, and again by hearing of the wonderful life and miracles of the hermit Antony. He reached a state of conviction in which he just could not act: he had desired continence but not yet. And then came the critical moment in the garden. As Augustine wrestled in thought he heard a child say, 'Take up and read, Take up and read'; *tolle lege, tolle lege.* He took up the volume of Paul which he was reading and found Romans xiii. 13, 'Let us walk honestly, as in the day; not in rioting and drunkenness, not in chambering and wantonness, not in strife and envying.' Such a sudden voice was to a pagan as to a Christian guidance from without. To Augustine it meant the certainty which he had almost but not quite reached: it was like a long convalescence at the end of which it is sometimes some casual circumstance which at last enables a man to realize that he is well. All was now plain and settled and he could meditate on the Psalms and go to Ambrose and at his direction read Isaiah.

This is a conversion which rests in the last resort

on the permanence of an early impression and of the religious atmosphere with which his mother had invested his childhood. Christianity had at most times his vote to be true if it could. So there was an emotional background for conversion. At the same time the Christianity which he had known as a boy was not theologically profound: this was natural for what a boy hears, but was no doubt typical of the Christianity of Africa at the time, in which the heart was stronger than the head. So his memories were not equal to the intellectual atmosphere in which he found himself as he grew up. Adolescence brought to him, as to so many, not only its welter of vague inquisitive desire which does not exactly know what it wants, but also its generous if incoherent aspirations after new truths. So his quest ran its way to an intellectual conviction, and this conviction gradually acquired an emotional strength sufficient to bring him to decisive action. The story is like the familiar type of conversion discussed in the first chapter, in that Christianity is throughout presupposed and present in the subject's subconsciousness, but it is unlike it in that it is not a conversion from indifference; it is a progress in a continuous line; it is like a chemical process in which the addition of a catalytic agent produces a reaction for which all the elements were already present.

We have now surveyed one chapter in the long history of conversion. We have seen something of the general characteristics of conversion, of the rise and spread of religious movements, of the fears and desires which arouse men's interest in these movements. We have seen something of what religious practices meant to the average citizen of the Roman Empire. We have seen how he was prepared to avail himself of new cults as additional means of ensuring protection against various dangers here and hereafter, and how this use of the novel did not, except in rare cases, mean any rejection of the familiar and any renunciation of a man's past, ethical or religious, any theology or any membership of an oecumenical organization with an oecumenical creed. We have also learned that a reorientation of life was commonly involved in adhesion to the tenets of a philosophical school, and that in this there was a definite element of repentance and of conversion. We have passed to the growth of the Christian body, and remarked on its peculiar individuality in the world of the time, on the renunciation which it required of older ways of worship. We have studied its requirements and found them not wholly strange and yet cast in a strange form which rested on strange foundations, and we have made an attempt to see how that form and those demands appeared both to the man in the street and to certain folk of more striking individuality who felt impelled to set their experiences on record.

In the light of this survey the advance of Christianity stands out as a phenomenon which does not stand alone but has parallels which make its success not wholly incomprehensible. There were other forms of belief at the time which won adherents among men who were not called to them by anything in their antecedents. And yet these very analogies enable us to see the differences the more clearly. The other Oriental religions in Roman paganism, as Cumont calls them on the title-page of his famous book, were neither

Oriental nor religious in the same degree. They had not brought a compact body of doctrine or of accessible sacred literature from the Nearer East with them: in so far as they appealed to men who did not come from the lands of their origin it was in forms which were fully hellenized, at least fully hellenized in matters of fundamental thought and above all in their expectations of the hereafter. This is true in spite of the exotic appearance which they had and sometimes artificially adopted for purposes of effect. Christianity avoided the exotic in externals and retained it in doctrine, in its doctrine of the last things and of the hereafter, in its sacred literature, available to all and sundry but not accommodated to classical style and classical thought, in its peculiar and unbending view of history. The Oriental mystery religions were not Oriental in the same sense as Christianity. Neither were they religions in the same sense. Theology might be and was applied to them: beliefs and hopes and interpretations clustered around them, but they were fluid and the interpretations came from outside, from Greek speculation and from the earlier habits of the Greek mind in religious things. And, as we have seen, there was no body of faithful throughout the world, no holy Isiac or Mithraic church—no Isiacs even, except as the members of a local association, with a devotion and belief which an Isiac from elsewhere could recognize.

Greek philosophy was applied to Christianity as to its unequal competitors. But, as applied to Christianity, it was applied to what was already much more of an entity. In Christianity it was used for the interpretation of a body of doctrine widely held by men speaking Greek and Latin. In its rivals it was used to give substance and meaning to what was essentially a cult and a mythology. This may sound a little less than just to Mithraism, which had in its origins a dualism and a cosmic expectation. Yet it must be borne in mind that Mithraism reached the Mediterranean world in a casual and sporadic way, as the worship of groups of Persians left without a country, and not starting with anything like the original urge of Zoroastrianism, which lay centuries and centuries behind. As we know it, the early theological element is very much obscured, and the core of the matter has become individual deliverance: certainly the cosmic expectation and the doctrine of the resurrection have faded. Christianity represents just such a movement as might have resulted from Zoroastrianism had it come into being at the beginning of our era and been promptly forced to leave Persian soil while still in its first vigour. So Christianity was different. And yet it was capable of being made intelligible and it was removed from Judaea early enough to become part of the larger world.

This is one chapter in the history of conversion. There are many more—the extension of Christianity to the natives of Britain and Germany and Scandinavia, the rise of Islam, the extension of sects in the Middle Ages, the choice of individuals during the Reformation and the Counter-Reformation, the phenomena of modern revivalism, and the rise and expansion of Buddhism. All these things we see as movements governed and directed by political and other considerations conditioned by the intellectual atmosphere of the times. All of them turn largely on difficult and nicely balanced decisions made by individuals on the questions of man's relations with the unseen and the unknowable.

All of them we know in part and understand in part. Which of us has any accurate idea of what is going on in the mind of the average churchgoer? How far does he himself know? And if this is so with the present, how much more so is it with the past? If we cannot estimate the exact measure of honesty in the leaders of certain movements in our own times, how can we judge precisely how far Alexander of Abonutichus was charlatan and how far by his own lights prophet? In the period in which we have, for a little, tried to live, the accidents of survival have left us bright patches of light here and there and but fitful gleams to guide us from one to another. One of the greatest of scholars has said:

> 'The tradition yields us only ruins. The more closely we test and examine them, the more clearly we see how ruinous they are; and out of ruins no whole can be built. The tradition is dead; our task is to revivify life that has passed away. We know that ghosts cannot speak until they have drunk blood; and the spirits which we evoke demand the blood of our hearts. We give it to them gladly; but if they then abide our question, something from us has entered into them.'

Any one who has tried to get at the realities of ancient thought and belief knows how true this is. Our interpretation must be in a considerable measure a personal interpretation, based on a balance of probabilities but informed by the spirit which we bring to it. Yet the facts increase, and any detached observer who compares the picture which recent study has made available with that of even twenty or thirty years ago cannot but feel confident that we have drawn nearer to the truth. So we must go on. We cannot but think that even partial truths about a central period of human thought are worth attaining; we cannot but hope that posterity will see a little more, and that the mistakes and gropings of the present will lead to a deeper understanding. We cannot but so think and so hope. And yet there will be always something lacking in our interpretation; it will always fall short of completeness, and we shall know it;

> Bold Lover, never, never, canst thou kiss,
> Though winning near the goal.

'Here we have no final revelation of truth,' said John Inglesant, and this applies to any of our attempts to follow the history of man's gropings after ultimate reality just as fully as it must needs to these gropings themselves.

NOTES

Our knowledge of ancient religion rests upon very varied material. With the exception of some (but not all) mathematical writers, there is hardly a work of Greek or Roman literature which does not in a way bear upon religious matters, just as there is hardly an important Greek public building of the fifth or fourth century B.C. which is not in some way associated with the worship of the gods. Religion in Greece and Rome was not a distinct and separate aspect of life, but something which ran through all its phases. We have therefore an abundance of literature about religion. We have, however, very little religious literature, in the sense of works written by devotees for devotees.[1] This is a natural consequence of the absence of hierarchy and theology.

Ancient literature was produced by a small class of educated persons who wrote for their like. It shows us the high points of ancient religious thinking. But it leaves us very much in the dark about the habits of mind of the ordinary man and it fails to describe many features of practice precisely because no one needed to have them described. If we had only the authors we should be in the position of one who had to know about religious things in the nineteenth century from Emerson and Arnold and Browning. They would not take the place of the Missal and the Book of Common Prayer and the hymns of Moody and Sankey.

This gap in our knowledge is to a large extent filled by inscriptions, papyri, and archaeological finds. We have the remains of the external apparatus of religion, the places of worship and images and votive offerings; we have the records of the building and rebuilding and personnel and accounts of temples, of communal and individual piety which seemed to deserve the immortality of stone or bronze, representations, often idealized, of processions and sacrifices and other holy rites; we have coins which indicate the cults which had in the cities minting them an official standing so clear that the city would allow them to appear as its divine representatives. (An alliance between two cities was often expressed by a greeting between their leading deities.)

The notes which follow seek only to indicate some of the ancient sources on which the text depends and certain modern books and articles of special importance for our present purpose. The student who wishes to follow these questions further will find full bibliographical indications in Franz Cumont, *Les Religions orientales dans le paganisme romain*, ed. 4, 1929; J. Geffcken, *Der Ausgang des griechisch-römischen Heidentums*, 1920 (with *Nachträge*, 1929); G. Wissowa, *Religion und Kultus der Römer*, ed. 2, 1912; A. von Harnack, *Die Mission und Ausbreitung des Christentums*, ed. 4, 1924 (the first edition is available in an English translation); F. Überweg–K.

[1] Cf. my remarks in *Journal of Biblical Literature*, lii (1933).

Praechter, *Die Philosophie des Altertums*, ed. 12, 1926; the encyclopaedias of Pauly-Wissowa, Roscher, and De Ruggiero mentioned below; G. Kittel, *Theologisches Wörterbuch zum Neuen Testament* (in publication 1932–). An admirable survey of recent study is afforded by Fr. Pfister, *Die Religion der Griechen und Römer* (*Bursians Jahresberichte über die Fortschritte der klassischen Altertumswissenschaft*, ccxxix (1930), issued separately as a book), one of the most useful of works on ancient religion: the literature is discussed at intervals by L. Deubner and O. Weinreich in *Archiv für Religionswissenschaft* [last in xxiii (1925)], annually by H. J. Rose in *Year's Work in Classical Studies*, and (as far as Hellenistic things are concerned) by me in *Journal of Egyptian Archaeology*.

ABBREVIATIONS

AJA American Journal of Archaeology.

Arch. Delt. Ἀρχαιολογικὸν Δελτίον.

ARW Archiv für Religionswissenschaft.

BCH Bulletin de correspondance hellénique.

BMC Catalogue of Coins in the British Museum (followed by the name of the region).

CIL Corpus Inscriptionum Latinarum, edited by the Berlin Academy (cited by volume and number).

CQ Classical Quarterly.

CR Classical Review.

C.R. Ac. Inscr. Comptes rendus de l'Académie des Inscriptions et Belles-Lettres, Paris.

Cumont, *TM* Franz Cumont, *Textes et monuments figurés relatifs aux mystères de Mithra.*

Cumont, *Rel. Or.* Franz Cumont, *Les Religions orientales dans le paganisme romain*, ed. 4.

Dess. H. Dessau, *Inscriptiones Latinae Selectae* (cited by number).

Ditt. *OGI* W. Dittenberger, *Orientis Graeci Inscriptiones Selectae* (cited by number).

Ditt. *Syll.* W. Dittenberger, *Sylloge Inscriptionum Graecarum*, ed. 3 (cited by number).

EGC A. D. Nock, 'Early Gentile Christianity and its hellenistic background', in *Essays on the Trinity and the Incarnation*, edited by A. E. J. Rawlinson (1928: about to be reissued).

ERE Encyclopedia of Religion and Ethics, edited by James Hastings.

Harnack, *Miss.* Harnack, *Die Mission und Ausbreitung des Christentums*, ed. 4.

HTR Harvard Theological Review.

IG Inscriptiones Graecae, edited by the Berlin Academy (cited by volume and number).

IGR R. Cagnat, &c., *Inscriptiones Graecae ad res Romanas pertinentes* (cited by volume and number).

JHS Journal of Hellenic Studies.

JRS Journal of Roman Studies.

JTS Journal of Theological Studies.

Manteuffel G. Manteuffel, *De opusculis graecis Aegypti e papyris ostracis lapidibusque collectis* (Travaux de la Société des Sciences et des Lettres de Varsovie, Classe I, 12; Warsaw, 1930).

ML W. H. Roscher, *Ausführliches Lexikon der griechischen und römischen Mythologie.*

Not. Notizie degli scavi.

P. Oxy. B. P. Grenfell–A. S. Hunt, *Oxyrhynchus Papyri* (cited by number of papyrus).

PW Pauly-Wissowa–Kroll, *Realencyclopädie der classischen Altertumswissenschaft.*

Reitzenstein, *HMR* R. Reitzenstein, *Die hellenistischen Mysterienreligionen*, ed. 3 (1927).

De Ruggiero, *Diz.Ep.* E. de Ruggiero, *Dizionario epigrafico di antichità romane.*

RHR Revue de l'histoire des religions.

Wissowa, *RK* G. Wissowa, *Religion und Kultus der Römer*, ed. 2.

Academies, other than that of Paris, are normally cited with *Abh.* (Abhandlungen), or *SB* (Sitzungsberichte), followed by the name of their home.

NOTES

I. THE IDEA OF CONVERSION

p. 1. For the germ of a distinction between the natural and the supernatural in the animal world, cf. E. Westermarck, *The Origin and Development of the Moral Ideas*, ii. 582 ff.; for the general psychological factors underlying rudimentary religion, cf. Br. Malinowski's essay in *Science, Religion, and Reality*, ed. J. Needham.

p. 3. The passage quoted is from *Corpus Hermeticum*, i. 26 ff. An interesting private inspiration appears in the foundation of the shrine at Philadelphia, discussed p. 216: Zeus gave to Dionysius in a dream commands for the purifications and sacrifices (Ditt. *Syll.* 985).

p. 7. On the psychological aspects of conversion, cf. W. James, *The Varieties of Religious Experience*, 189 ff.; the passage quoted p. 8 is from p. 209; J. Jastrow in Seligman-Johnson, *Encyclopaedia of the Social Sciences*, iv. 353 ff.

p. 10. On Greek words applicable to religion, cf. U. von Wilamowitz-Moellendorff, *Der Glaube der Hellenen*, i. 15 f.; on the rarity of actual atheism, A. B. Drachmann, *Atheism in Pagan Antiquity.*

p. 11. For the story of the *flamen Dialis* cf. Livy, xxvii. 8 (209 B.C.).

p. 12. The idea of purification was emphasized in the Dionysiac mysteries (Servius on *Georgic*, i. 166) and in the Thracian rites of Zeus Sabazios (Iamblichus, *De Mysteriis*, iii. 10), perhaps as a result of Orphic ideas; but it was not the final goal of initiation.

II. THE IDEA OF CONVERSION AND GREEK RELIGION BEFORE ALEXANDER THE GREAT

p. 17 f. The invitation of the Athenians to the Greeks as a whole (about 423 B.C.?) to send first-fruits to Eleusis represents an attempt to gain political prestige (Ditt. *Syll.* 83; L. R. Farnell, *Cults of the Greek States*, iii. 156 f.). For Pan, cf. Herodotus, vi. 105.

pp. 18 ff. Χρᾶσθαι θεοῖσι: Hdt. i. 172. Cf. in general I. M. Linforth, *University of California Publications in Classical Philology*, ix. 1 (1926), 1 ff. There is an instructive story in Hdt. ii. 18. The dwellers in Marea and Apis on the Libyan edge of Egypt felt that they were Libyans, not Egyptians, and found Egyptian animal-worship burdensome: they wished to eat cows and sent to consult Ammon. He ruled that they were dwellers in Egypt; *quorum regio eorum religio*.

The letter of Gadates: Ditt. *Syll.* 22. A foreigner might become more deeply interested: Hdt. iv. 76 tells of Anacharsis the Scythian, who after seeing the festival of the Mother of the gods (Cybele) at Cyzicus vowed to her that if he returned home safe and sound he would sacrifice to her as the Cyzicenes did and would establish an all-night celebration. He did so, and was put to death.

For the Brea decree, cf. Ditt. *Syll.* 67; for Naucratis, cf. D. G. Hogarth, *JHS*, xxv (1905), 115; for the story of Lindos, Chr. Blinkenberg, *Die lindische Tempelchronik*, 34 ff., and P. Roussel, *BCH*, lv (1931), 96 f. (whose comment I borrow).

p. 20 f. Decree for men of Citium: Ditt. *Syll.* 280. Cf. J. de Prott–L. Ziehen, *Leges Graecorum Sacrae*, i. 119, No. 42 (privilege granted to Thracians, clearly for worship of Bendis, 'according to the oracle from Dodona'); W. S. Ferguson, *Hellenistic Athens*, 216 ff., thereon: on Athenian religious associations, cf. Ferguson, *Classical Philology*, v (1910), 257 ff. The influence of trade is seen in the fact that early alien cults are particularly common at Corinth (Wilamowitz, *Glaube*, ii. 6). On the naturalization of Adonis, cf. W. R. Halliday, *Cambridge Ancient History*, ii. 638: he probably came from Cyprus rather than from Phoenicia.

p. 21 f. On the spread of Apollo's cult, cf. M. P. Nilsson, *History of Greek Religions*, 201 ff.; Wilamowitz, *Glaube*, ii. 26 ff.: for the creedlike oracle, Hdt. i. 47.

p. 22 f. On the hymn to Hecate, cf. Fr. Pfister, *Philologus*, lxxxiv (1928), 1 ff. For the idea that this is deliberate propaganda I am indebted to Professor Nilsson.

On the rare temples which are earlier than the seventh century, cf. D. S. Robertson, *A Handbook of Greek and Roman Architecture*, 51 ff.; on the emergence of life-sized cult-images, V. Müller, *PW*, *Supp.*, v. 490 ff.; K. Lehmann-Hartleben, *Die Antike*, vii (1931).

pp. 24 ff. On the antecedents of the Dionysiac movement, cf. M. P. Nilsson, *The Minoan-Mycenaean Religion and its Survivals in Greek Religion*, 492 ff.; on the opposition which it encountered, Nilsson, *The Mycenaean Origin of Greek Mythology*, 133, 172, and Wilamowitz, *Glaube*, ii. 66. Compare the legend

of Scyles, done to death by the Scythians for his devotion to the orgies
of Dionysus (Hdt. iv. 79 f.). For the inscription from Cumae, cf. A.
Sogliano, *Not.* 1905, 377 ff., E. Gabrici, *Monumenti Antichi*, xxii (1913),
573: οὐ θέμις ἐντοῦθα κεῖσθαι ἱ μὲ τὸν βεβαχχευμένον. The enthusiasm
excited by Dionysus in Thrace is shown by the story in Cassius Dio, liv.
34. 5; in 11/0 B.C. Vologaeses, a priest of his among the Bessi, revolted
and drove Rhoemetalces into flight, 'stripping him of his forces without
a battle by belief arising from the god'. For an illustration of the civic
status of the cult, cf. O. Kern, *Inschriften von Magnesia*, 139 f., No. 215,
on the introduction of Dionysus' worship at Magnesia on the Maeander.
The inscription records that three Maenads were summoned from Thebes
in accordance with an oracle: each founded a *thiasos*. This is a document
of historical antiquarianism: the oracle is called an 'ancient oracle'.

pp. 26 ff. On Orphism in general, cf. O. Kern, *Orphicorum Fragmenta*;
A. Boulanger, *Orphée*; Nilsson, *Minoan-Mycenaean Religion*, 509 ff.; G .W.
Dyson in *Speculum Religionis . . . presented to Claude G. Montefiore*, 19 ff. On
the origin of its literature, cf. L. Malten, *ARW*, xii (1909), 417 ff.; A. D.
Nock, in *Studies presented to F. Ll. Griffith*, 248 (on Hdt. ii. 81, τοῖσι
᾽Ορφικοῖσι καλεομένοισι καὶ Βακχικοῖσι, ἐοῦσι δὲ Αἰγυπτίοισι καὶ Πυθα-
γορείοισι; Wilamowitz, *Glaube*, ii. 189, n. 1, argues that the shorter
text, omitting καὶ . . . Αἰγ., is right; but Herodotus goes on οὐδὲ γὰρ τούτων
τῶν ὀργίων μετέχοντα, where ὀργίων cannot well refer to Πυθ., but can to
᾽Ορφ. and Βακχ., and the omission is easily explained as due to homoeo-
teleuton).

p. 26 f. For the mood of the sixth century, cf. Nilsson, *History*, 201 ff.;
for the story of Orpheus and sun-worship, cf. [Eratosthenes] *Cata-
sterismi*, 24.

Pindar fr. 137; perhaps, however, written for an Athenian initiated at
Eleusis and reflecting the Eleusinian hope (Wilamowitz, *Pindaros*, 155).

For the fragment of Alexis, cf. Athenaeus, iv. 164 c.

p. 28 f. On the passage of Theophrastus, cf. H. Bolkestein, *Religionsgeschichtliche Versuche und Vorarbeiten*, xxi. 2, 52 ff.; for the Gurob fragment, cf. Kern, 101 ff. The possibility of, so to speak, self-ordained
ministers is illustrated by Hdt. iv. 76, mentioned p. 276 above: Anacharsis
himself celebrates the festival of the Mother of the gods.

p. 30 f. On the fragment of Euripides (472 Nauck), cf. A. B. Cook,
Zeus, i. 648 ff. For the *lamellae*, cf. Kern, 104 ff.

The Ptolemaic text, dating from Philopator, in W. Schubart, *Einführung
in die Papyruskunde*, 352.

III. GREEKS IN THE EAST AFTER ALEXANDER

p. 33. On the cultural conditions of the period, cf. Ed. Meyer, *Blüte und
Niedergang des Hellenismus in Asien*; W. W. Tarn, *Hellenistic Civilization*;

Cambridge Ancient History, vii, viii; M. Rostovtzeff, in *Scientia*, February, 1933; on the religious moods of Greece proper, cf. K. Latte, *Die Antike*, i (1925), 146 ff.

p. 34. On Doura, F. Cumont, *Fouilles de Doura–Europos*: Baur–Rostovtzeff–Bellinger, *The Excavations at Doura Europos*, 1929– . On Susa, F. Cumont, *Mémoires de la Mission archéologique en Perse*, xx (1928), 77 ff. and *C. R. Ac. Inscr.* 1930 ff.

p. 35. Royal cult of Anahita: Berossus fr. 56 in P. Schnabel, *Berossos und die babylonisch-hellenistische Literatur*, 275 (fr. 16 in Müller, *Frag. hist. gr.* ii. 509); on dubious tradition ascribing such activity to Cyrus, cf. C. Clemen, *PW*, *Supp.* v. 683.

pp. 35 ff. For cults of 'all the gods' in the new cities, cf. F. Jacobi, ΠΑΝΤΕΣ ΘΕΟΙ (Diss. Halle, 1930), 114 ff.; for Selucid policy in Mesopotamia, cf. M. Rostovtzeff, *Yale Classical Studies*, iii. 6 f.; C. F. Lehmann–Haupt, *Klio*, xxii (1928), 396 f. For the adaptation of local and Greek myths, cf. Lucian, *De Dea Syria*: this happened in Egypt in the identification of Isis with Io, and in the localization of the Perseus story (Hdt. ii. 91). For Ptolemaic calendars, cf. Fr. Bilabel, *Neue Heidelberger Jahrbücher*, 1929, 1 ff. On branding at Hierapolis, cf. U. Wilcken, *Festgabe Deissmann*, 1 ff.; on Sarapis, U. Wilcken, *Urkunden der Ptolemäerzeit*, i. 7 ff. The legend of the bringing of the image from Sinope is summarized p. 50 above: M. Rostovtzeff, cited by O. Weinreich, *Neue Urkunden zur Sarapisreligion*, 7, has drawn attention to the existence at Sinope of an underworld god, Darzales. I suspect that Sinope was brought into the story in order to give to Sarapis a supposed neutral origin, neither Greek nor Egyptian, and also one at a suitable distance. For the awakening of Sarapis, cf. Porphyry, *De abstinentia*, iv. 9; for the paeans of Demetrius, Diog. Laert. v. 76; for the Menander fragment, P. Oxy. 1803 and O. Weinreich, *Aegyptus*, xi (1931), 13 ff.; for the festival of Sarapis, Mommsen, *CIL*, i (ed. 2), p. 317 (not later than Flavian period in Italy; G. Wissowa, *Apophoreton überreicht von der Graeca Halensis*, 51).—On the relation of the new mysteries to older Egyptian mysteries, cf. E. Briem, *Zur Frage nach dem Ursprung der hellenistischen Mysterien*, *Lunds Universitets Årsskrift*, N. F. Avd. i. 24, 5 (1928), 43 ff.; P. Roussel, *Rev. ét. gr.* xlii (1929), 158 ff.; R. Reitzenstein, *ARW*, vii (1904), 406 ff.; A. D. Nock, *Ricerche Religiose*, vi (1930), 394 ff.; *HTR*, xxv (1932), 341 f., and art. 'Mysteries' in *Encyclopaedia of the Social Sciences*. With the emergence of Lucius, cf. the Coptic-Ethiopic *ordo confirmationis*, in which the neophyte, clothed in white, is acclaimed by the people: O. Michels, *Jahrb. f. Liturgiewissenschaft*, viii (1928), 76 ff. It is a welcome indication of the presence and familiarity of the rite in Egypt, as is also Athanasius, *Vita Antonii* 14 (Migne xxvi, p. 864 c), προῆλθεν ὁ 'Αντώνιος ὥσπερ ἔκ τινος ἀδύτου μεμυσταγωγημένος καὶ θεοφορούμενος.

On the multiplication of mysteries in general in Graeco-Roman times, cf. Cumont, *Rel. Or.* 223, n. 17: *Greek and Latin Inscriptions of Sardis*, ed. by W. H. Buckler–D. M. Robinson (*Sardis*, vii), i. 46, No. 21, l. 4 Ἑρ[μεῖ καὶ] | ['Ηρακλεῖ τ]οῖς κατὰ παλα[ίστραν] | [θεοῖς τ]ά τε μυστή[ρια ἐπι]- | [τελέσαν]τα πολυτελῶς, where it is hard to guess what the mysteries were; Ditt. *Syll.* 985, l. 41 (text mentioned, pp. 216, 275 above) refers to 'seeing the mysteries performed'.

On the *Praises of Isis*, cf. W. Peek, *Der Isishymnos von Andros und verwandte Texte*: a transposition of its ideas into the third person is found at the end of the Hermetic treatise called *Kore Kosmou*.

On the detachment of Christianity from its old periphery, cf. Harnack, *SB Berlin*, 1913, 177, n. 2. Christianity claimed to be the rightful heir to the legacy of Israel: the cult of Isis and Sarapis in the world at large claimed the authority of Egyptian tradition, but did not unchurch its origin.

p. 41. On Cybele, cf. H. Graillot, *Le Culte de Cybèle*; on Timotheus, Th. Zielinski, *La Sibylle*, 83; on mysteries of Attis, *Sardis*, vii. i, 38, no. 17, l. 6 (μυστήριον Ἄττει, meaning a hall of initiates, probably belonging to a confraternity; about A.D. 200).

pp. 41 ff. On the development of Persian religion, cf. Cumont, *Les Mystères de Mithra* (ed. 3); Fr. Saxl., *Mithra*; A. D. Nock, *Gnomon*, vi (1930), 32 ff., and in Foakes Jackson–Lake, *Beginnings of Christianity*, v. 164 ff. The Persians in Asia Minor included not only officials but also nobles holding large estates (M. Rostovtzeff in *Anatolian Studies presented to Sir William Ramsay*, 372 ff., a reference which I owe to Mr. C. F. Edson). Such men came into close relations with Greek culture and employed Greek artists; cf. the Dascylium relief (Cumont, *Rel. Or.* 135, fig. 10), and a funerary stele in G. Mendel, *Catalogue des sculptures* (de Constantinople) iii. 275 ff. For the Cappadocian inscription about Bel, cf. M. Lidzbarski, *Ephemeris für semitische Epigraphik*, i (1900–2), 66 ff.; for the Nemrud Dagh inscription, Ditt. *OGI*, 383; for the Sagarios inscription, H. Grégoire, *C.R. Ac. Inscr.* 1908, 434 ff.; for stories of Magian asceticism, cf. Porphyry, *De abstinentia*, iv. 16; A. D. Nock, *JHS*, xlix (1929), 113. Free development on an Iranian basis is illustrated by the divine types on Indo-Scythian coins (W. W. Tarn, *JHS*, xxii (1902), 276).

It is possible that the Mithraic communion is a generalization of something originally (*a*) expected at the end of the world, (*b*) thought to belong to kings (as in the Scythian objects discussed by M. Rostovtzeff, *Iranians and Greeks in South Russia*, 104 ff.).

p. 44. The emotion excited by the repulse of the Gauls at Delphi is illustrated by representations of the event on Chiusine ash-urns and Calenian pottery (*Not.* 1931, 497; cf. ib., 1897, 302, the decoration of a temple at Sassoferrata).

pp. 45 ff. For Asoka I follow the translation of Vincent A. Smith, *Asoka* (ed. 2), 173 ff., 156 ff.; cf. E. Hultzsch, *Corpus Inscriptionum Indicarum*, i. 69 f., 28 f.; W. W. Tarn, *Antigonos Gonatas*, 336 ff., and R. Mookerji, *Asoka* (with references, p. 33, for the Yavana missionary, 104, for column in honour of Vasudeva by Heliodorus, about 140 B.C.). For a survey of Gandhara art and its analogues, cf. W. Weber, *Die Antike,* i (1925), 101 ff.; on Buddhist influence in the frontier regions, cf. W. W. Tarn, *JHS*, xxii (1902), 271 ff. The mime is P. Oxy. 413. Bardaisan may have known something of Buddhism; cf. E. Bickel, *Diatribe in Senecae Fragmenta*, i. 146 ff. Plotinus joined the Eastern expedition of Gordian in a desire to acquire first-hand knowledge of Persian and Indian philosophy (Porphyry, *Vita Plotini*, 3).

IV. THE OPPOSITE CURRENT

pp. 48 ff. On the nature of foreign groups and on the religious consequences of their mode of life, cf. G. La Piana, *HTR*, xx (1927), 249 ff. They did not altogether hold aloof from the worship of the communities in which they settled; thus a Syrian woman at Vesontio restored a temple *Deo Mercurio Cissonio*, that is, to a local god identified with Mercury (*CIL*, xiii. 5373). We are here concerned with the incoming cults which attracted attention and not with individual devotion which made no impress on others, e.g. the invocation by a Dalmatian of his native deity Medaurus at Lambaesis in Africa; *Sancte Medaure domi et sancte hic* (Buecheler, *Carmina Latina epigraphica*, 1527. 3). It is important that, as Cumont emphasizes (*Rel. Or.* 21), Epona is the only deity originating in the Western provinces whose cult had any substantial success in the world at large. She was, for instance, worshipped in Moesia (Y. Todoroff, *The Pagan Cults in Moesia Inferior* (Sofia, 1928), 184 f.). But she filled the need for a special deity guarding horses and mules.

For the Eretrian evidence on Isis worship, cf. N. Papadakis, *Arch. Delt.* i (1915), 115 ff. (p. 186, the inscription quoted in the text); for the importance of Greeks coming from Egypt, cf. P. Perdrizet, *BCH*, xviii (1894), 418, and P. Roussel, *Les Cultes égyptiens à Délos*, 280; for Achaeus, W. S. Ferguson, *Hellenistic Athens*, 386; for Syrians at Rome, La Piana, 314ff.

For the Zoilus letter, cf. C. C. Edgar, *Zenon Papyri*, i. 55 ff., No. 59034; A. Deissmann, *Licht vom Osten* (ed. 4), 121 ff.; E. R. Bevan, *Later Greek Religion*, 69 f. Cnidus was at this time very probably in Ptolemaic hands. For the Sarapis story, cf. Tacitus, *Hist.* iv. 83 (noting *Aegyptiorum antistites sic memorant*); E. Schmidt, *Religionsgeschichtliche Versuche und Vorarbeiten*, VIII. ii. 49 ff. For the vision of Naulochus, cf. Hiller von Gärtringen, *Inschriften von Priene*, 139, No. 196; for punishment for delay, Livy, ii. 36. The anger of the Egyptian gods became proverbial.

If we should take the piety of Zoilus seriously, we should say that his experience was suggested by the tradition.

pp. 50 ff. For the Delian inscription, cf. *IG*, xi. 4, 1299: P. Roussel, *Les*

Cultes égyptiens à Délos, 71 ff.; O. Weinreich, *Neue Urkunden*, 31 ff. For the *therapeutae*, Roussel, 84 ff. For the authorization needed to buy the site, cf. p. 20 above; Ditt. *Syll.* (ed. 2), 666, records a Samian decree of the second century B.C., permitting the priest of Isis to beg for the goddess. For the claim to immemorial antiquity, cf. Apul. *Met.* xi. 5 of the Ploi-aphesia, 'diem qui dies ex ista nocte nascetur aeterna mihi nuncupavit religio', and Euripides, *Bacchae*, 201 ff., where Tiresias, defending the then new cult of Dionysus, says: 'The traditions of our fathers, which we have as coeval with time, will not be overthrown by any argument, even if it has been the invention of the keenest wit.' For the later history of Sarapis on Delos, cf. Roussel, 253 ff.; W. S. Ferguson, *Athenian Tribal Cycles in the Hellenistic Age* (*Harvard Historical Monographs*, i), 155 ff.

pp. 54 ff. For the dream interpreter of Memphis, cf. O. Rubensohn, *Festschrift Vahlen*, 1 ff. For cult society and public worship at Athens and Rhodes, cf. Roussel, 258. The view here adopted of the place of political considerations in the spread of the cult is taken from T. A. Brady's forth-coming work, *The Reception of Egyptian Cults by Greeks during the last three centuries before Christ.*

For Magnesia, cf. O. Kern, *Inschriften von Magnesia*, 84 f., No. 99; for Priene, Hiller von Gärtringen, *Inschriften von Priene*, 138, No. 195; for Magnesia in Thessaly, *IG*, ix. ii. 1107 (there is here an association of *hypostoloi*); for Eretria, *Arch. Delt.* i (1915), 148; for Athens, W. S. Ferguson, *The Athenian Secretaries*, 46. We find what was probably an annual priesthood at Philippi under the Empire (P. Collart, *BCH*, liii (1929), 80, No. 4 Κάστωρ Ἀρτεμιδώρου ἱερητεύσας θεοῖς).

On the introduction of the Osiris drama at Athens, cf. A. Rusch, *De Serapide et Iside in Graecia cultis* (Diss. Berlin, 1906), 10 f.; at Rome, Mommsen, *CIL*, i (ed. 2), p. 333 f. An association of initiates at Prusa made a thank-offering to Sarapis and Isis, probably in the second century A.D. (G. Mendel, *BCH*, xxiv (1900), 366 ff.).

For the sense of *soter, soteira*, cf. Roussel, 289 ff.; *EGC*, 87 ff.; P. Oxy. 1380, 235 ('Thou (Isis) didst make the Dioscuri *soteres*'); Apion in his letter to his father speaks of Sarapis as having saved him in peril at sea (Wilcken–Mitteis, *Grundzüge und Chrestomathie der Papyruskunde*, 1. ii. 565 f., No. 480). The description of initiates is quoted from Apul. *Met.* xi. 9. Payment for initiation is mentioned by Philo, *De specialibus legibus*, i. 323 (ii, p. 261 Mangey). Some charge was made for admission to the dramatic festival of Adonis, if with Glotz we so interpret the *deikterion* of two obols mentioned in a papyrus referring to this celebration (*Revue des études grecques*, xxxiii (1920), p. 208).

p. 57 f. For an instance of the liquidation of a guild, cf. Dess. 7215*a* (funerary college of freedmen and slaves working in the gold-mines in Dacia; extinguished in A.D. 167). G. La Piana, *Harv. Theol. Rev.* xviii

(1925), 268 ff., has remarked on the importance to Pope Victor of his possession of the catacomb: only those in communion with him were sure of burial. For Isis saving the universe, cf. Kaibel, *Epigrammata graeca*, 985, 4 (Philae); for the Delian references, cf. Roussel, 197 f., 173; for Boeotia, Thalheim, *PW*, vii. 98; for Tithorea, Nilsson, *Griechische Feste*, 154 f. p. 59 f. For names derived from Men, cf. N. Papadakis, *Arch. Delt.* i (1915), 156. For the Beroean inscriptions, cf. A. K. Orlandos, *Arch. Delt.* ii (1916), 144 ff.

Mr. C. F. Edson has kindly contributed the following remarks: 'Dexilaos, the father of Apollonides, bears a pure and characteristic old Macedonian name of a distinctly aristocratic flavour. Proper names compounded of *-laos* are quite common in early Macedonia (O. Hoffmann, *Die Makedonen*) and occur in the royal family itself, e.g. Menelaos, son of Alexander I, Archelaos, son of Perdiccas II, and Agelaos (this last among the names of the royal family in the treaty between Athens and Perdiccas in 422 B.C., P. Davis, *AJA*, second series, xxx (1926), 181, fragment *c*, line 52). Menelaos also appears in the dynasty of Lyncestis (Hoffmann, op. cit., 165 f.). Apollonides is therefore to be considered of true Macedonian stock. In the list of *hieromnemonoi* to Delphi in 178 B.C. (Ditt. *Syll.* 636) there appears as one of Perseus' two representatives a Σιμωνίδης 'Απολλωνίδου Βεροιαῖος. 178 is almost a generation after the date given to Apollonides' dedication by Orlandos, and it is therefore very possible that Simonides is the son of Apollonides the priest of Atargatis. If such be the case, the family of Apollonides and Simonides was of some prominence. It is in any case significant that at the end of the third century the priest of Atargatis in Beroea was a native Macedonian.'

For Aphrodite Syria Phistyis, cf. *IG*, ix. 417, and the new *ed. min.* pt. i, fasc. 1, No. 95, with Klaffenbach's analysis of the material; W. J. Woodhouse, *Aetolia*, 201. This Aphrodite was worshipped in a temple which she appears to have shared with Ματὴρ τῶν θεῶν καὶ Παρθένος, the latter perhaps a younger consort given to Cybele on the analogy of Persephone's relation to Demeter (Klaffenbach, p. 52; but cf. K. Latte, *Gnomon*, ix (1933), 409).

For Thuria, cf. N. S. Valmin, *Inscriptions de la Messénie*, Nos. 1 and 2 (*Kungl. humanistiska Vetenskapssamfundet i Lund, Årsberättelse*, 1928–9), 108 ff. On the ritual theatres, cf. Valmin, 133; Cumont, *Fouilles de Doura-Europos*, 185, 188, 202 f., and *Syria*, v (1924), 354 ff.

U. Wilcken, *Festgabe Deissmann*, 3, has remarked that the Macedonian soldier, Machatas, whom we find erecting in 222 B.C. a shrine at Pelusium in the Fayoum to the Syrian goddess and Aphrodite Berenice had a wife Asia, probably of Oriental origin. (But the parallel figure Astarte had been worshipped in Egypt from the time of Amenophis IV; cf. H. Ranke, *Studies Griffith*, 412 ff.)

p. 61. For the Jewish attitude towards Gentiles, cf. G. F. Moore, *Judaism*, i. 22; for the date of Job, Kautzsch–Bertholet, *Die heilige Schriften des alten Testaments* (ed. 4), ii. 50.

pp. 61 ff. For the language of the Jews in Rome, cf. I. Zoller, *Ricerche Religiose*, viii (1932), 461 ff.; for a list of known synagogues, Krauss, *PW*, iv A. 1293 ff. (to which Doura-Europos is now to be added); for the impression which a synagogue would make on an outsider, G. F. Moore, i. 284. Josephus in passages (*BJ*, ii. 119 ff.; *AJ*, xviii. 11 ff.) very likely based on Nicolaus of Damascus treats the Pharisees, Sadducees, and Essenes as philosophical schools, differentiated by their attitude on fate (G. F. Moore, *HTR*, xxii (1929), 371 ff.); Augustine, *Ciu. Dei*, vi. 11, quotes from Seneca, 'illi tamen causas ritus sui nouerunt: maior pars populi facit quod cur faciat ignorat'.

For proselytes in Antioch, cf. Josephus, *BJ*, vii. 45. For grave inscriptions of Jewish proselytes, cf. N. Müller, *Inschr. d. jüdischen Katakomben am Monteverde*, 74, No. 77. Epigraphy warns us against exaggeration of the success of this movement (G. La Piana, *HTR*, xx (1927), 390).

For 'fearers of God', cf. E. Schürer, *SB Berlin*, 1897, 200 ff.; Moore, i. 325 ff. Apul. *Met.* ix. 14 seems to refer to a woman belonging either to this type of religion or to Christianity; 'tunc spretis atque calcatis diuinis numinibus in uicem certae religionis mentita sacrilega praesumptione dei, quem praedicaret unicum, confictis obseruationibus uacuis fallens omnis homines'; Epictetus (ii. 9. 19 ff.) mocks at half-hearted proselytes. For anti-Semitism, cf. I. Heinemann, *PW, Supp.* v. 3 ff., and the questions addressed to would-be proselytes in Palestine in the second century of our era (Moore, i. 333 f.); for Jewish quietism, Michel, *Theol. Stud. u. Krit.* cii (1930), 302 ff. (apropos of *Letter to Aristeas* and its approximation to Stoicism).

p. 63 f. For pagan following of Jewish religious customs, cf. Josephus, *Contra Apionem*, ii. 282; Philo, *De uita Moysis*, ii. 20 ff. (ii. p. 137 M, mentioning also the Day of Atonement).

For the proseucha, cf. Ditt. *OGI*, 742. For worshippers of Hypsistos, cf. Schürer, l.c.; E. H. Minns, *Scythians and Greeks*, 620 ff.; Cumont, *Hypsistos* (1897), and article in *PW*, ix. 444 ff. For Sabazios–Sabaoth, cf. Cumont, *C.R. Ac. Inscr.*, 1906, 63 ff., *Musée Belge*, xiv (1910), 55 ff., *Rel. Or.* 60 ff., 228.

V. THE PATH TO ROME

p. 66 f. For the Puteoli text, cf. *IGR*, i. 420; K. Latte, *Die Religion der Römer* (A. Bertholet, *Religionsgeschichtliche Lesebuch*, ed. 2, fasc. 5), 37, n. 82. For the Tyrian letter, cf. G. La Piana, *HTR*, xx (1927), 257 ff. Wissowa, *RK*, 86, draws attention to the marble basis in the Forum, inscribed *Numini deae Viennae*, and obviously set there by a group of men

from Vienne. So later the cult of St. Menas was established on the road
to Ostia in A.D. 589 by an Alexandrian corporation (L. Duchesne, *Bull.
soc. arch. d'Alexandrie*, xii (1910), 5).

For the Syrian colony on the Janiculum, cf. La Piana, 314. For
Eunus, cf. F. Jacoby, *Die Fragmente der griechischen Historiker*, ii A, 288
(No. 87, F. 108; probably Posidonius). For Sulla's vision, Plut. *Sulla*, 9.
A. von Domaszewski, *Westdeutsche Zeitschrift*, xiv (1895), 58, has stressed
the importance of the movement of centurions from unit to unit. Cen-
turions could afford to make dedications. For Maioumas, cf. Joannes
Lydus, *De Mensibus*, iv. 80, p. 133, Wünsch; for Sarapis at Puteoli, *CIL*,
x. 1781, i. 6. For Delos, cf. M. Bulard, *La Religion domestique dans la
colonie italienne de Délos*; for Italian interest in exotic cults, cf. J. Hatzfeld,
Les Trafiquants italiens dans l'Orient hellénique, 357 ff.

p. 68 f. For the Romanization of Cybele, cf. J. Carcopino, *Mél. d'archéol.
et d'hist.* xl (1923), 135 ff., 237 ff.; La Piana, *HTR*, xx (1927), 289 f.
Carcopino makes a strong case for the view that the cult at Pessinus itself
was given a more worldly character. On the banishment of the slave, cf.
Julius Obsequens, 44 (104); on the festal cycle, cf. Wissowa, *RK*, 322;
on the *Initium*, Mommsen, *CIL*, i (ed. 2), p. 314; H. Graillot, *Le Culte de
Cybele*, 174, 337 f.; for initiations, cf. also a text from Cyme, of the first
century of our era, mentioning initiates and the purchase of an underground room for worship, published by J. Keil, *Jahreshefte*, xiv (1911),
Beibl. 133 ff.

p. 69 f. On the *taurobolium*, cf. Wissowa, *RK*, 322 ff.; *EGC*, 118 f. The
rebirth is physical; at the end of paganism it may have acquired moral
connotation, cf. *Carmen contra paganos*, 62 (A. Riese, *Anthologia latina*, ed. 2,
i. 22), 'uiuere cum speras uiginti mundus in annos'. *Criobolium* was
perhaps introduced from some other Thracian cult, e.g. that of Sabazios;
perhaps it was a cheaper substitute.

For the Julianic text, cf. H. J. Rose, *JHS*, xliii (1923), 194 ff.; xlvi
(1926), 180 ff.

For belief in the efficacy of blood, cf. F. J. Dölger, *Vorträge der Bibliothek
Warburg*, 1923/4 (published 1926), 196 ff. For the earliest *taurobolium*, cf.
Dess. 4271; R. M. Peterson, *Cults of Campania*, 156 f.; for its time of year,
J. Toutain, *Cultes païens dans l'Empire romain*, ii. 84 f.

In the Baths of Caracalla there is a Mithraeum, outside which is a pit
probably dug for the purpose; so at Trier (S. Loeschke, *Die Erforschung
des Tempelbezirkes im Altbachtale zu Trier*, 35, Abb. 9). If this attachment
of cult was made, it may be suggested that it was due to the fact that
Mithraism alone among the mystery-religions did not possess a cult-
drama symbolizing a cosmic process, and to the possibility of a connexion
being made between the rite and the cosmogonic role of the bull, from
which life came.

For the authority of the *quindecimuiri*, cf. Dess. 4131 (Lyons); in *CIL*, x. 3698, they confirm the right to insignia of *sacerdos Matris deum Baianae* at Cumae (17 August 289); ib. 3699, they have some authority over the guild of *dendrophori* at Cumae (A.D. 251); R. Paribent, *Not.*, 1916, 324, has found a probable indication of their control over Cybele's priesthood at Ostia.

For State interference in religious matters, cf. Mommsen, *Gesammelte Schriften*, iii. 389 ff.

The origin of the Bacchanalian movement is perhaps to be sought in the presence in Rome of many slaves from Tarentum, captured in 208 B.C. (T. Frank, *CQ*, xxi (1927), 128 ff.). It may again be due to contacts with Sicily, where the strength of the cult is shown by the vases from Centuripe discussed by G. M. A. Richter, *Metropolitan Museum Studies*, ii (1930), 187 ff. (second and first centuries B.C.). For the Senate's decree, cf. Dess. 18, and Ed. Fraenkel, *Hermes*, lxvii (1932), 369 ff.

p. 71 f. When Livy says (xxxix. 13. 11) of sexual and homo-sexual intercourse among these devotees *hanc summam inter eos religionem esse*, he may well be quoting mere scandal, but it is possible (*a*) that there was some queer sacramental valuation set on such acts, as in [Apuleius] *Asclepius*, 21, and in some gnostic sects, or (*b*) that there is a misunderstanding of some idea of intercourse with the god in initiation, for which material is to be found in A. Dieterich, *Mithrasliturgie*, 121 ff., with O. Weinreich's *addenda* in the third edition, 244 ff.; so a misunderstanding of Eucharistic language caused the Christians to be accused of cannibalism and a misunderstanding of their eschatological views caused them to be regarded as revolutionaries.

For the Tusculum inscription, cf. Cumont–Vogliano, *AJA*, 1933. On Dionysiac mysteries in general, cf. Cumont, *Rel. Or.* 195 ff.

For new temple foundations at Rome, cf. Wissowa, *RK*, 354 ff., 596 ff.

p. 74 f. For a Mithraic portico, cf. Cumont, *TM*, i. 58. We have, ib. ii. 100, *inscr.* 35, the epitaph of a freedman of Severus, Caracalla, and Geta, described as *sacerdos inuicti Mithrae domus Augustanae*; that means of the Emperor's household, who presumably formed a sodality. The Mithraeum at Trier is in the sacral area, but two altars erected in it by Martius Martialis pater have the phrase, *in suo posuit* (G. Loeschke, *Tempelbezirk*, 36).

For *Capitolia*, cf. Wissowa, *PW*, iii. 1539; for that at Oxyrhynchus and for the cult of Juppiter Capitolinus at Arsinoe, Wilcken, *Grundzüge*, I. i. 116.

VI. HOW EASTERN CULTS TRAVELLED

p. 77. For Mithraists refusing wreaths, cf. Tertullian, *De corona militis*, 15.

p. 78. The absence of theological explanations from mysteries is attested by Macrobius, *Saturnalia*, i. 7. 18, 'nam occultas et manantes ex meri ueri fonte rationes ne in ipsis quidem sacris enarrari permittitur, sed si quis illas adsequitur continere intra conscientiam tectas iubetur'.

p. 79 f. Heliodorus, ix. 9, echoes Philo, *De uita Moysis*, ii. 195 (ii, p. 164 м), as Geffcken remarks (*Ausgang*, 277); there may have been some common source. On the Genesis quotation, cf. Heinemann, *PW*, *Supp.* v. 23 ff.; on Jewish Orphica, cf. O. Kern, *Orphicorum Fragmenta*, 260 ff.; on Gog and Magog, Fr. Pfister, in E. Hoffmann–Krayer and H. Bächtold–Stäubli, *Handwörterbuch des deutschen Aberglaubens*, iii. 910 ff.; for the supra-Hebraized form in *Corp. Herm.* i, there are analogies in the Septuagint (H. J. Cadbury in Jackson–Lake, *Beginnings of Christianity*, v, p. 422, n. 3).

p. 80 f. For the Ploiaphesia, cf. L. Deubner, *Athenische Mitteilungen*, xxxvii (1912), 180 ff.; for an Isiac procession, Cumont, *Rel. Or.*, pl. viii, 1; for a sacred dance, ib. viii. 2; for the adoration of sacred water, ib. vii. 2; for the Katochoi, U. Wilcken, *Urkunden der Ptolemäerzeit*, i. 52 ff.; for penitents, Ovid, *Ex Ponto*, i. 1. 51 ff.; for the hymns, Martial, ix. 29. 6, x. 48. 1.

For the portent of Cybele's anger, cf. Cassius Dio, xlviii. 43. 4; for the impression made by her processions, cf. the Metropolitan Museum bronze with an imaginative picture of Cybele in a car drawn by lions (G. M. A. Richter, *Bronzes of the Metropolitan Museum*, 128) and the representation of a procession on an altar, Cumont, *Rel. Or.*, fig. 3 (facing p. 52), and ib. 224, n. 28, on the confraternity of *hastiferi*; for priestly insignia, cf. G. Calza, *Not.*, 1931, 514 f. (*occabus* or armlet, and mitre). For priestly diadems, cf. G. A. S. Snijder, *Oudheidkundige Mededeelingen uit's Rijksmuseum van Oudheden te Leiden*, Nieuwe Reeks, xiii. i (1932), 8 ff. The sanctity of priestly dress is seen in the way in which it facilitated Domitian's escape in A.D. 69 and that of Volusius in 43 B.C.: the latter dressed as the wearer of the Anubis attire (Appian, *Civil War*, iv. 47, § 200). Priestly devotion is shown by an epitaph at Ostia (*Not.*, 1913, 134, No. 14), *qui induxit arbores XVIIII.*

p. 82. For prophesying by priests of Cybele, cf. Polybius, xxi. 37. 5; J. Carcopino, *Mélanges d'archéologie et d'histoire*, xl (1923), 261 ff.; for the man who filled forty sacks, Ch. Fossey, *BCH*, xxi (1897), 60 (epitaph at Kefr-Haouar in Syria); for religious *agyrtai* in general, Pollux, vii. 188 and p. 281 above. For threats by such priests, cf. Persius, v. 186 f.; for the fear of the curse, Pliny, *Natural History*, xxviii. 19, 'defigi quidem diris precationibus nemo non metuit'.

p. 83. Celsus in Origen, *Contra Celsum*, vii. 9 (p. 55 of O. Glöckner's separate edition).

p. 84. Aristides, *Oratio viii* (vol. i, pp. 88, 95, Dindorf = xlv. 15, 29, vol. ii, pp. 356, 360, Keil). Cf. O. Weinreich, *Neue Urkunden zur Sarapisreligion*, 3 ff.; A. Boulanger, *Aelius Aristide*; Wilamowitz, *SB Berlin*, 1925, 339.

p. 84. P. Oxy. 1382, re-edited by Manteuffel, 92. For miraculous gifts of drinking water, cf. Plutarch, *Quaest. graec.* 54 with W. R. Halliday's note, p. 205 (Aphrodite on Samos); the Lindian story, p. 20 above; and a miracle of S. Frances Xavier in the Roman Breviary for December 3 (Lectio vi) 'tantum marinae aquae signo crucis conuertit in dulcem, quantum quingentis uectoribus, qui siti adigebantur ad mortem, diu suffecit: qua in uarias quoque regiones asportata, aegri plurimi subinde curati sunt'.

p. 85 f. For the Wâdi Fatîre incident, cf. J. Vogt, *Die alexandrinischen Münzen*, i. 85 ff.

For Vespasian, cf. Suetonius, *Vesp.* 7; Tacitus, *Hist.* iv. 81.

For the Ekdysia, cf. Antoninus Liberalis, 17.

For Artemon, cf. Artemidorus, *Onirocritica*, ii. 45, p. 148. 25 Hercher.

p. 86. P. Oxy. 1381, re-edited by Manteuffel, 86 ff. Ll. 135, 158, are difficult; in 161 I read ἐπεγνώκει[ν], as Reitzenstein, in 178 μακρολογού-μ[ε]νο[ν], as K. Fr. W. Schmidt; in 172 φυσικῶ . . . λόγῳ refers to the common ancient allegorization of myth as describing natural phenomena (K. Latte, *Die Religion der Römer*, 38).

p. 89. On acclamations, cf. E. Peterson, ΕΙΣ ΘΕΟΣ; for the story of Cyprian, *Acta Sanctorum*, Sept. vii, p. 244 A. In Epictetus, i. 16. 16 f. we have μέγας ὁ θεὸς ὅτι . . . with repetition. For the *libelli*, cf. Augustine, *Ciu. Dei*, xxii. 8. He says that there were seventy in less than two years at Hippo Regius.—For Isis at Menouthi, cf. Zacharias Scholasticus, *Life of Severus* (ed. M.–A. Kugener in *Patrologia Orientalis*, ii. 18 ff.). We may note the promise made by Propertius to Bacchus of what he will do if by the god's bounty he is vouchsafed sleep (iii. 17. 19 f.); 'quod superest uitae, per te et tua cornua uiuam, uirtutisque tuae, Bacche, poeta ferar'.

pp. 90 ff. For the recording of miracles and for literary works about them, cf. Pfister, *PW, Supp.* iv. 298 ff.; P. Roussel, *BCH*, lv (1931), 73, No. 2, l. 1 and his discussion; A. Wilhelm, Πρακτικὰ τῆς ᾿Ακαδημίας ἐν ᾿Αθήναις, vi (1931), 319 (sanctuary at Themisonium saved from the Gauls). For the people sharing in the joy, cf. Ditt. *Syll.* 1173. 5, 10 (wonders of Asclepius at Rome). For the fragments of Aelian, cf. Hercher's edition, ii. 195 ff.; for the dialogue about Delphi, Manteuffel, 95, No. 6; for the *Heroicus*, S. Eitrem, *Symbolae Osloenses*, viii. Ditt. *Syll.* 867 (about A.D. 160), a decree of the people of Ephesus, records that temples and altars have been erected to their own Artemis in many places because of her manifest epiphanies.

For confession inscriptions, cf. F. Steinleitner, *Die Beichte im Zusammenhang mit der sakralen Rechtspflege in der Antike*; *EGC*, 73 f.; W. H. Buckler–D. M. Robinson, 'Greek and Latin Inscriptions of Sardis' (*Sardis* VII. i), 97 f. Nos. 95 f.; W. H. Buckler, *CR*, 1933, 7 f.

That a miracle did not always produce adhesions we have seen at

Delos (p. 53). In the same way Mohammedans made pilgrimage to Christian monasteries famous for miracles (A. Fischer, *Berichte d. sächischen Gesellschaft d. Wissenschaften*, lxxxi (1929), iii. 2). The supernatural aid to be gained was valued, without men concluding that any reorientation was necessary.

For the papyrus catechism (second century A.D.), cf. Fr. Bilabel, *Philologus*, lxxx (1925), 339.

For the hymn of Artemidorus, cf. H. Herter, *De Priapo* (*Religions-geschichtliche Versuche und Vorarbeiten*, xxiii), 233 ff. Cf. the inscription of Caecilius Donatianus, p. 136. For Manichee hymns, cf. C. Schmidt, *Ein Mani-Fund in Ägypten*, 30 (*SB Berlin*, 1933, 31); for Augustine's psalm, H. J. Rose, *JTS*, xxviii (1927), 383 ff.

p. 92 f. Among works of art particular importance attaches to a group discussed by Fr. Saxl, *Mithra* (pt. i, chs. 2–3), and B. Schweitzer, *Archäeo-logisches Jahrbuch*, 1931, in which a deity is represented frontally, and this representation is set in a framework of small scenes showing divine actions or attributes.—The earlier cult of Asclepius at Abonutichus is shown by coins; Waddington–Babelon–Reinach, *Recueil général des mon-naies grecques d'Asie mineure* (ed. 2), i. 167*, Nos. 4, 4a.

p. 97. Horace, *Satires*, i. 5, 97; Campbell Bonner, *Trans. Am. Phil. Ass.* xli (1911), 82; *AJA*, 2nd series, xxxiii (1929), 368 ff.; Heron, *Pneumatica*, i. 38, p. 175, Schmidt, 17, p. 99 (cf. M. Bertholet, *Journal des savants*, 1899, 271 ff.; A. Delatte, *La catoptromancie grecque et ses dérivés*, 201). On a sup-posed wonder in the Sarapeum at Alexandria, cf. W. Weber, *Drei Unter-suchungen zur ägyptisch-griechischer Religion*, 9 ff.

VII. THE APPEAL OF THESE CULTS

p. 100. For ancient criticism of astrological ideas, cf. Cicero, *De divina-tione*, ii. 87, with A. S. Pease's note; A. D. Nock, *Sallustius*, lxx ff. For astrology and the spread of the idea of causality, cf. M. P. Nilsson, *History of Greek Religion*, 282. For the desire to escape from fate, cf. P. Wendland, *American Journal of Theology*, xvii (1913), 345 ff.

p. 101. For the view that worship is useless, cf. Maximus of Turin, *Oratio contra paganos* (edited by A. Spagnolo–C. H. Turner, *JTS*, xvii (1916), 321), 'aiunt pagani fato omnia fieri et nihil preces, nihil orationes ualere'. For Attis, cf. A. D. Nock, *Sallustius*, li; Hippolytus, *Refutatio*, v. 9. 9.

p. 101 f. Belus as *fortunae rector*; Dess. 4333. For Sarapis and Moira, cf. Manteuffel, 93 ff. (cf. 23 ff.); for the Praises of Isis, W. Peek, *Isishymnos von Andros*, 22, ll. 171 f.; 74 f. The Hermetic fragment is in Lactantius, *Institutiones diuinae*, ii. 15; the note of Servius is on *Aen.* iv. 694. Iamblichus, *De mysteriis*, viii. 7, says that we worship the gods as deliverers from fate. Libanius, *Oratio i*, 43, says that an adversary accused him of having dealings with a man who had authority over the stars (ἀνδρὶ τυραννοῦντι τῶν ἄστρων), by which he did good to this man and evil to that, as rulers do by means of their guards. Philostratus, *Ap. Ty.* v. 12, also refers to charlatans who claimed by their craft to alter or undo what is fated, contrasting their conduct with that of his hero, who foretold the future by direct revelation. According to Firmicus, *Math.* ii. 30. 5, the Emperor alone is above fate: this could be deduced from high doctrines about his position, but looks like an attempt to avoid the common association of the art with treasonable attempts.

p. 102 f. For religious promises in regard to the after life, cf. A. D. Nock, *HTR*, xxv (1932), 344 ff.; for the wife of Praetextatus, Buecheler, *Carmina latina epigraphica*, 111, 23; for Pliny's views on survival, *Natural History*, vii. 188 ff.

p. 103 f. For the attainment of a nature like god, cf. K. Preisendanz, *Papyri graecae magicae*, iv. 220 (i, p. 78).

Philo, *Quaestiones in Exodum*, ii. 29; R. Reitzenstein, *Die Vorgeschichte der christlichen Taufe*, 113. For the prayer for defence, *P. gr. mag.* i. 215 (i, p. 12); cf. xiii. 613, 635, 712 (ii, pp. 116 ff.).

p. 104 f. For ancient ideas of possession, cf. J. Tambornino, *De antiquorum daemonismo* (*Religionsgeschichtliche Versuche und Vorarbeiten*, vii. 3), and Menander's *Hiereia*, of which P. Oxy. 1235 gives the plot (it is pretended that a servant is possessed, and he is brought to a priest for treatment).

For the fear of bewitchment, cf. Buecheler, *Carmina latina epigraphica*, 1604 (a woman, long sick, died *carminibus defixa*). On daimones, cf. p. 222 ff.

p. 106. On rings with Harpocrates, cf. Pliny, *Natural History*, xxxiii. 41 (the phrase is significant; *uiri quoque portare incipiunt*). If Sergius Paulus sent for Paul and Barnabas his motive was no doubt in part curiosity: so also with Paul's being brought before the Areopagus (as F. C. Burkitt, *JTS*, xv (1914), 462).

For this interest in Egypt, cf. Hist. Aug., *uita Seueri*, 17. 4.

pp. 108 ff. For the letter of Thessalus, cf. P. Boudreaux, *Catalogus codicum astrologorum graecorum*, VIII. iii. 132 ff.; Cumont, ib. VIII. iv. 253 ff.; F. Boll, *Zeitschrift für die neutestamentliche Wissenschaft*, xvii (1916), 139 ff.; Cumont, *Revue de philologie*, xlii (1918), 85 ff., and *Monuments Piot*, xxv (1921/2), 77 ff.

The motive of the smuggling in of paper is perhaps parodied by Apul. *Met.* vi. 25 ff. (Lucius, when in the shape of an ass, regrets that he had not a stilus and tablets to take down the story of Cupid and Psyche). For parallels, cf. R. Reitzenstein, *HMR*, 127 ff.

For the Rabbinic parallel, cf. A. H. Goldfahn, *Monatschrift f. Gesch. u. Wiss. d. Judentums*, xxii (1873), 52.

For the Mandulis text, cf. Preisigke, *Sammelbuch griech. Urk. aus Ägypten*, 4127. I am about to print a discussion in *HTR*, and append for convenience a restoration:

ἀκτινοβόλε Δεσπότα, Μανδοῦλι, Τιτάν, Μακαρεῦ, σημῖα σοῦ τινα λαμπρὰ

θεάμενος, ἐπενόησα καὶ ἐπολυπράγμοσα ἀσφαλῶς ἰδέναι θέλων, εἰ σὺ ἲ(= εἶ) ὁ
ἥλιος. ἀλότριον ἐμαυτὸν ἐποιησάμην πάσης κακείας καὶ πάσ[ης ἀθέ]οτος
καὶ ἀγνεύσας ἐς πόλυν χρόν[ον τὰ πρέποντα ἔ]τι θείας εὐσεβείας ἵνεκ[εν]
ἐπεθυσάμην καὶ ἐνθεασάμενος ἀνε[πάην]. νεύω[ν γὰρ κατ]έδειξάς μοι
σεαυτὸν ἐν τῷ χρυσ . . . . . καφος Δι . . τ . . . ρωντα τὸν οὐρανιω.ωλον και
στοπ . . . ν Δεμματα κατὰ Δεινὸν νυκτιδρόμον . . νια α.πιατον ποιησάμενος,
ἐν ᾧ καὶ ἁγίῳ τῷ τῆς ἀθανασίας ὕδατι λουσάμενος φαί[νη Δεύτερ]ον.
ἦλθες κατὰ καιρὸν ἀνατολὰς ποιο . . . εἰς τὸν σὸν σηκόν, ξοάνῳ τε σῷ καὶ
ναῷ ἔμπνοιαν παρέχων καὶ Δύναμιν μεγάλην. ἔνθα σε ἔγνων, Μανδοῦλι,
ἥλιον τὸν παντεπόπτην Δεσπότην, ἁπάντων βασιλέα, Αἰῶνα παντοκρά-
τορα. ὦ τῶν εὐτυχεστάτων λαῶν τῶν κατοικούντων, ἣν ὁ ἥλιος Μανδοῦλις
ἀγαπᾷ, τὴν ἱερὰν Τάλμιν, ἥτις ἐστὶν ὑπὸ τὰ σκᾶ[πτρα τῆς εὐε]θείρας μυρι-
ωνύμου Ἴσιδος.

p. 110 f. For Cyprian of Antioch, cf. *Acta Sanctorum*, Sept. vii. 222 ff.

For *all knowledge*, cf. Preisendanz, *P. gr. mag.* v. 256 ff. (i, p. 190),
a threat to the gods, 'unless I learn the things in the souls of all men,
Egyptians, Greeks, Syrians, Ethiopians, and every race and every tribe,
unless I learn the things that have been and are to be, unless I learn their
crafts and occupations and works and lives and the names of them and
of their fathers and mothers and brothers and friends and the dead': *Orac.
Sibyll.* viii. 56 (of Hadrian) καὶ μαγικῶν ἀδύτων μυστήρια πάντα μεθέξει.
For the date of the kernel of the magical papyri, cf. A. D. Nock, *Journal
of Egyptian Archaeology*, xv (1929), 225 ff.

For Porphyry and the Clarian Oracles, cf. id., *Revue des études anciennes*,
xxx (1928), 280 ff.

p. 112. Maximus Tyrius, xi. 6, p. 134 Hobein. Cf. Epictet. ii. 7; Lucan,
ix. 566 ff., on the wise man's freedom from any need of oracles: Cicero,
De diuinatione, ii. 11, remarks that you do not consult an oracle on moral,
philosophical, or political issues. But Diocletian and his colleagues consulted Didyma on the persecution of the Christians (H. Grégoire,
Mélanges Holleaux, 81 ff.).

For the text of Nearchus, cf. Wilcken–Mitteis, *Grundzüge und Chrestomathie*, I. ii. 148, No. 117. The quotation from Philodemus; *Concerning
the Gods*, i, col. x, p. 17, cf. 57, ed. Diels (*Abh. Berlin*, 1915, vii). Cf.
Philostratus, *Apoll. Ty.* iii. 42, and Reitzenstein, *HMR*, 237. Aristotle
fr. 45, p. 1483 a 19, Berlin ed. For the wisdom of the founders of
mysteries, cf. Sallustius 3 (and *Prolegomena*, xliii ff.).

p. 114 f. With this passage from Apuleius, *Apologia*, cf. *Met.* iii. 15, where
Fotis, about to reveal the magic secrets of her mistress, expresses her fear
but says 'sed melius de te doctrinaque tua praesumo, qui praeter generosam
natalium dignitatem, praeter sublime ingenium, sacris pluribus initiatus
profecto nosti sanctam silentii fidem'; in Lucian, *Menippus*, 2, M. pretends
that he must not reveal what he saw in the underworld, and his friend

replies that he can keep a secret and has been initiated; cf. Achilles Tatius, v. 26.

Libanius, *Oratio* xxiv, 36; Buecheler, *Carmina latina epigraphica*, iii. 25. Cf. Iamblichus, *Vita Pythagorae*, 18; A. D. Nock, *JHS*, xlv (1925), 88 f.

p. 116. Philo, *De specialibus legibus*, i. 320 (ii, p. 260 м); possibly influenced by Wisdom vi. 22, to which Canon W. L. Knox drew my attention. On the Chaldaic oracles, cf. W. Kroll, *De oraculis Chaldaicis* (*Breslauer philologische Abhandlungen*, vii. 1); J. Bidez, *Revue belge de philol. et d'hist.* vii (1928), 1477 ff. There were other private mysteries; cf. A. D. Nock, *JHS*, xlvi (1926), 50 ff., for a Hecate rite embedded in the Orphic *Argonautica* (fifth century A.D.).

p. 117. For the gnostic gem with a quotation from the *Poimandres*, cf. Campbell Bonner, *HTR*, xxv (1932), 362 ff.

p. 119. On knowledge of God, cf. R. Bultmann, in G. Kittel, *Theologisches Wörterbuch zum Neuen Testament*, i. 122.

VIII. THE SUCCESS OF THESE CULTS IN THE ROMAN EMPIRE

This chapter seeks to state the broad lines of development. I hope to return to the religious periodization of the Roman Empire, and to attempt something of the sort for the Hellenistic age.

p. 122. On the divisions of Roman society, cf. Friedländer–Wissowa, *Darstellungen aus der Sittengeschichte Roms* (ed. 10), i. 104 ff.

p. 124. On the period from Augustus to the death of Nero, cf. M. Rostovtzeff, *Mystic Italy*; A. D. Nock in *Cambridge Ancient History*, x.

p. 125. For the Narcissus episode, cf. Cassius Dio, lx. 19, 2.

On social change, cf. M. Rostovtzeff, *Social and Economic History of the Roman Empire*, 97 ff., 107; on the disappearance of the surviving old families from the government of the Imperial (as contrasted with the senatorial) provinces, E. Groag in *Strena Buliciana*, 253 ff.

For the Egyptian gods, cf. H. Mattingly, *BMC Roman Empire*, ii. xlix, 123, 149 (all bronze: also lxxxviii. 345, coin showing temple of Sarapis); J. Vogt, *Alexandrinischen Münzen*, i. 43 f. (who shows an increase from this time of Graeco-Egyptian types: on Alexandrian coins they appeared first under Nero; ib. 104 f.); *Not.*, 1893, 267 ff., and 1904, 118 ff.; A. D. Nock, *Theology*, xvi (1928), 156 f.

p. 126 f. On the second century, cf. Friedländer–Wissowa, iii. 119 ff.; on Antinous, W. Weber, *Drei Untersuchungen*, 19 ff.; Vogt, 106; on the possibly posthumous issues, Mattingly–Sydenham, *Roman Imperial Coinage*, ii. 335, 398 ff.; on the *equites singulares*, *CIL*, vi. 31138–51.

p. 127 f. On the rise of men from the Eastern provinces to prominence in Rome, cf. W. Weber, *Abh. Berlin*, 1932, v. 65 ff.; on the coin with RELIG AVG, W. Weber, *SB Heidelberg*, 1910, vii.

p. 129 f. On effects in soldiers' dedications of Imperial policy, cf. A. von Domaszewski, *Westdeutsche Zeitschrift*, xiv (1895), 59 ff.; on the Roman reaction, cf. A. D. Nock, *HTR*, xxiii (1930), 258 ff.; on Aurelian, Wissowa, *RK*, 367; on the Arval brothers, Wissowa, *PW* ii. 1467; for the dedication to Mithras, Dess. 659 (and cf. *Not.*, 1917, 272, No. 23, a *templum dei Solis* built at Como by a *corrector Italiae* at the order of Diocletian and Maximian); on the general state of worship in the third century, Geffcken, *Ausgang*, 20 ff.

p. 130. For the temple of Romulus, cf. Platner–Ashby, *Topographical Dictionary of Ancient Rome*, 450; for the decline in dedications in the West to Oriental deities, cf. C. H. Moore, *Trans. Am. Phil. Ass.* xxxviii (1907), 109 ff. *passim*. (The worships did not disappear: Ammianus Marcellinus, xvi. 12. 25, records that the name of Agenarichus had been changed to Serapio because his father had been long kept in Gaul as a hostage and had learnt *Graeca quaedam arcana*.)

p. 131. J. Toutain, *Les Cultes païens dans l'empire romain*, ii; ib. iii. 4 ff., his reply to Cumont's criticisms, *RHR*, lxvi (1912), 125 ff. Cumont, *Les Mystères de Mithra* (ed. 3), gives a map of the distribution of Mithraic worship; Turchi, *Le religioni misteriosofiche del mondo antico*, one including also Dea Suria, Cybele, Isis, Dionysus, and the Samothracian deities; W. Weber in Laqueur–Koch–Weber, *Probleme der Spätantike*, 81, one for Dionysus and Artemis Ephesia in Asia Minor (for the spread of the latter, cf. Ditt. *Syll.* 867); C. Bosch, in *Archäologische Anzeiger*, 1931, 455, a map of the Demeter cult in Asia Minor; J. Juster, *Les Juifs dans l'empire romain*, a survey of the dissemination of Judaism; Harnack, *Mission*, one of that of Christianity on the eve of its triumph.

p. 131. On the part played by troops raised in Syria, cf. G. La Piana, *HTR*, xx (1927), 286.

p. 132. F. Behn, *Das Mithrasheiligtum zu Dieburg*; A. D. Nock, *Gnomon*, vi (1930), 30 ff. F. Drexel, *Römisch-Germanische Kommission*, XIV Bericht (1922, published 1923), 62, suggests that Mithraism was brought by the eighth legion to Germany, on its transference from Moesia in 70. C. H. Moore, *Harvard Studies in Classical Philology*, xi (1900), 58, remarks that there is no evidence that imported divinities made any appeal to native Britons. For his percentage calculation, cf. *Trans. Am. Phil. Ass.* xxxviii (1907), 145 ff.

p. 134. For Rome, cf. Apuleius, *Met.* xi. 26; Ammianus Marcellinus, xvii. 4. 13.

For the Caracallan altar, cf. Cumont, *C.R. Ac. Inscr.* 1919, 313 ff.; *Rel. Or.* 79, fig. 5. To avoid misunderstanding I should remark that the acclamation, *There is one Zeus Sarapis*, made by those who hear the account of the miracle of Sarapis and commonly used as a formula of power to aid (e.g. on amulets) is not a creedal statement but a cry of enthusiasm, perhaps best rendered 'There is no god like Zeus Sarapis'. It is an acclamation, of the type studied by E. Peterson, ΕΙΣ ΘΕΟΣ. Thus in the Orphic liturgical text found at Gurob (O. Kern, *Orphicorum Fragmenta*, 102, No. 31, l. 23), we read, 'There is one Dionysus', but the context is full of other deities. Perhaps the formulation of *One Zeus Sarapis* at Alexandria is due to the constant opposition of the citizens and the Jews, in which Sarapis was the religious rallying point of the first. Thus, in P. Oxy. 1242 the two parties came before Trajan, the Greeks bearing a bust of Sarapis, the Jews some holy object. During proceedings the bust sweated, there were tumults in Rome, many shouts were raised, and all fled to the high parts of the hills (W. Weber, *Hermes*, l (1915), 47 ff.; O. Weinreich, *Neue Urkunden*, 18 f.). In Egypt there were struggles between different villages which were said to arise from a dislike of another's gods (e.g. [Apul.] *Ascl.* 37; W. Scott, *Hermetica*, iii. 234), but the animosity was no doubt local in its essence. Nevertheless, it is significant that in a rhetorical exercise, Πρὸς Ἱππόμαχον (Cramer, *Anecdota Parisina*, i. 165 f.; A. Bohler, *Sophistae anonymi protreptici fragmenta*, Diss. Strassburg, 1903), a Roman governor is represented as saying to the Egyptians that they must not be divided about the gods or reckon that one god is distinguishable from another.

There is a possible indication of exclusiveness in a passage of Eunapius, *Life of Maximus* (p. 52, ed. Boissonade, 1822), from which it appears to follow that a Mithraic pater was under oath not to preside over other *teletai*. This may be true of a pater, but the inscriptions prove that Mithraists as a whole were not exclusive (Cumont, *TM*, i. 331, n. 4), and we have noted the presence in Mithraea of statuettes of native deities (p. 133).

Attention has been called to electioneering scribbles on a wall at Pompeii, *All the Isiacs support Gnaeus Salvius Sabinus for the position of aedile*, and *Popidius Natalis, a client of Pansa, and the Isiacs support Cuspius Pansa for the position of aedile* (*CIL*, iv. 787, 1011). This represents probably a congregational rather than a sectarian spirit: the canvassers are members of a guild. The Roman fear of the danger of political combinations arising from men who introduced strange cults was not wholly groundless.

p. 135. For the hierarchic organization of Maximinus, cf. J. Maurice, *Numismatique Constantinienne*, iii. ix ff. The pagan mood of the moment is illustrated by a priestly inscription from Acmonia in Phrygia (Cumont, *Musées royaux du Cinquantenaire. Catalogue des sculptures et inscriptions antiques*, ed. 2, 158 ff., No. 136).

For the term *mons Vaticanus*, cf. Dess. 4131; *CIL* xiii. 7281. The Mother of the gods was called *Mater deum magna Idea Palatina* at Marseilles (*CIL*, xii. 405) and at Nemausus *matri deum mag[nae Idaeae Phrygi]ae Palatinae* occurs in a taurobolic inscription of A.D. 255 (*Année épigraphique*, 1910,

No. 217). One of the two precincts of Isis at Corinth was called *In Canopus* (Pausanias, ii. 4. 6), and there is a dedication at Carthage ἐν Κανώβῳ θεῷ μεγίστῳ (*CIL*, viii. 1003).

p. 136. There is a puzzling inscription at Rome (*CIL*, vi. 377; Dess. 3051), 'aram Ioui Fulgeratoris ex precepto deorum montensium Val. Crescentio pater deoru omnium et Aur. Exuperantius sacerdos Siluani cum fratribus et sororibu dedicauerunt'. *Pater deoru omnium* looks like a pretentious title invented by a small sodality.

For the Carvoran inscription, cf. Buecheler, *Carmina latina epigraphica*, 24.

p. 137. For *pantheus* and kindred representations, cf. F. Jacobi, ΠΑΝΤΕΣ ΘΕΟΙ (Diss. Halle, 1930), 121 ff.

IX. THE CONVERSION OF LUCIUS

Professor D. S. Robertson has very kindly helped me with difficult passages in Apuleius, xi.

p. 138. We know the original from the *Ass* of Lucian.

p. 139. For this wreath, cf. the statue of a priestess of Isis at Cyrene wearing a large garland across her right shoulder and left arm (E. Ghislanzoni, *Notiziario Archeologico*, iv (1927), 166 f., fig. 9).

p. 145. Two small bath-houses are in the group of buildings attached to the Iseum at Eretria (N. Papadakis, *Arch. Delt.* i (1915), 129).

p. 146. For this platform, cf. the prothesis with platform at the back of the same Iseum (ib. 120, 118, fig. 4).

p. 147. For the intimate relationship between Lucius and the priest who initiated him, cf. *CIL*, xi. 574 (Forum Popili), 'Fullonia L. f. Tertulla sacror. Isidis locum dedit C. Telegennio Sperato sacerdoti VIvir. Aug. telestinis eius posterisque eorum' (a burial-place to be shared by the priest, his initiates, and their descendants); *BCH*, xxiv (1900), 366 f. (Prusa) οἱ περὶ Λεωνίδην Ἑρμησιλάου ἱερέα μύσται καὶ Δεκατισταί.

p. 150. For *myrionyma*, cf. Dess. 4376a &c.; for *una quae es onmia*, ib. 4362. For a revised text of P. Oxy. 1380, cf. Manteuffel, 70 ff. It has been thought that the absence of any mention of Alexandria indicates that the basis of the first part of the text is an older Egyptian document, but it is preferable to suppose that Alexandria was named in the beginning which is lost. The papyrus gives for Paphos, l. 86, ἀγνήν, Δῖαν, ἠπίαν, and does not expressly name Aphrodite to correspond to Venus in Apuleius.

pp. 152 ff. For dedications *ex imperio*, &c., cf. A. D. Nock, *JHS*, xlv (1925), 95 ff.; for vocation, *HTR*, xxiii (1930), 255 f., and A. Alt, *Der Gott der Väter*: the Dolichenus text is Dess. 4316.

X. THE LAST PHASE

p. 156. Cf. Tertullian, *De spectaculis*, ii. 3 (p. 41 Boulanger), 'plures denique inuenias quos magis periculum uoluptatis quam uitae euocet ab hac secta'. For this chapter as a whole cf. J. Geffcken, *Ausgang*.

p. 156. Προσκαρτέρησις; B. Latyschev, *Inscr. Ponti*, ii, No. 52; E. Schürer,
SB Berlin, 1897, 202 f. Cf. καρτερία, Joseph, *C. Ap.* ii. 123, of Greeks
adopting Jewish customs.

p. 157. J. Bidez, *Vie de Porphyre*, 6 ff.

Julian, *Orat.* iv, p. 130 c; *Ep.* 106, Bidez–Cumont; *Orat.* vii, p. 234 c.
Cf. in general J. Bidez, *Vie de l'Empereur Julien*.

p. 158. For Pegasius, cf. Julian, *Ep.* 79.

p. 159. Julian, *Ep.* 84 b, pp. 116 f., Bidez–Cumont; Augustine, *Ep.* 91
(202), 5; Cumont, *Rel. Or.* 181 ff.

Hartel's edition of Cyprian, iii. 302 ff.

XI. CONVERSION TO PHILOSOPHY

p. 168. On the Basilica, cf. J. Carcopino, *La Basilique pythagoricienne de la
Porte Majeure*.

p. 169. The story of Hipparchia can be traced back to Menander fr.
117–18, Kock: that is nearly contemporary evidence. On *parrhesia*, free
speech, cf. E. Peterson, *R. Seeberg Festschrift*, 283 ff. In the Dio passage
we may note the phrase πολλὴν σπερμολογίαν συνείροντες, for the parallel
to σπερμολόγος, Acts xvii. 18, indicates the expectation of Paul formed
by an educated group with no special information. For the number of
Cynics, cf. Philo, *De plantatione*, 151 (i, p. 352, Mangey); for their continued
existence in the time of Julian, J. Bidez, *Vie de l'Empereur Julien*, 248 ff.

p. 172. The remains of Diogenes of Oenoanda have been edited by
J. William in the Teubner Series. I cite fr. II, col. ii. 7, p. 5, col. iv. 3,
p. 6; XXIII, col. ii, p. 29. Cf. Virgil, *Catalepton*, 5. 10, *uitamque ab omni
uindicabimus cura*.

p. 173. For Polemo, cf. S. Mekler, *Academicorum philosophorum index
Herculaneus*, 46 ff. It is of importance for the study of monasticism that
Epictetus iii. 12 has to warn men against useless forms of self-discipline,
and refers to the uncritical admiration thus excited. An ironic comment
on the pretensions of philosophers is afforded by a bronze vase found at
Herstal in Belgium (end first/early second century A.D.). It shows us
austere philosophers engaged in their researches; on the cover we see the
same philosophers pursuing the homosexual tastes ascribed in Lucian to
the sage who had taken her lover from Drose (Cumont, *Ann. soc. arch.
Bruxelles*, xiv (1900), 401 ff.; *Comment la Belgique fut romanisée*, ed. 2,
92, fig. 63).

Dio tells his story, *Orat. xiii*. Cf. H. von Arnim, *Dio von Prusa*, 234 ff.;
O. Hense, *C. Musonii Rufi reliquiae*, xxiv f.

p. 174 f. Euripides fr. 910 Nauck; Democritus fr. 118 (Diels, *Vorsokratiker*,
ed. 4, ii. 83); W. W. Jaeger, *Aristoteles*, 53 ff.; F. Boll, *Vita contemplativa*
(ed. 2). Augustus wrote *Hortationes ad philosophiam* (Suet. *Aug.* 85).

p. 176. Celsus, pp. 60, 48, Glöckner. The impression made by the memory of Epictetus is shown by a curious inscription at Yazülü (J. R. S. Sterrett, *Wolfe Expedition to Asia Minor* (Papers American Sch. Class. Stud. Athens iii (1888)), 315 f., No. 438), with a summary of philosophic principles: the only freedom is that which lies in you; Zeus is our father; Epictetus, an eagle among men, was born of a slave mother.

On the idealization of philosophers, we may note that the gnostic sect of Carpocratians kept images of Christ together with images of philosophers, Pythagoras, Plato, Aristotle, and others, 'et reliquam obseruationem circa eas similiter ut gentes faciunt' (Irenaeus, *Aduersus haereses*, i. 20. 4, vol. i, p. 210 Harvey).—For the influence of philosophic legend on saint legend, cf. K. Holl, *Gesammelte Aufsätze zur Kirchengeschichte*, ii. 249 ff.; R. Reitzenstein, *SB Heidelberg*, 1914, viii.—Of the philosopher as thaumaturge, Apollonius of Tyana, Iamblichus, and Proclus are all illustrations: but in Philostratus, *Apollonius*, vii. 16, we find the sober Musonius credited with the discovery of a spring on Gyara.

p. 176 f. On the place of philosophy in education, and on its general standing and character under the Empire, cf. A. D. Nock, *Sallustius*, ch. i. For philosophic impostors, cf. Cassius Dio, lii. 36. 4.

p. 178. For the philosopher in the household, cf. Friedlander–Wissowa, *Sittengeschichte Roms* (ed. 10), iii. 283 ff.; on Greek confidential companions in general, cf. W. Kroll, *Neue Jahrbücher*, 1928, 312; for the importance of philosophic personality in the unspeculative atmosphere of Rome, R. Hirzel in V. Gardthausen, *Augustus*, i. 1297.

p. 179. For the Memphis library, cf. Wilcken–Mitteis, *Grundzüge und Chrestomathie*, i. ii. 182 ff., No. 155.

p. 179 f. ἐπιστροφή; Epictetus, ii. 20. 22, in the last sense quoted. Cf. Porphyry *Ad Marcellam* 24, πιστεῦσαι γὰρ δεῖ ὅτι μόνη σωτηρία ἡ πρὸς τὸν θεὸν ἐπιστροφή; Sallustius, xiv, p. 28. 2, τῆς πρὸς τὸ θεῖον ἐπιστροφῆς (of prayers and sacrifices which set us right after sin); Iamblichus, *De mysteriis*, i. 13, δύναται οὖν ἡ ἐξίλασις ἡμᾶς ἐπιστρέψαι πρὸς τὴν κρείττονα μετουσίαν. Cf. E. R. Dodds on Proclus, *Elements of Theology*, 15. In the Septuagint ἐ. is used of turning to God, in a general as well as in a specific sense (cf. Preuschen–Bauer, *Griechisch-deutsches Wörterbuch zu den Schriften des Neuen Testaments*, 469; A. H. Dirksen, *The New Testament Concept of Metanoia*, Diss. Cath. Univ. Washington (1932), 151); in Acts xv. 3, τὴν ἐπιστροφὴν τῶν ἐθνῶν. Hence *conuerti, conuersio* in and after Tertullian.

On *metanoia*, cf. W. W. Jaeger, *Göttingische gelehrte Anzeigen*, 1913, 590 f.; K. Latte, *ARW*, xx (1921), 281, n. 1; J. S. Boughton, *The Idea of Progress in Philo Judaeus* (Diss. Columbia, 1932: Jewish Publication Society of America: Philadelphia), 154 ff. In Cebes Metanoia acts once to save a man: we have not the recurrent repentance of Judaism.

p. 181. Epicurus, fr. 523, p. 318, Usener. It is significant that

Diogenes of Oenanda, fr. xxxiii, col. iii. 10 ff., pp. 41 f., argues against determinism because it would destroy moral responsibility. This implies the common but fallacious belief that the world must be such as *I* think it ought to be.

p. 182. For the metaphor of initiation, cf. Dio Prus. xii. 33; Epictet. iii. 24, 13 ff. Porphyry, *De abstinentia*, ii. 49, speaks of the philosopher as the priest of the universal god.

p. 183. On Persius III, cf. A. E. Housman, *CQ*, vii (1913), 16 ff. Ideas of this sort are parodied by Petronius, e.g. chs. 1–5 and 88, on the relation of literary and moral decadence, which agree closely with Philo, *De plantatione*, 157 ff. (i, p. 352, Mangey; cf. A. D. Nock, *CR*, 1932, 173), and 55 on luxury. It is hard to resist the conjecture that Petronius had Seneca in mind. At the end, by his way of dying, he parodied Stoic death-bed scenes.

XII. THE SPREAD OF CHRISTIANITY AS A SOCIAL PHENOMENON

p. 187. Claudius edict, l. 96, in H. I. Bell, *Jews and Christians in Egypt*, 25.

p. 188 f. For the book of the Damascus sect, cf. R. H. Charles, *Apocrypha and Pseudepigrapha of the Old Testament*, ii. 785 ff.; G. F. Moore, *Judaism*, i. 200 ff.; G. Hölscher, *Zeitschrift für die neutestamentliche Wissenschaft*, xxviii (1929), 21 ff. W. K. L. Clarke, *Theology*, xxi (1930), 331 ff., has remarked on the similarity of their organization with that described in *Didascalia Apostolorum*.

On the doctrine of the Spirit of Judaism, cf. the summary by Proksch in G. Kittel, *Theol. Wörterb. zum N.T.*, i. 104.

pp. 189 ff. On the meaning of *Hellenistes*, cf. H. J. Cadbury in Jackson–Lake, *Beginnings*, v. 59 ff.

On Paul, cf. Ed. Schwartz, *Characterköpfe aus der antiken Literatur* (ed. 3), ii. 97 ff. For the episode in Cyprus, cf. A. D. Nock in Jackson–Lake, v. 182 ff.; for the impression which he made at Athens, cf. p. 295 above.

p. 192. The Christians began by using rooms in private houses; then they built churches like those described in *Didascalia*, that of St. Gregory Thaumaturges at Neocaesarea in Pontus, and that at Doura (early third century). (For other evidence, cf. H. Leclercq in Cabrol–Leclercq, *Dictionnaire d'archéologie chrétienne et de liturgie*, iv. 2292 ff.) These churches were no doubt for the most part not recognizable as such from the outside, and certainly had none of the outward marks of a temple as commonly known; the church at Doura is based on the plan of the synagogue.

p. 193. We have a testimony to the impression made by martyrdom in Tertullian, *De spectaculis*, i. 5, p. 40, Boulanger, 'sunt qui existimant

Christianos, expeditum morti genus, ad hanc obstinationem abdicatione
uoluptatium erudiri, quo facilius uitam contemnant amputatis quasi
retinaculis eius nec desiderent, quam iam superuacuam sibi fecerunt,
ut hoc consilio potius et humano prospectu, non diuino praescripto
definitum existimetur'.

On the Jewish idea of martyrdom, cf. G. F. Moore, *Judaism*, ii. 105 ff.:
quotations in Strack–Billerbeck, *Komm. zum Neuen Testament*, i. 220 ff.
Zealots courted death and came by it in order to protest against the
conduct of Herod the Great.

pp. 194 ff. This evidence for the philosophic use of *martys* was put together
by J. Geffcken, *Hermes*, xlv (1910), 481 ff.; for the fascination of voluntary
death, cf. Fr. Dornseiff, *ARW*, xxii (1923/4), 133 ff.; for the development
of Christian terminology, H. Delehaye, *Sanctus*, 74 ff., and literature
collected by A. Wilhelm, *SB Berlin*, 1932, 845 ff.

To the philosophic instances add Seneca, *De beneficiis*, vii. 8. 2, 'Deme-
trium rettuli, quem mihi uidetur rerum natura nostris tulisse temporibus
ut ostenderet nec illum a nobis corrumpi nec nos ab illo corrigi posse';
Philo, *Quod omnis probus liber est*, 92 (ii, p. 459 м). χρὴ ... μάρτυρας βίους
τῶν κατὰ μέρος ἀνδρῶν ἀγαθῶν παραγαγεῖν, οἳ σαφέσταται πίστεις
ἐλευθερίας εἰσί.

Porphyry, *Against the Christians*, fr. 63 (ed. Harnack, *Abh. Berlin*, 1916,
i. 84 f.), contrasts the attitude of Apollonius favourably with that of
Christ. The fate of Socrates and Pythagoras figures among the misdeeds
of paganism also in Constantine, *Oratio ad Sanctos*, 9, p. 163, Heikel (in
the first volume of the Berlin Eusebius); that of Socrates in *Martyrium
Pionii*, 17; Tertullian, *Ad nationes*, i. 10.

p. 197. For the exciting of sympathy, cf. Tacitus, *Annals*, xiv. 42 ff.;
Cicero, *Ep. ad fam.* vii. 1. 3 (in 55 в.с. Pompey showed elephant-baiting at
the last day of his games, 'extremus elephantorum dies fuit, in quo admi-
ratio magna uolgi atque turbae, delectatio nulla exstitit; quin etiam miseri-
cordia quaedam consecuta est atque opinio eius modi esse quandam illi
beluae cum genere humano societatem'); Cassius Dio, xliii. 19. 2–4 (sight
of Arsinoe in chains in Caesar's triumph in 46 в.с. moves the people to pity).

p. 198. Clemens Alexandrinus, *Stromata*, iv. 4, § 17. 1 (ii, p. 256 Stählin).
The whole of his treatment of martyrdom is instructive: he compares
these suicides with the Gymnosophists and produces numerous pagan
analogies for the heroism of true martyrs, men and women alike.

On the fascination of voluntary death, cf. Tertullian, *Apol.* 50; *Ad
nationes*, i. 18.

p. 199. For this topic in the novel, cf. K. Kerényi, *Die griechisch-oriental-
ische Romanliteratur*, 95 ff.; A. D. Nock, *Gnomon*, iv (1928), 485 ff. It
involves an element of vicarious sadism.

p. 200. Julian, p. 301 в; *Ep.* 89, p. 141. 14, Bidez–Cumont.

p. 201. This desire for an eternity of memory appears conspicuously in many foundations, as for instance a woman's bequest at Gythion, A.D 161–9, for an annual benefaction 'that my liberality to the gymnasium and the city may abide forever. . . . For I shall seem to be immortal' (B. Laum, *Stiftungen in der griechischen und römischen Antike*, ii. 11 ff., No. 9, ll. 11, 16, 56). Tertullian remarks (*De testimonio animae*, 4) 'nam omnibus fere ingenita est famae post mortem cupido'.

The same theatrical mood is conspicuous in the tragedies of Seneca, and in the popular 'Martyr Acts' at Alexandria recording the various proceedings in which men maintained the city's rights (e.g. Wilcken, *Grundz. u. Chrest.*, i. ii. 34 ff., No. 20). I would raise the question whether the increasing popularity of frontality in art under the Empire is to be connected with this egocentricity.

p. 202. Celsus, i. 2, p. 1; iii. 55, p. 19, Glöckner.

p. 203. The contrast of free Christian prayer with stereotyped Roman prayer is stated by Tertullian, *Apol.* 30; for worship directed to Jesus, cf. E. C. Ratcliff, *J.T.S.* xxx (1929), 30 ff.

p. 204. Hefele–Leclerq, *Histoire des conciles*, i. ii. 715 (decree of synod in 341); cf. C. H. Kraeling, *Journal of Biblical Literature*, li (1932), 157; for the iconostasis, K. Holl, *ARW*, ix (1906), 365 ff. (*Ges. Aufs.* ii. 225 ff.).

I quote Celsus from O. Glöckner's text (Lietzmann, *Kleine Texte*, No. 151), i. 9, p. 2; iii. 17, p. 16; iii. 50, p. 18; iv. 10, p. 22; vi. 22, pp. 44 ff.

Origen's reply apropos of Mithras must be quoted, vi. 22 (ii, p. 93), Koetschau, 'Why did he set forth Mithraic mysteries rather than any other mysteries with their story? They do not appear to be specially valued among the Greeks in comparison with those of Eleusis or those transmitted to people who on Aegina are initiated in the rites of Hecate. Why rather, if he wanted a barbarian rite, did he not take the Egyptian mysteries, *a source of pride to many*, or the Cappadocian rites of Artemis in Comana, or those of the Thracians, or those of the Romans themselves who initiate the noblest descendants of the senate?'

p. 206. iii. 59, p. 20; vi. 11, p. 42.

pp. 207 ff. For the Decian texts, cf. J. R. Knipfing, *HTR*, xvi (1923), 345 ff.; for the view of Christianity as apostasy, the pagan (possibly Porphyry; Wilamowitz, *Zeit. neut. Wiss.* i (1900), 101 ff.) summarized by Euseb. *Praep. euang.* i. 2. 2–4; for the petition to Maximinus, E. Diehl, *Inscriptiones latinae christianae veteres*, 1; for the policy of Decius, A. D. Nock, *HTR*, xxiii (1930), 251 ff.; for the name of Jesus in magic, K. Preisendanz, *Papyri graecae magicae*, iv. 3019 f. (i, p. 170); for charges against Christians, J. P. Waltzing, *Le crime rituel*.

XIII. THE TEACHINGS OF CHRISTIANITY AS VIEWED BY A PAGAN

p. 213. This motive of curiosity is invoked by Augustine, *Sermo cxxxii*. In speaking of the Eucharist he says to catechumens: 'Disputo, non dissero. Ecce Pascha est, da nomen ad baptismum. si non te excitat festiuitas, ducat ipsa curiositas; ut scias quid dictum sit, Qui manducat carnem meam, et bibit sanguinem meum, in me manet, et ego in illo.'

p. 213 f. On catechetical discipline and on lists of sins to be renounced, cf. H. Leclercq, *Dict. arch. chrét. lit.* ii. 2530 ff. For *Egyptian Church Order*, (ch. 34), cf. R. H. Connolly in *Texts and Studies*, ed. J. Armitage Robinson, viii. 4, 183.

p. 216 f. Musonius, pp. 63 ff. Hense; Dio, vii. 133 ff.; Ovid, *Amores*, ii. 14; Martial, ix. 41.

For temple requirements, cf. *EGC*, 69 ff.

For the Philadelphia text, cf. Ditt. *Syll.* 985; O. Weinreich, *SB Heidelberg*, 1919, xvi.

On conscience, cf. Fr. Zucker, *Syneidesis-Conscientia*; on Greek ideas of sin, K. Latte, *ARW*, xx (1921), 254 ff.

p. 219. The real spirit of this world appears in the tale of the death of Septimus Severus (*SHA, Seu.* 23), 'ultima uerba eius dicuntur haec fuisse: "turbatam rem publicam ubique accepi, pacatam etiam Britannis relinquo, senex ac pedibus aeger firmum imperium Antoninis meis relinquens, si boni erunt, inbecillum si mali". iussit deinde signum tribuno dari "laboremus", quia Pertinax, quando in imperium adscitus est, signum dederat "militemus".'

Dess. 4316 *fratres carissimos et collegas hon(estissimos)*; *brethren* again in the oath of a mystery confraternity (probably Mithraic), preserved in a papyrus and interpreted by Cumont, *HTR*, xxvi (1933).

p. 220. For a desire to live up to a standard, cf. Juvenal, xiii. 19 ff., 120 f., where the question is that of keeping one's temper and serenity.

p. 221. The Jews regarded pagan gods as (1) angels set by God over the seventy peoples of the world, (2) devils, (3) (the Hellenistic Jews) deified dead men, (4) nothing; (Strack–Billerbeck, *Kommentar z. N.T.* iii. 48 ff.). On *daimon, daimonion*, cf. R. Heinze, *Xenokrates*, 78 ff.; J. Geffcken, *Zwei griechischen Apologeten*, 219 ff.; J. Tambornino, *De antiquorum daemonismo*, 69 ff.; M. Pohlenz, *Vom Zorne Gottes*, 129 ff.; Andres, *PW, Supp.* iii. 267 ff.; W. Bousset, *ARW*, xviii (1915), 134 ff.; M. P. Nilsson, ib. xxii (1923/4), 363 ff.; Cumont, *Rel. Or.* 280, 295 f.; A. Miura–Stange, *Celsus und Origenes (Beih. z. Zeit. neut. Wiss.* iv), 93 ff.; Wilamowitz, *Glaube*, i. 362 ff.; F. J. Dölger, *Antike und Christentum*, iii (1932), 153 ff.; Nock, *HTR*, xxiii (1930), 261 f. The subject is not exhausted.

p. 225. Varro, *Frag.* i. 55, p. 163, 59, p. 164, 10 b, p. 146, 30, p. 155 ed. Agahd (*Fleckeisens Jahrbücher*, Supp. XXIV).

pp. 227 ff. On the significance of ruler-worship, cf. A. D. Nock, in *Cambridge Ancient History*, x. On the Japanese Christians and the Byzantine precedent, cf. L. Bréhier–P. Batiffol, *Les Survivances du culte impérial romain*.

p. 231. For Alexander, cf. Walz. *Rhetores Graeci*, ix. 336 f.; for Aristides, cf. J. Amann, *Zeusrede des Ailios Aristides*; for the Clarian oracle, p. 111 above.

p. 232. For God as shaper of world out of existent matter, cf. Justin, i. 59; Athenagoras, 15 f. Quotations from Origen in H. Usener, *Das Weihnachtsfest* (ed. 2), 13. [But I now doubt their relevance to this point.]

p. 232 f. On bipaternity, cf. H. Usener, *Kleine Schriften*, iv. 259 ff.; Br. Meissner, *Babylonien und Assyrien*, i. 46.

p. 233. Thus in Virgil, *Aen.* ii. 604 ff. Venus lifts from the eyes of Aeneas all that dims mortal sight and shows him the divinities who are active in the fall of Troy, Neptune, for instance, overthrowing its walls with his trident: that was, so to speak, the spiritual interpretation. Ovid, *Metamorphoses* xv. 750 ff., says of Julius, 'neque enim de Caesaris actis ullum maius opus quam quod pater exstitit huius'. Now he adopted Octavian, and did not beget him. Yet Ovid cannot well be showing his wit on this theme: Augustus was *Diui filius*. This concept of two planes of reality is important for Egyptian and other magic; cf. Bell–Nock–Thompson, *Magical Texts from a bilingual papyrus in the British Museum* (*Proc. Brit. Acad.* xvii, 1932), 25 ff.

We find this again in the thinking of Christians, who believed themselves to have the sole and complete interpretation of phenomena by revelation and read this revelation into all that they saw. Thus in the *Acts of Philip* and among the Messalianists reality is set forth in terms of myth, and mental processes are represented as enacted in external happenings (E. Peterson, *Oriens Christianus*, 1932, 172 ff.). It is so in Manichaeism, with its doctrine of the suffering Jesus who hangs on every tree. Joannes Damascenus, *De haeresibus*, 49 (Migne, xciv, 707), describes a sect of Pepuziani who glorified Pepuza, which lay between Galatia and Cappadocia, and believed it to be Jerusalem. In the central movement, the dramatization of the liturgy tended in this direction: compare the antiphons for the eve of the Epiphany in Usener, *Kleine Schriften*, iv. 431.

p. 235. Celsus, v. 6, p. 33 Glöckner.

Cf. Cumont, *ARW*, ix (1906), 323 ff.; M. Zepf, ib. xxv (1927), 225 ff.

p. 236. 'general ideas', i.e. the ideas sanctioned by the consent of humanity. Cf. A. D. Nock, *Sallustius*, xli; F. H. Sandbach, *CQ*, xxiv (1930), 44 ff. This passage of Gregory should be a warning against the assumption that an Anthropos myth, such as we find in the *Poimandres*, was widespread.

Celsus v. 2, p. 33, Glöckner, expresses himself strongly against the possibility of the descent of a god or a son of god; against the idea that deified kings were thought to be avatars of gods, cf. A. D. Nock, *JHS*, xlviii (1928), 30 ff. Glycon (p. 94 above) is not exactly an exception; there was commonly a somewhat vague relation between a deity and the animal or bird linked with him and sometimes thought to be a manifestation of him.

p. 241. Didymus, *De Demostheni commenta*, col. xi. 7; F. W. Hall, *Companion to Classical Texts*, 39.

p. 243. For Zarathustra, cf. Chr. Bartholomae, *Die Gatha's des Awesta*, ix, 18, p. 64; for the doctrine of periods, Theopompus ap. Plut. *De Iside et Osiride*, 47, p. 370 B.

p. 245. For these prophecies, cf. W. W. Tarn, *JRS*, xxii (1932), 135 ff.; R. Reitzenstein–H. H. Schaeder, *Studien zum antiken Synkretismus*, 38 ff.
For Mithraism cf. Cumont, *RHR*, ciii (1931), 29 ff.

p. 246. For the epitaph *non fui, fui, non sum, non desidero*, cf. Cumont, *Musée Belge*, xxxii (1928), 73 ff.

p. 247. Usener, *Epicurea*, p. 65. 12.

p. 250. Justin, *Apol.* i. 46. In Eusebius, *Triakontaeterikos*, 4. 2, p. 202, Heikel, all wisdom is due to this Logos.

p. 251. Cf. F. M. Cornford, *The Laws of Motion in Ancient Thought*, 29 ff. For the resulting method of argument, cf. Sallustius, ch. 7, 13, 20. The idea of symmetry was raised to the principle of *isonomia*; Cicero, ascribing it to Epicurus, defines 'eam esse naturam ut omnia omnibus paribus paria respondeant' (*De natura deorum*, i. 50; J. B. Mayor's note shows its popularity). Cf. a Philonic mode of argument discussed by E. R. Goodenough, *Yale Classical Studies*, iii (1932), 122, 150.

XIV. THREE TYPES OF CONVERSION
JUSTIN, ARNOBIUS, AUGUSTINE

p. 260. Symmachus, *Relatio pro ara Pacis*.

The letter of Maximus in Augustine, *Ep.* 16.

Cf. Cumont, *Rel. Or.* 300, n. 22. There were, of course, waverers: cf. Constantine, *Oratio ad Sanctos*, *11*, p. 165, Heikel.

p. 270. Wilamowitz, *Greek Historical Writing and Apollo*, 26.

INDEX

Abonutichus 93 ff.

Abstinence 142. *See* Fast.

Acclamations 292 f.; after miracle, for Isis 140; for Sarapis 84, 89; for Zeus Panamaros 90; in Christian texts 89; in mystery, for Osiris 39; for Sarapis 134.

Achilles Tatius 199 f.

Acts 254.

Adhesion 7.

Adonis 21, 41, 236, 281.

Aegina 299.

Aelian 91, 127 f.

Agathodaimon 40.

Agdistis 216.

Agrarian rites 22, 133, 226 f.

Alexander, son of Ammon 232.

Alexander legend, Judaizing insertion in 79.

Alexander of Abonutichus 93 ff., 128.

Alexandria 38, 85, 126 f., 169, 293.

Allegory 159, 264.

Ambrose 264.

Anahita (= Anaitis) 35, 42; punishes sin 91.

Anatolian cults 41, 132.

Angels 223, 235; gods as 111, 231 f.

Anger of Sarapis 50; of Isis 80; of Cybele 81.

Anthropomorphism, rise of 23; limitations 222, 231; alleged against Christianity 263.

Antioch, proselytes at 62; Christianity at 190, 204.

Antiquity claimed by cults 53, 73, 281.

Apamea, Judaizers at 64.

Aphrodita Syria, see *Dea Suria*.

Aphrodite, the Semitic 20.

Apollo, rise of 21 ff.; known to Darius 19; worshipped by Orpheus 27; sons of 232; epiphanies 90; oracle at Charos 111 f., 231.

Apollonius of Tyana 91, 93, 129, 195 f., 298.

Apuleius 14 f., 38 f., 114 f., 138 ff., 283.

Archigallus 69 f.

Aretalogos (teller of miracles) of Sarapis 54, 89.

Aristides the rhetorician 83 f., 231.

Aristophanes 27.

Arnobius 226, 257 ff.

Art, religious 74, 92 ff., 102, 124, 288.

Asceticism, Orphic 26; Pythagorean 167; Magian 43; Brahman 47; of Egyptian priest 87; trend to 174, 252 f., 295.

Asclepius introduced at Athens 18; at Rome 68; manifested as Glycon 93 f.; (= Imouthes) seen by Thessalus 109.

Asoka 45 ff.

Associations, religious 20 f., 276; of aliens at Athens 20; for Dionysus 26, 31, 73; in Egypt 36; Mithraic 44, 300; Judaizing 63 f.; on Delos for Sarapis 52 f.; at Rome for Cybele 68; for Juppiter Dolichenus 66, 219; for Isis 149; at Pompeii for Isis 293; for Bellona 82; relation to temples 52, 149; oath of 300.

Astrology 100 ff., 229, 259, 262 f., 289; measures against 74.

Atargatis, see *Dea Suria*.

Athena, miracle at Lindos 20.

Athens, introduces cult of Bendis 17 f., of Pan 18, of Asclepius 18; religious policy in colonies 19; foreign groups at 20; private cults of Zeus Sabazios and Cotytto 20, of Adonis 21; Men in 59; Orphism in 26; *exegetai* of Apollo at 21; sends priest of Sarapis to Delos 54.

Attis 37, 41, 101, 236; mysteries of 279; at Rome 69.

Augustine 159, 184, 259 ff.; contrast with Julian 158.

Augustus 124, 232, 240, 257 f., 295.

Babylonia 34 f., 100.

Bacchanalia 71 ff.

Baptism 220, 260 f.

Bath before initiation 145.

Bellona 75, 82.

Bendis, 17 f., 276.

Birthdays, 232.

Blood, efficacy of 70.

Body and soul 26, 247 ff.

Brethren, 63, 219, 300.

Buddhism 9, 46 f., 280; contrast with Orphism 31.

Cappadocia 42 f.

Caracalla 129, 134.

Cassius Dio 129 f.

Castration 37.

Cebes 180 f.

Celsus 83, 204 ff., 224, 235.

Cemetery, Bacchic 25.
Chaldaic Oracles 102, 111, 117, 158.
Chaplains, philosophic 178.
Christian meeting-places 202, 297.
Christianity, demands of 213; promise
 of 13; and the mysteries 57, 205 f.;
 and philosophy 179, 186; and needs
 of time 210 f.; and popular feeling
 192, 207 ff., 255.
Church 241 f.
Cicero 184.
Civic religious duties 11, 227 f.
Claros 111 f.
Claudius 69.
Clementine Homilies 108.
Coinage expresses religious ideas 85,
 125 ff., 272.
Commagene 42.
Commands of gods 72, 148, 152 ff.;
 of Helios Saraptenos 66; of Isis
 139 f., 142 ff.; of Sarapis 49 ff., 86;
 of Zeus 275; of mountain-gods
 294.
Commission for foreign worships at
 Rome 68, 71, 74, 132.
Common chest, forbidden in edict on
 Bacchanalia 73.
Communion, Mithraic 279.
Communities, Orphic 30; Hermetic
 117.
Composite divine types 137.
Conflict, against Dionysus 25; at
 Delos 51 ff., 59; at Rome 134; in
 Egypt 293.
Conquest, effects of 5 f.
Conscience 217 f.
Contemplation 174 f.
Continuity of private rites 29 f.
Conversion 7, 134; preparation for
 266; to Hermetism 118; to philo-
 sophy 173, 179; from Christianity
 157; in Acts 154; of Dion of·Prusa
 173 f.
Cornutus 129, 182 f.
Cosmogony 88, 164 f., 232.
Cotytto 20.
Credulity 90, 241.
Creeds 214.
Creedlike statement of Apollo's
 power 22; of birth of Dionysus 25;
 about *Dea Suria* 136.
Criobolium 70.
Cult-images 23.
Cumae 25.
Cures by Asclepius 54; by Sarapis
 84 ff.; by Imouthes 86 f.; Christian
 89.
Curse, fear of 76, 286.

Cybele 37, 41, 59, 81 f., 126 f., 132 f.,
 159 f., 276, 293 f.; at Rome 68 f.
Cycles, theory of 244 ff.
Cynics 168 ff.
Cyprian of Antioch 110.
Cypriots at Athens 20.

Daimones 221 ff.
Damascus, covenanters of 188.
Dea Suria (= the Syrian goddess,
 Atargatis, Aphrodita Syria, Venus
 Caelesta), at Beroea 59; at Phistyon
 59; at Thuria &c. 60; at Puteol 71;
 at Rome 75; at Carvoran 136; in
 Fayoum 282; inspires prophecies of
 Eunus 66; begging priests of 82;
 Nero's interest in 106.
Death, prevention of 102; and initia-
 tion 143; fascination of 198.
Deification of Antinous 126; of son of
 Maxentius 130; of Plato 175; of
 dead men 221; of kings 237; from
 gratitude 257 f.
Delos, Syrian deities on 49; Sarapis
 and Isis on 51 ff., 58; Italians on 67.
Delphi 19, 22, 25, 112, 173, 279.
Demeter 22 f.
Diogenes of Oenoanda 172.
Dion of Prusa 43, 169, 173 f.
Dionysus 23, 27, 193 f., 276 f.; at
 Rome 71 ff.; miracles 97; visions
 206; initiations 114 f.; commissions
 priest 154; and after-life 102.
Divinity, attempt to secure 103.
Dogma, Julianic 159; philosophic 181.
Domitian 126.
Doura-Europos 34.
Dramatic instinct 9.
Dream, simultaneous 139; interpre-
 ters 54, 89. *See* Commands, Visions.
Dress of initiate 145 f., 148.

East, source of wisdom 239, 280.
Economic and religious change 130.
Ecstasy, Dionysiac 24, 72.
Education 176 f.
Egypt, religion in 5, 97, 205, 206;
 Greeks in 19, 36 f.; interest in 106.
Egyptians at Athens 20; at Eretria 48;
 on Delos 51, 54; assistant in ritual
 at Priene 55.
Elagabal 75 f., 129.
Elagabalus 129.
Eleusis 22 f., 41, 116, 275 f.
Emesa 128 f.
Emotions underlying religion 9, 162;
 heightened in crisis 18, 44, 226;
 appeal to, by philosophy 181.

Endurance 156.

Epictetus 170, 176 ff., 181, 183, 194 f., 230, 248, 296.

Epicureanism 171 ff.

Epicurus 247, 258.

Epimenides 26.

Epiphanies 90. *See* Vision.

Epithets: Pythian, Delian 21; Phistyis 59 f.; of Cybele 293 f.

Epona 280.

Eternity 231, 235; of memory 299.

Eucharist 204, 234.

Eunus 66.

Euripides 25, 27, 30.

Eusebeia 10.

Exclusiveness, Jewish 61; supposed, in Mithraism 293.

exegetai of Apollo 21.

Exorcism 104.

Faith 181, 185, 205, 213.

Fanatics of Bellona 82.

Fast before vision 108; before initiation 144.

Fate 100 ff., 247, 283, 288, 296 f.; it is superior to 139.

Fear of curse 76, 286; of Sabbath 78; of bewitchment 105.

Flavian period 125 f.

Foreign groups 6, 65, 280; merchants 48; at Athens 20, 276; Greeks at Memphis 33; Italians on Delos 67; Jews in Asia Minor 62; Syrians at Rome 66; Tyrians at Puteoli 66; from Vienne at Rome 283 f.; from Alexandria 284; need authorization for temple 20, 53.

Fortune 140 f.

Freedmen in Dionysiac association 73; and Oriental cults 131 f.

Freedom 174.

Generalizations, love of 233.

Gifts before initiation 145.

Glycon 94.

Gnosis 119, 290.

Gnostics 92, 104, 119, 253, 296.

God the Father 229 ff.

God, son of 232 ff.

Gods, all worshipped together, 35, 111; astral 101; born 232; coming on earth 236 f.; dying 234; masters of fate 101 f.; and universe 165; in Eastern belief 154; Christian views of 221 ff.; Jewish views of 300; philosophic views of 223 f., 231; definition 91; Greeks and foreign 19. *See* Identification.

Golden Age 244 f.

Grace 249.

Greece, incoming of Indo-Germans 6.

Greek Church 234.

Greek civic religion 17 f.; national religion 18; attitude towards foreign gods 18 ff., 34; religious temper 31.

Gregory of Nyssa 236.

Groups, philosophic 166.

Hadrian 126.

Hecate, propaganda for 22, 92; contact with Mithraism 44; gives oracles 111; mysteries 117; initiation 299; rite 291; identified with Isis 151.

Helios Saraptenos 66.

Hellenization of East 36.

Hermes 23.

Hermetic writings 3 f., 12, 79, 88, 102 f., 117, 224, 235, 237, 251, 279.

Heron 97.

Hesiod 22.

Hierapolis 37.

Hierarchy 135.

History and cult 234 f.

Holy places 135, 293 f.

Honesty and miracle 96 ff.

Honour from deity 109, 144.

Horace 11.

Humanity, escape from 103, 237.

Hymns, Homeric 23 f.; Orphic 30 f.; for Sarapis 38; for Isis 80, 152; for Hecate and Priapus 92; means of propaganda 92.

Hypsistarii 63 f.

Hypsistos (Highest God) 63.

Iao (Jehovah) 62 f., 111.

Identification of gods 19, 136 f., 150 f., 280.

Idolatry 221.

Image of Sarapis 50; of Isis 146.

Immorality alleged against Bacchanalia 72; against Isis cult 74, 153; against Christians 209; against philosophers 295.

Immortal fame, desire of 201, 299.

Immortality. Popular ideas 28, 103, 246; interest 108, 259; in Judaism 61; ensured by Orphic life 26 f.; by religious rites 13, 23, 39, 77, 102 f.; by magic 118; by help of Isis 139; by acceptance of revelation 4.

Imouthes 86 ff.

Impersonal view of deity 222, 231, 260.

Incarnation 236 f.

India, contacts with West, 46 f.; mention in Isis text 151.

Indian suicide at Athens 201.

Inferiority feeling 212.

Initiate's relation to priest 147, 294.

Initiations 12, 40; Dionysiac 26, 31, 72 ff.; Graeco-Egyptian 39, 56 f., 278; Mithraic 43; of Cybele and Attis 69, 279, 284; enjoined by Isis 142; preceded by abstinence 142; secrecy of 214, 290; free from death 103; cost of 56 f., 143, 148 f., 282; successive 114 f.; philosophy compared with 182, 185.

Inquisitiveness 105 ff., 145, 167, 289, 300.

Insignia, priestly 71, 127, 136, 286.

Inspired individual 112.

Intellect, loss of faith in 120.

Intermediary deities beings 222 ff., 235.

Intolerance 11, 21, 25, 165.

Isiacs at Pompeii 293.

Isis in Egypt 38 ff.; at Athens 20; at Eretria 48; at Samos 282; at Priene 55; in Boeotia 58; at Cenchreae 138; at Tithorea 153; at Rome 74 f., 124 ff., 147; at Beneventum 126; in Western provinces 131; name of ship 127; in Statius 106; in Apuleius 14, 138 ff.; in Oxyrhynchus text 150 ff.; identified with Fortune 141; with other deities 150 ff.; 'of many names' 144, 150; superior to Fate 102, 139; saviour 56 ff.; indicates day for initiation 143, and those who may enter temple 153; ritual of 80; begging priests of 82, 282; miracles of 85 f., 89, 138 ff.; duration of worship 160; *Praises of* 40, 102, 279.

Istrus 90.

Iulia Domna 128.

Jerusalem; church at 187 ff.

Jesus, name in magic 209; the Gospel picture and the mission 210; death 234; teaching 242.

Jonah 61.

Josephus 78 f., 153.

Judaism, promise of 13; and Seleucids 35; in world at large 61 ff., 187; proselytizers banished from Rome 74; later expulsion 74; how spread 77 ff.; exorcisms 104; organization 241 f.; martyrs 193; privileges 227 f.; concept of God 230; view of pagan gods 300; Plutarch on 105.

Judaizing groups 63 f.

Judgement 242.

Julian 70, 157 ff., 185, 224.

Juppiter Dolichenus 66, 75, 155, 219.

Justin Martyr 213 ff., 221, 228, 238 f., 250, 255 ff.

Katochoi 80, 153.

Kerygma 188.

Kindness of Roman mob 298.

Kingdom of God 242 ff.

Knowledge and piety 119 f.

Lapsed Christians 156.

Law, universal 101.

Leading, divine 136, 265. *See* Vocation.

Lectures 176 ff.

Legends, Apolline 21 f.; philosophic 176.

Lindos 20, 90.

Literature, ancient 272; Roman 123; on religion 105 f.; *religious* Orphic 26 ff., 251; Dionysiac 31; Egyptian 38; Jewish 78 ff.; miracles of Sarapis 84; dissemination thereof 89; on Imouthes 86 ff.; Christian miracles 89; prophetic 239, 251; personal statement 115.

Liturgy, Egyptian 38 ff.; language Greek, for Cybele and Attis 41; of mysteries 78; Isiac book 144.

Love for the brethren 219 f.

Lucian 93 ff., 107, 220, 256 f.

Luxury 218.

Ma 67.

Mag 42 f., 107.

Magic 43, 74, 97, 110, 206, 229.

Magical papyri 62 f., 117 f., 209.

Magnesia on the Maeander 55.

Maionmas festival at Ostia 67.

Mandulis 109 f., 289 f.

Manichaeism 92, 252 f., 259, 263.

Manumission, religious 58 f., 63, 156.

Marcus Aurelius 128.

Martyrdom 193 ff., 298.

Maximus of Madaura 260.

Memphis 33, 38.

Men 59, 91.

Mendicant priests 82 f., 205, 281; philosophers 169.

Mercenaries 23, 59.

Merchants 20, 23, 48.

Messianic ideas 228.

Methods of Christian mission 191 ff.

Milan 264.

Miracles of Athena on Lindos 20; of Apollo 22; of Sarapis and Isis 51 f., 83 ff., 138 ff.; at Epidaurus 54;

Miracles (*cont.*).
Dionysiac 73; Christian 89; of Antony 265; recording in temples 90 f., 287; confute scepticism 91; prove deity 91; produce or fail to produce adhesion 53, 254, 287 f.; artificial 97. Cf. *Aretalogos*.

Mithraism, origins 41 ff., 60 f., 269; at Rome 75, 77, 128, 130; in West 132 f.; communion 214, 279; *taurobolium* 71, 284; Greek ideas in 245 f.; myth 235 f.; places of worship 75, 285; confraternity 300; supposed exclusiveness 293; mention in Statius 126; rivalry with Sarapis 134; Greek view of 299; comparison with Christianity 14, 206, 268.

Monotheism, trend to 223.

Morality of Christianity and paganism 206, 215 ff., 284.

Mother-goddess, Lydian 91.

Municipal interest in Oriental cults 132.

Mysteries of Eleusis 22 f., 116; of Dionysus 72; of Osiris and Isis 38 ff., 142 ff.; of Mithras 44, 299; of Syrian goddess 60; of Hecate 117; at Abonutichus 96; private 116 f., 291; Neoplatonic 158; multiplication of 279; no explicit theology in 285 f.; source of enlightenment 113 ff.; promise of 12; and Eucharist 204.

Myth 11, 159, 233, 301.

Naassenes 115 f.

Nanaia 34.

Neoplatonism 158, 181.

Neopythagoreanism 116, 168.

Nero 106.

Novel, Greek 198 ff.

Obedience 139, 144, 170.

Oracles at Abonutichus 93 ff.; at Dodona 276; and general issues 111, 290; international standing 19; decline 112, 223; sought for Lysander 232; due to *daimones* 223. *See* Delphi.

Organization 135, 241 f.

Oriental religions in Roman paganism 267 f.

Origen 204, 299.

Orpheus 26 f., 113.

Orphism 12, 26 ff., 277.

Osiris 38 ff., 56, 147.

Ostanes 223.

Ostia 67, 70.

Otherness, feeling of, in Orphism 31; in Hermetism 117 f.; in Judaism 61 f.; in Isis worship 80; in Magi 44; in Mithraism 77.

Ovid 85, 124, 216.

Pagani 227.

Paganism and Christianity 160 ff., 249, 259 ff.

Palmyra 36.

Pan 18.

Pantheus 137.

Past, view of 113 f.

Pastophorus 147, 149.

Paul 190 ff., 295.

Paulina 153.

Penance 80, 159, 287.

Peregrinus 201, 220.

Persecutions 130, 192, 196 f., 208 f.

Persians and alien religions 19 f., 35; in Asia Minor 42, 60 f., 279.

Persius 182 f.

Pessimism 246.

Pessinus 41, 68.

Philadelphia 216 f.

Philo 79, 103, 116, 240.

Philosophers as tutors and advisers 178; as saints 175 f.

Philosophy, esoteric and exoteric 167; literature 179; in education 176 f.; values of 173; postulates 251 f.; a unity 173; relation to religion 120 f., 165; necessary for piety 120, 186; an initiation 182, 185; appeal to emotions 181; disappointment by 107 f., 255 ff.

Philostratus 129.

Phrygia 64.

Phylarchus 90.

Pindar 22, 27, 155.

Pirates 44.

Plato 27, 166, 175, 222 f., 232, 256.

Ploiaphesia (opening of sailing) 57, 141.

Poimandres 3, 9.

Political influences in spread of cults 55 (Ptolemaic), 134 (Rome).

Poor attitude of 212, 242, 246.

Porphyry 111, 157, 184 f., 224.

Porta Maggiore basilica 168.

Possession 104, 289.

Prayer 101.

Priapus 92.

Priene 55.

Priests, Greek and Eastern 34, 164; public and private 30, 71; Roman 11, 127; hereditary 154; Orphic 28; of Asclepius at Epidaurus 54; Atargatis

Priests (*cont.*).
at Beroea 59, 282; of Cybele 71, 82, 285 f.; mouthpiece of Imouthes 87; Isis 80, 143, 153, 281; Mithraic 44, 75; of Sarapis, hereditary or annual 51, 53 f., 56; of Syrian goddess 75 f., 82 f.; of Judaizing group 63; dignitaries 135 f.; forbidden in Bacchanalia edict 73; interpret dreams 54, 89; treat possessed 289; relation to worshippers 63; relation to initiates 144, 147, 294.
Private shrines 116; 74 (Egyptian deities); 75 (Mithras); 216 f. (Agdistis, &c.); 282 (Syrian goddess and Aphrodite Berenice).
Processions of Bellona 82; Cybele 81 f., 286; Isis 57, 80, 139 f.; of Syrian goddess 60.
Progress 113 f.
Proof-texts 237 ff., 250 f.
Propaganda in Hesiod 22; in Homeric hymns 22 f.; of Asoka 46; Jewish 78 f.; relating miracles 83 ff.; of Alexander of Abonutichus 95; Christian 249 ff.; reasons for 16.
Prophecies 94, 240.
Prophecy, argument from 237 ff., 254, 258.
Prophesying, in Dionysiac ecstasy 72.
Prophet 2; movement in Judaism 61; of *Dea Suria* 66; Syrian, described by Celsus 83; Alexander of Abonutichus 93 ff.
Prophetess, Syrian 83.
Prophetic intellect in Philo 103; tone in Orphism 26; in early philosophers 165.
Proselytes 61 f., 109.
Provincials in West and Oriental cults 131 ff.
Ptolemaic policy 36, 55.
Purity, ritual 10, 12, 206, 216; in Orphism 30; before Dionysiac initiation 72; before vision 109 f.
Puteoli 66 f., 71.
Pythagoreanism 27, 31, 96, 167 f.

Rationalism, limitations of 225.
Reality and copy 243.
Rebirth by mystery 12, 39; after supposed death in rite 143 f.; by *taurobolium* 70 f., 284; by magic 118; of Lucius 141.
Recantation 11, 160.
Recitation of miracles 89.
religio 67; *Augusta* 128.
Religion 1; primitive 8; Greek 10,

18 f., 36 f.; personal 26; Eastern 34; ancient and modern 160 ff.
Repentance 4, 61, 180, 213, 242, 296.
Resurrection 242 ff.
Revelation, desire for 107 ff.
Rings, Harpocrates 106.
Rites, pagan, demonic copy of Christian 221 f.; freeing from human limitations 103, 118.
Rome, religious policy 67 ff., 196 f.; religious influence 76, 134; social divisions 122 f.; religious change at 124 ff.; Judaizers at 64; Syrians at 66; Christians at 187.
Ruler-worship 227 ff.

Sabbath 63 f., 78.
Sacrifice 101, 224 ff., 235.
Sailors, delivered by Sarapis 84; cf. 88.
Sallustius 186, 234, 243, 247.
Salvation 9; in Orphism 26; by philosophy 181, 185; rival ways 206; in Apologists 222.
Sarapis 35 ff., 50, 278; festival 39; functions 58, 84; at Memphis 38, 86; at Alexandria 38, 126, 293; in Greek cities 49 ff.; at Puteoli 67; at Rome 75, 126, 129 f., 134; miracles 51 f., 84 f.; acclamations 84, 292 f.; *soter* 56; superior to Fate 102; S. and Mithras 134. *See* Katochoi.
Sarcophagi 74.
Scepticism 10 f., 91.
Secrecy 214 f., 290.
Sect, genesis of 28.
Seleucid religious policy 35.
Seneca 168, 182.
Sermon 78, 177 f.
Severan dynasty 128 f.
Sexual life 1, 215 ff., 252 f., 285.
Shorn devotees 80, 148 f., 160.
Sibyl 239.
Sick souls 26, 220.
Sin 8, 12, 15, 91, 145, 160, 220, 224.
Slaves 66, 73, 131 f., 285. *See* Manumission.
Snake, Asclepius 94.
Social and religious change 125 ff.; standing of priest of Atargatis 282.
Socrates 21, 165 f., 174, 194, 196.
Soldiering, holy 141.
Soldiers 67, 127, 131 f.
Soter, Soteira (= Saviour) 56, 59.
Soul 26, 31, 44, 119, 247 ff.
Spirit 188 f., 221, 238, 241.
Stage, metaphor of 174, 201 f.
Stars 100 f., 144, 289 f.
Stephen 189.

Stoicism 170 f., 183 f., 197 f., 218 f., 221, 230 f., 244, 250.

Sun worship 27, 67, 75 f., 118, 130, 157, 292 (*see* Helios); initiate arrayed like 146.

Superstition 28, 72, 82, 127, 162.

Susa 34.

Suspension of judgement 263.

Symbol, Dionysiac 114.

Symmetry, assumption of 251 f.

Synagogue 62, 78, 283, 297.

Syria 35 f.

Syrian deities on Delos 49; at Rome 49, 66, 75; in Western provinces 131 (see *Dea Suria*); custom of saluting rising Sun 67.

Syrians on Delos 49; at Rome 49.

Syriscus 90.

Taurobolium 69 ff., 127, 132, 284.

tclete (= solemn rite) 28.

Tellthusa 85 f.

Temples, Greek 23; in Egypt 36; Bacchanalia 73; of Isis 74, 80, 142; of Mithras 75, 132, 285; of Sarapis 49, 51; civic record in 60; miracles recorded in 90; centres of piety 135; Lucius dwells in precinct of 142; instruction in 159.

Tests imposed on Christians 207.

Thankfulness 4, 146.

Theatricality 71, 197 ff.

Theology 106 f., 136 f., 150 ff., 285 f.

Thera 92.

Thessalus 108 f.

Third day after initiation 146.

Thrace, Athenians in 19.

Thracian cults 18 ff.

Thracians at Athens 276.

Time-sense 234 f.

Timotheus 38, 40 f.

To a senator 159 f.

Tradition 1 f., 161, 225 f.; in Syria 36.

Transcendence 223, 235.

Transformation by philosophy 182.

Tyrians 66.

Unbelief 11, 161.

Universalism 23, 58, 150 ff.

Varro 225.

Vatican sanctuary of Cybele 69 f.; derivatives 135, 293.

Venus Erycina 68.

Vespasian 85, 125 f.

Virgil 233, 244.

Visions 67, 87, 108 ff., 138, 142, 145, 149, 153 f., 206.

Vocation 2 f., 50, 61, 152 ff., 170; cf. 70.

Votives 92 f., 154 f.

Water, miraculous 84 f., 287.

Ways of life 167 ff.

Witnessing to doctrine 185, 194 ff.

Women, accessibility to religious propaganda 127.

World, concept of 99 ff., 235.

World to come 61.

Worship 202 ff., 226.

Yoke of service 141.

Zeus 90, 230 f.

Zeus Panamaros 90.

Zeus Sabazios 20, 64.

Zoilus 49.

Zoroastrianism 9, 43, 243 f., 269.

PRINTED IN GREAT BRITAIN
AT THE UNIVERSITY PRESS, OXFORD
BY VIVIAN RIDLER
PRINTER TO THE UNIVERSITY